To Gary

Page 1:
Camille dressed as an
Oriental, 1886 or 1887

Page 2:
Camille Claudel at twenty
in 1884, photographed
by César

Left:
The atelier at rue Notre-
Dame des Champs, with
Camille in the center,
Jessie and William
Elborne at the right,
1886 or 1887

Editor: Barbara Burn
Designer: Darilyn Lowe Carnes

Library of Congress Cataloging-in-Publication Data
Ayral Clause, Odile.
    Camille Claudel: a life / Odile Ayral-Clause.
        p. cm.
    Includes bibliographical references and index.
    ISBN 0–8109–4077–9 (HC) / 0–8109–9076–8 (book club: pbk.)
    1. Claudel, Camille, 1864–1943. 2. Women sculptors—France—Biography. I. Title.
NB553.C44 A97 2002
730'.92—dc21
[B]   2001046507

B
CLAUDEL
A
9-2002

Copyright © 2002 Odile Ayral-Clause

Printed and bound in the U.S.A.
10 9 8 7 6 5 4 3 2 1

Harry N. Abrams, Inc.
100 Fifth Avenue
New York, N.Y. 10011
www.abramsbooks.com

Abrams is a subsidiary of

LA MARTINIÈRE
GROUPE

CONTENTS

PREFACE

AS RECENTLY AS twenty years ago, in France, Camille Claudel was known only to a handful of admirers. The brief moments of applause she had enjoyed during her lifetime had never led to important commissions, and the sales of her pieces remained few and far between. The exhibitions of her sculpture before and after her death were so poorly attended that they mostly attracted the few idealistic critics who stubbornly persisted in praising the sculptor. Yet these circumstances were to change so suddenly that in the space of a few months Camille Claudel would take on the stature of a mythical figure.

It was one of the tragic ironies of Claudel's posthumous fame that the man who had spent many years of his life uncovering documents about her and tracking down her lost works—Jacques Cassar—died before he was able to complete his task.[1] As a result, Claudel was first rediscovered in 1982 through a work of fiction.[2] Two years later, a major exhibition organized by Bruno Gaudichon and Monique Laurent drew large crowds to the Musée Rodin in Paris and to the Musée Sainte-Croix in Poitiers. Claudel's legend had begun and, with it, the misunderstandings and fallacies that all legends seem to attract.

Camille Claudel displayed many of the characteristics that contribute to the weaving of myths: she was beautiful, talented, witty, and fiercely independent; she was connected to some of the most visible artists and writers of her era; and she even had a romance with Auguste Rodin, the greatest sculptor of the nineteenth century. But hidden among the magnificent gifts nature had bestowed upon her was the seed of an illness that eventually brought her to a mental asylum. This facet of her life, as well as her relationship with Rodin, has been the focus of much romantic speculation and misrepresentation.

It is my intent, in this biography, to dispel the myths enveloping Claudel and to rely on the patchwork of documentary evidence left behind—journals, letters, art reviews, reports from government officials, medical records, interviews, and so on. Many documents have disappeared and have probably been destroyed, and the complete medical records are not yet accessible to the public, but enough is available to help reconstruct Claudel's upbringing, her years of creation, her endless struggles against the art world, her disintegration, and, finally, her survival in the asylum.

Another objective of this book is to give a voice to the women artists who lived in Paris at the turn of the nineteenth century and who, like Claudel, struggled to overcome the limitations imposed upon them. Contemporaries of Claudel, including Cecilia Beaux, Marie Bashkirtseff, Kathleen Kennet Scott, Hélène Bertaux, and many others, give testimonies to their experiences, which were often both frustrating and exhilarating. The British artists who shared Claudel's studio—particularly Jessie Lipscomb—provide a fresh vision of Claudel's fascinating but difficult personality. Lipscomb was herself a gifted portraitist, and like Claudel she became Rodin's assistant.

Like most biographies, this one is a stepping-stone toward a better understanding of its protagonist and of the art she produced. Lost documents and even lost works keep reappearing; they shed new light upon the sculptor and help correct previous misinterpretations. The remarkable second edition of Claudel's catalogue raisonné written by Anne Rivière, Bruno Gaudichon, and Danielle Ghanassia, includes the newly discovered correspondence and medical records from the Ville-Evrard asylum, as well as a clear presentation of the correspondence and medical records from Montdevergues. Without such documents, it would have been impossible to understand Claudel's life in the asylum. Although the sculptor herself burned some of the correspondence she received, other documents will undoubtedly turn up to help further bridge the gap between the real Camille Claudel and the myth created around her.

THE TRAIN CARRYING Jessie Lipscomb Elborne and her husband, William, rolled across the colorful countryside in the south of France toward the ancient walled city of Avignon. The English couple had planned this detour on their way to Italy in order to reach the Montdevergues asylum, a nearby hospital for the mentally ill. There, Camille Claudel, a friend of Jessie's youth and her studio partner in Paris, was expecting to see Jessie again after forty-two years of silence. It was 1929, and Camille had already spent fifteen years in Montdevergues and one in the Ville-Evrard asylum. During these years, the Great War had brought its wave of devastation to both sides of the Channel, but it is doubtful that Camille had a clear understanding of it. In asylums, time stops and is spent in waiting; at this point, Camille was waiting to see Jessie, her loyal—if long-lost—English friend.

The reunion was recorded by Jessie's husband, William, an amateur photographer who also produced gelatin silver prints of their earlier times together. Two photographs, one of Camille alone and the other with Jessie, show the aged women sitting by the door of a stone building. Camille, aged sixty-five, is dressed in a long coat, her hair covered with a hat and her hands folded over her arms, as she stares directly at the camera. Softness has remolded her once-haughty expression, but her dignity is still evident. No sign of madness mars her dreamy eyes. Jessie, sixty-eight, has placed one of her hands on Camille's lap and appears to stare into her own thoughts. The Paris of the 1880s, the Paris of dreams and endless possibilities, the Paris that drew the young artists together and led them to Auguste Rodin's atelier was long gone, but it remained vivid in the women's minds. The years Jessie had spent raising her four children in England had never erased the brightness of those early days. For Camille, their brightness had turned into a brutal irony. "I have fallen into an abyss," she wrote from Montdev-

Camille Claudel and Jessie Elborne at Montdevergues Asylum, 1929.
Photographed by William Elborne

ergues to a friend. "I live in a world so curious, so strange. Of the dream that was my life, this is the nightmare."[1]

Of the dream that was my life. . . . As Camille sat beside Jessie in the asylum, the Paris years must have swelled toward her in a rush of poignant memories.

CAMILLE CLAUDEL AND her family moved to Paris from the Champagne region in 1881. The fifth-floor apartment they rented at 135 bis boulevard Montparnasse was located in a rapidly changing area that had been recently integrated into the city. As late as the 1860s, the quartier Montparnasse had retained its countryside feeling, with windmills visible everywhere and remains of the old Mount Parnasse still standing. By the 1880s, absorbed into the city, the quartier Montparnasse, which includes such famous streets as rue Notre-Dame des Champs and rue de la Grande Chaumière, was turning into an artists' quarter where one could find quiet and inexpensive studios.[1] As such, it did not betray any sign of the bohemian life that is often associated with artists and that could have alarmed Madame Claudel. The family settled down, but without Camille's father, who remained behind in the small town of Wassy-sur-Blaise, where he held a position as registrar of mortgages. Thus, Madame Claudel headed a household that included Camille, her brother, Paul, and her younger sister, Louise.

Camille and her mother contrasted sharply in both appearance and personality, differences that would bring them into conflict throughout their lives. Camille was visually striking, as is evident in a well-known photograph taken by César, which displays the troubling beauty of the twenty-year-old woman whose haunting gaze seems to challenge the viewer. To her brother, Paul, later a famous poet and playwright, this photograph represented the quintessential Camille. As an old man, he recalled with much emotion: "this splendid young woman, in the triumphal glow of beauty and genius. . . . A superb forehead over two magnificent eyes of a dark blue that we rarely see outside of novels . . . this large mouth, more proud than sensual, this powerful mass of chestnut hair, the true chestnut called auburn by the English, and which fell down her back. An impressive air of courage, directness, superiority, gaiety. One who was endowed with much."[2]

Paul failed to mention a small physical imperfection, a slight limp that, according to a friend, may have contributed to Camille's drive to look for perfection in her art; but his recollection mirrors the stunning portrait left by César.[3] Yet César's photograph also reveals pride, willfulness, even arrogance. Camille's comportment with others could be unpredictable and often tempestuous. Paul spoke of "her horribly violent character," of the "cruel influence" she had over his young years. He also remembered how everyone had to endure her "ferocious gift for sarcasm."[4] Even the Claudels' faithful servant Eugénie claimed that she "had the worst temper in the family."[5]

Self-control was not a Claudel quality. As Paul confessed in his *Mémoires improvisés:* "Everyone quarreled in the family: my father and my mother quarreled, the children quarreled with the parents, and they quarreled much with each other."[6] Conflict was therefore a daily occurrence in this environment, and Madame Claudel bore it with resignation. She was a sullen, unassuming woman, with a rural rather than bourgeois character. After her death, Camille remembered "the spirit of forbearance that exuded from her person, her hands crossed over her knees in an expression of complete self-sacrifice: everything pointing to humility, to a sense of duty pushed to the extreme."[7] Born Louise-Athanaïse Cerveaux, Madame Claudel had been brought up by her father, Dr. Athanase Cerveaux, after her mother's early death. Sadly, this motherless childhood appears to have crippled her emotionally, shaping her into a rigid woman unable to express feelings of tenderness: "Our mother never kissed us," said Paul.[8]

Louise-Athanaïse belonged to the well-established French bourgeoisie. Her father and her grandfather owned substantial property in the Champagne region, to which she became sole heir after her brother's death in 1866. Like many middle-class French women of this era, Louise-Athanaïse had a sense of duty, which pushed her to keep busy all day long in the house or in the garden, and to seek no frivolous forms of entertainment. Short on tolerance, she was also of limited intellectual curiosity. As a mother, she identified with her younger daughter, Louise, a rather conventional young woman; unfortunately, she never understood her more gifted children, Paul and Camille. Thus Paul rightly wondered: "How could this

Madame Claudel, c. 1862

Louis-Prosper Claudel, c. 1862

woman whose character was mostly humility and simplicity have two children like my sister Camille and me?"[9]

Camille was much closer to her father, Louis-Prosper Claudel. She
left a delicate charcoal drawing of him at the age of seventy-nine: smiling
eyes above a fine, long nose, a short white beard, a graceful hand bent over
his pencil, the expression of a sensitive intellect. Like Camille, Louis-Prosper
was imaginative, quick-tempered, and endowed with a sarcastic sense of
humor. As a product of the French middle class, he had received a human-
istic education in a Jesuit school and possessed a substantial classical library.
Although he had a few assets in the Vosges area, where he was born, they
were modest; therefore his work as registrar was his main contribution to
the family resources. This may explain why he was compulsively thrifty and
rather conservative in his political views.[10] Yet this conservative, thrifty man
understood his children's dreams and would become a crucial force behind
their artistic achievements. For their sake, he accepted separation from his

family, high expenses, and even social reproof. As far as Camille was concerned, he proved to be a very liberal father, and until his death in 1913, he remained her staunchest supporter.

Camille was born on 8 December 1864 in Fère-en-Tardenois, a small town nestled among the fields and rolling hills of the Champagne region. Her parents, married two years earlier, had lost their first child, a two-week-old boy, so Camille became the oldest child of a family that grew to include her sister, Louise, born in 1866, and her brother, Paul, born two years later. By the time of Paul's birth, the family had moved eight kilometers away to Villeneuve-sur-Fère, a village that would be remembered with much nostalgia by Camille and with conflicted feelings by Paul. Although Louis-Prosper Claudel's occupation forced the family to move on a regular basis, the Claudels spent their summers in Villeneuve, where they eventually inherited the comfortable house acquired by Louise-Athanaïse's father. Hence, for the children, Villeneuve remained a place of vacation and an anchor of stability.

Hidden away from major country roads, the village clustered its humble houses around a large rectangular square shaded with lime trees. "Villeneuve is a harsh and forbidding country," Paul Claudel wrote, "a country of plowed fields and forests, which have none of the Champagne cheerfulness and none of the pleasantness of the wine towns sleeping under the sun in the cozy folds of the river Marne. It rains a lot in Villeneuve, and when it does, it is a hard, violent, almost passionate rain. The wind is terrible. It makes the rooster of the steeple go round and round, and the weathervane of our home screech."[11] Villeneuve's Gothic church sat strangely to the side, away from the square, and its imposing silhouette sometimes unsettled visitors. "A church that suffocates the village in its shadow," the writer Jules Renard commented after a visit to Paul Claudel, "and these devout people who see us always, always, as strangers."[12] Villeneuve's four hundred inhabitants were mostly farmers and artisans, or workers for the local plaster and clay businesses. "They hated one another," Paul wrote bluntly, "especially relatives. Violence, grievances, long-mulled-over acts of revenge. Now and then, awful scenes. The best of them were lazy or eccentric."[13] In this environment, the Claudels appeared sophisticated and wealthy and thought of themselves as "immensely superior to everyone else."[14]

The fountain and square in Villeneuve, France

But for the children Villeneuve meant the stark, rugged country surrounding the old village and hiding its many treasures. For little Camille, the treasure was clay, the thick red clay that workers turned into roof tiles. Camille's grandfather had built on his property a kiln that could hold 25,000 tiles.[15] Although the girl had no interest in tiles, she saw that clay could be molded into fascinating shapes, which when baked would remain permanent. Camille's curiosity quickly turned into games, games into serious creation, and, finally, creation into a consuming pursuit, remembered by Mathias Morhardt, a journalist and Camille's first biographer, as "a violent passion . . . that she despotically imposed upon everyone."[16] She forcibly enrolled as assistants the ill-advised people who happened to be around her, usually her brother and sister, giving them the tasks of finding clay or preparing the plaster and also acting as models. When they tired of these games and ran away, Camille would turn to the servants. One, in particular, the young maid Eugénie, became her most efficient assistant.

In spite of their numerous squabbles, Camille and Paul were very close, drawn together by their imaginative minds. Paul would follow his older sister in her wanderings, sometimes as far as la Hottée du Diable—the Devil's Basket—a stunning landscape of massive rocks shaped by erosion. Some rocks had been molded into caves, others had adopted the shapes of animals or mythological beings. According to legend, this was the work of the Devil. Having agreed to build a convent in one night in exchange for the soul of the contractor, the Devil stuffed an enormous basket with huge stones, and went to work. But a rooster, awakened by the noise, started crowing. The Devil ran off, dropping all his stones in his panic and leaving a fantastic landscape behind him.[17]

This landscape had a profound impact upon both Camille and Paul, an impact that later finds its echoes in their art. Paul set the third act of his play *La Jeune fille Violaine* in a similar place. Years later, he confessed: "It is there that I conceived *Tête d'or* and that I became aware of my vocation. . . ."[18] As for Camille, the strange natural sculptures she observed at la Hottée du Diable were the first examples of an art that would soon absorb all her attention.

By the time she was twelve, Camille already stood out among her schoolmates in the Catholic school she attended in the near-by town of Épernay. Her art teacher, Mère St. Joseph, would proudly show her pupil's drawings to the other girls—portrait heads, for the most part. The teacher might have been more reserved if she had known of Camille's budding passion for sculpting, but the rudimentary art education provided in the school did not reveal this facet of the girl's interests.

La Hottée du Diable, near Villeneuve

Camille Claudel in 1878

As Camille grew older, she enriched her artistic education with literature and old engravings. Alone, and with the help of an anatomical model, she created Greek characters such as Oedipus and Antigone, historical figures such as the revered Napoléon or the dreaded Bismarck. The writer Mathias Morhardt, who became Camille's friend and protector for many years, was able to view the last surviving piece of these early works—a sculpture of David and Goliath, made when Camille was about thirteen. He greatly admired the romantic ardor animating this group, especially in David's splendid gesture of victory underlined by his knotty, robust muscles.[19]

This work also attracted the attention of the sculptor Alfred Boucher after the Claudel family moved to Nogent-sur-Seine in 1876. Boucher was from Nogent and, like Camille, had first started to sculpt as a child. A scholarship to the École des Beaux-Arts helped him mature into a successful sculptor who exhibited regularly at the Salon in spite of his young age. Boucher frequently returned to Nogent, which was only a hundred kilometers away from Paris, and the small town kept no secrets from him. Intrigued by Camille's sculptural activities, he eventually dropped by to visit her studio. What he saw impressed him, and since he had a generous nature, he returned to give her the much-needed guidance that she had yet to receive.[20]

Nogent proved to be unusually good to Camille, for it was in this town that she also benefitted from the instruction of Monsieur Colin, an outstanding teacher hired by the Claudels for their children's education. Under the guidance of this intelligent tutor, Camille was able to go beyond the standard education usually given to women. In *Mémoires improvisés*, Paul Claudel speaks with much enthusiasm of the influence of this man upon his life:

> For three years, to tell the truth, he set up the real bases of my education. He taught me Latin, spelling, and math, at least what I know of them, in a solid and fundamental manner that never left me, only because he had good methods, took good care of us, and had found ways to make learning interesting.
>
> These three years left me wonderful memories. And then, from time to time, he read us something which I thought splendid, for example excerpts from Aristophanes—of course, he did not read everything—*la Chanson de Roland, le Roman de Renart*, texts that are not usually read to children, and which enraptured us, my sister and me.[21]

Under these exceptional circumstances, Camille benefitted from the same education as her brother. The readings she discovered during this period led her to question the social values of the French middle class, and eventually caused her to reject established religious beliefs. Hence, Paul would later blame her for steering the Claudel family away from religion.[22]

Although Camille progressed rapidly under the supervision of her two mentors, Colin and Boucher, she faced an important limitation in Nogent: the lack of facilities offering serious advanced studies in art for women. In many provincial towns, art instruction was provided by schools of design modeled after the École Gratuite de Dessin pour les Jeunes Filles in Paris. Most of these schools, however, focused on giving women the tools to earn a living either in manufacturing or in teaching, and none of them permitted women access to nude models.[23] Propriety was an important concern, but the lack of confidence in women's ability to produce any kind of serious art work played a major part in upholding this tradition.

In the nineteenth century, the naked body was the standard of all art. Of this esteem for the nude, a contemporary critic would write: "Artists are trained from boyhood to look upon the successful painting of the nude as the proof of their proficiency; if they can do that, they can do anything; if they cannot do that, they can do nothing; the painting of the nude is the Alpha and Omega, the beginning and the end of art."[24] When women were barred from nude studies, they were de facto excluded from the mainstream of art and from the commissions available at the time.

Fortunately, Paris offered a variety of private schools and artists' ateliers where women had the opportunity for serious art study, as well as access to nude models. Boucher and Colin knew that a move to Paris was a necessity for their gifted protégée. Colin was also aware that Paul, a brilliant student in literature, would soon require the instruction of a prestigious school.

It is easy to imagine Louis-Prosper Claudel anxiously wavering between the evidence indicated to him by these two teachers and the sacrifices implied by a move to Paris. While Paul could be admitted to a boarding school, such a possibility did not exist for Camille. And it was inconceivable for a young woman of the French bourgeoisie to live alone in Paris. On the other hand, Louis-Prosper Claudel could not leave his position as registrar; he would have to stay behind in Wassy, where he had just been transferred. Therefore, his children's education meant splitting up the family, as well as expensive material arrangements.

According to Paul, Camille's passionate pleadings eventually swept away her father's hesitations: in 1881, Madame Claudel reluctantly moved with her three children to the Montparnasse apartment, Paul was enrolled in the prestigious lycée Louis-le-Grand, and Camille started her studies at the Académie Colarossi.[25]

CAMILLE WAS ONLY seventeen when she first strolled through the streets of Paris in 1881. The excitement she felt as she discovered the city can only be imagined, for she did not keep a diary. Fortunately, other artists related their dreams and daily work in great detail, as well as their successes and disappointments. Together these testimonies create a lively portrait of a city that had been on the verge of collapse only a few years earlier.

The year 1870 saw the defeat of the French army by the Prussians at Sedan. Emperor Napoléon III, who had been maneuvered into the war by

Camille Claudel at twenty in 1884,
photographed by César

the Prussian leader Otto von Bismarck, was forced to surrender. Three days later, Empress Eugénie fled Paris and the Second Empire was over, but not the war. The city of Paris was about to endure the worst siege of its history, a siege that lasted through a bitter cold winter claiming thousands of lives. Discouraged, the French government finally accepted the peace conditions demanded by Bismarck, conditions so humiliating that they led the Parisians to rise against their own government. The Commune, an egalitarian creation of the people of Paris, ruled for two months, until it was crushed by the government then centered in Versailles. During these months of insurrection, barricades were raised, people were executed, and fires were lit all over the city. Theaters, churches, libraries, and government buildings burned, including the Hôtel de Ville and the Palais des Tuileries. Ten years later, when Camille arrived in Paris, the ruins of the Tuileries remained untouched and would not be removed until 1889.

A number of Parisian artists, incriminated in the uprising of the Commune, had to flee into exile. The amnesty granted to the Communards in 1880 allowed these artists to return to France and participate in the proliferation of public monuments built to the glory of the new Third Republic. Indeed, the Republic had finally vanquished royalty and the empire, barely overcoming its rivals after the Commune and ironically owing its survival to the royal heir himself, the count of Chambord. Undeniably, his obsession with the white flag of the old regime—as opposed to the democratic blue, white, and red flag—discouraged his supporters, thus ensuring the permanent establishment of France as a republic.[1]

The Universal Exhibition held in 1878 turned into a huge celebration of the Republic and a demonstration of Paris's recovered grandeur. Paris's two million inhabitants took to the streets to sing, dance, eat, and admire the new electric street lights around the Étoile area, as well as the rich displays of the exhibition. At last, in 1880, the tricolor flag was declared the flag of the Republic, "La Marseillaise" its national anthem, and "Liberty, Equality, Fraternity" its motto.

Having paid its enormous war debts in record time, the French government proceeded to restore what had been destroyed during the war and to build an oriental-inspired white church on the heights of Montmartre in expiation for "the crimes of the Commune." But the crushing humiliation of the defeat by the Prussians would not be easily forgotten. Many Frenchmen

Camille Claudel: *Bust of Paul Claudel at Age 16*. Bronze, 1887. Museums of Tourcoing, Toulon, Avignon, Toulouse

experienced the loss of Alsace and Lorraine as a form of castration; the need to reaffirm their manhood, as well as their patriotism, would be one of the catalysts shaping social and political events after 1870. In art, inflamed republican pride led to statuary mania. Every small town wanted its statue of the Republic or Liberty, each traditionally represented by "a woman of the people" with aggressive features and a robust body. Another immensely popular figure was Joan of Arc—the most revered French heroine—who appeared on many squares as a reminder of the immortal spirit of France. It was during this period of republican enthusiasm that Frédéric-Auguste Bartholdi created his Statue of Liberty, whose head was completed in time for the Universal Exhibition of 1878. The finished statue was sent to the United States in 1885 and inaugurated in New York a year later. For a while at least, the art of sculpture must have seemed a goldmine in the eyes of the budding artists.

Camille could not have chosen a better time to move to Paris. The city was vibrant, industrious, and bustling with artistic activities. The studios had moved to the streets, the streets to the studios, and art was truly engaged in contemporary life. The artist, according to critic Albert Wolff, "has thrust his head foremost into the bustle of the world and participates in the activity of elegant Paris; he has his day when his studio is transformed into a salon where he receives the elite of polite society."[2]

When the American painter May Alcott-Nieriker, sister of the writer Louisa May Alcott, arrived in Paris in 1879, she found almost every block on the Right Bank around the boulevards Clichy and Rochechouart and their intervening streets given over entirely to studios: "All Paris, however, is apt to strike a newcomer as being but one vast studio," she declared, "particularly if seeing it for the first time of a morning, either in summer or winter, between seven and eight o'clock, when students, bearing paint-box and *toile*, swarm in all directions, hurrying to their *cours*. . . ."[3] Another American painter, Cecilia Beaux, who rented a studio on rue Notre-Dame des Champs, also noted that "the immense value to the student, in Paris, lies in the place itself. He cannot step out of the *cours* without having his crass judgments in regard to art developed, adjusted, poised. Everything is there. . . . The student may get, once and for all, in Paris, an inescapable sense of relation, not to be found elsewhere, and idealism has never been less sentimental, except perhaps in Greece."[4]

Of course, the rich museums of the city, especially the Louvre, the Luxembourg, and the Cluny, were also places where students could sketch from famous works of art and be inspired by them. But for many artists, the streets, with their Parisians and their studios, represented the strongest attraction. In fact, because permission from the authorities was required in order to sketch in the open air, artists who did not receive a *carte d'étude*, that is, an oval green card from the École des Beaux-Arts, had picked up the habit of hiring a *fiacre* (hackney carriage) by the hour in order to sketch from there.[5]

Art studios had been part of the Paris landscape for a long time. Many male students entered well-known artists' ateliers, private institutions, or government schools in order to prepare for admission to the most prestigious art school in France, the École des Beaux-Arts. Admission to this school was rigorous and often biased, but it was the only door leading to the competition for the Prix de Rome, with fame and commissions reserved for the winner. Jean-Baptiste Carpeaux was among its fortunate winners, but Alfred Boucher and Jules Dalou were unsuccessful, and Auguste Rodin did not even make it to the École des Beaux-Arts.

For women, the Prix de Rome was not an issue, considering that tradition prohibited their entry to the École des Beaux-Arts. Consequently, they were forced to seek alternative training that permitted both serious art studies and access to the nude model. During the second half of the nineteenth century, an increasing number of artists' studios offered suitable alternatives. One of the most famous belonged to Charles Chaplin, the first artist to open his atelier exclusively to women, thus eliminating the matter of propriety when teaching life classes. For his British students, Chaplin's rigorous teaching methods offered a sharp contrast to the superficial approach they had too often met in England: "Leave titles and description to the English who don't understand anything about art," he condescendingly wrote to Louise Jopling. "Painting must have a life of its own, without the help of anecdotes and stories."[6]

Not all ateliers were as well managed as Chaplin's, and students had to be careful in their choices. May Alcott-Nieriker warned that many were badly run, overcrowded, and expensive.[7] The best and most popular ateliers were run by private art academies such as Julian or Colarossi. "A year or two at Julian's, the Beaux-Arts, or Colarossi's," Clive Holland wrote, "is worth a cycle of South Kensington [now the Royal College of Art], with all its correctness and plaster casts."[8]

Julian's was the first academy to be run as both an extensive business venture and a serious art school. It was founded in 1868 by Rodolphe Julian with the intention of preparing students for admission to the École des Beaux-Arts. Realizing that more money could be made if the school were open to women, Julian created a special class for them in 1873. Four years later, nude models were made available to both male and female students and, over the next few years, the Académie Julian became so popular with foreign women that it eventually comprised seventeen studios on both sides of the Seine.[9] Julian's success was simple: he identified a neglected side of art instruction, and he provided what was necessary to change it. Along with access to nude models, the school offered the services of prominent artists who visited the studios twice a week and reviewed the students' work. These masters played a crucial part in sustaining the confidence of their female students, who were too often discouraged by the bias they encountered in the art world. "In Art, as in Religion," Cecilia Beaux wrote, "Faith is necessary—indispensable, in fact. What the student above all needs is to have his resources increased by the presence of a master whom he believes in, not perhaps as a prophet or adopted divinity, but one who is in unison with a living world, of various views, all of whose roots are deep, tried, and nourished by the truth, or rather the truths that Nature will reveal to the seeker."[10]

Life at Julian's has been described by many former female students of the school, the most famous ones probably being Cecilia Beaux and Marie Bashkirtseff. In her journal written between 1877 and 1884, Marie Bashkirtseff was eloquent about the qualities and the shortcomings of Julian's. She particularly appreciated the collegial environment of the studios: "In the atelier," she said, "everything disappears; we have no name and no family; we are not our mothers' daughters any more, we are ourselves, we are individuals and we have art and nothing else in front of us."[11] On the other hand, she constantly complained about the overcrowded conditions of the studios, which made the place occupied by each student of utmost importance. Weekly competitions awarded the best places to the winners, while the other students scrambled about as best they could to view the model properly. As a result, Marie obsessed about winning. But what comes most clearly out of her journal are the differences between the way men and women artists were viewed by their teachers, even at Julian's. "These men feel contempt for us," she deplored, "and only when they find a strong and even a coarse composition are they happy, because these flaws are rare among women. It is the work of a man, they said of me. It is energetic; it is natural."[12] She bemoaned the fact that she could not attend the École des Beaux-Arts and declared that if she ever became rich, she would create a school for women. Most of all, she longed for the simple daily freedom enjoyed by her male counterparts, a longing echoed by many women artists of that era: "What I envy is the freedom to walk about alone, to come and go, to sit on the benches of the Tuileries and especially the Luxembourg gardens, to stop at artistic shop windows, to enter churches, museums, to stroll in the old streets in the evening; this is what I envy and this is the freedom without which one cannot become an artist."[13]

Marie Bashkirtseff eventually became interested in sculpture and took courses with Saint-Marceaux, a sculptor Rodin disdainfully called "a nullity."[14] As far as sculpting was concerned, another academy would have been more appropriate: the Académie Colarossi, where Camille Claudel would enroll in 1881. The Colarossi had been established in 1815 as the Académie Suisse, preceding the Académie Julian by fifty-three years, but its name was changed after an Italian named Philippo Colarossi took over its management. The school had two studio locations, rue de la Grande Chaumière on the Left Bank and avenue d'Eylau (renamed avenue Victor Hugo after the death of the poet) on the Right Bank. Rue de la Grande Chaumière provided "a veritable nest of ateliers located one above another," which could be reached by means of a steep stairway.[15] According to Marie Adelaïde Belloc, Colarossi (whom she called Collo Rossi) was a former Italian model endowed with a keen sense of business.[16] He was also a minor sculptor who exhibited a number of plaster busts at the Salon des Artistes Français during the 1880s. Once he took over the academy, Colarossi decided to imitate Julian's methods and even improve on them. Like Julian, he hired established artists to visit his ateliers, but he accorded more importance to sculpture than Julian did, and he secured the services of well-known statuary artists. One of them, Ernest Hiolle, winner of the Prix de Rome, would marry one of the Colarossi daughters, thus becoming a permanent member of the academy.

Colarossi was also aware of a serious problem found in other private

Numéro 436   PRIX DU NUMÉRO : 40 CENTIMES   5 Mai 1888

A. ROBIDA   JOURNAL
RÉDACTEUR EN CHEF   **La Caricature**   HEBDOMADAIRE

Abonnements d'un an, Paris et Départements : 20 francs. — Union postale : 25 francs. — Trois mois : 6 francs. — Bureaux : 7, rue du Croissant

LE SALON DE 1888, — par A. ROBIDA

Attaque annuelle de *Migraine pictureuse* ou *Céphalalgie intense du Vernissage.*
   Grande Exposition de printemps de nouveautés en toiles peintes et garnitures de cheminées ou places publiques en marbre, bronze ou plâtre. Consulter le plan des magasins, suivre les itinéraires des critiques autorisés pour savoir exactement ce qu'il faut regarder et admirer et ne pas se risquer à perdre des adjectifs admiratifs et distingués devant une toile d'un talent non patenté encore.

A cartoon poking fun at the 1888 Salon

schools: prohibitive fees. At the Académie Julian, the fees for women were not only high, they were also inequitable in relation to fees for male students, a state of affairs that angered women like Marie Adelaïde Belloc:

> M. Julian demands a double fee from women and only gives them in exchange half the teaching received by the men working in his studios. The reason for this is not far to seek. L'École des Beaux-Arts offers gratuitous instruction to any who care to avail themselves of it, so that the fees must be low to tempt them away from the government schools. Women, on the other hand, have no choice, and must pay for tuition in any case.[17]

At Colarossi's, admission was more equitable, since men and women paid the same fees in the Right Bank studio—40 francs for a month for half days as compared with 60 at Julian's.[18] The equity at Colarossi's could also be seen in the way classes were run. Many were mixed, with women working shoulder-to-shoulder with men. One morning a visitor observed that as many women as men were sketching a Spaniard dressed as a matador and that every possible nationality was represented in the studio. All were concentrating so much upon their work that they hardly noticed the visitor's presence.[19]

It is therefore not difficult to see why Camille Claudel chose the Académie Colarossi: it taught more modeling, it was cheaper, and it gave women the same opportunities as men. Moreover, the school allowed a great deal of scheduling flexibility, thanks to a curriculum that could be as short as a week and as long as ten months. Through the advanced purchase of individual drawing coupons, students could also drop in and draw whenever they wished.[20] And for those who preferred to work outside, Colarossi organized regular excursions to the countryside, especially to Brittany, which gave students the opportunity to join their teachers in outdoor painting and drawing activities.

The school eventually closed its doors about 1920, some time after a family quarrel. It seems that the Colarossi men, who were known as bons vivants, took their female students to Brittany a little too often for their wives' peace of mind. Suspicion led to jealousy, and jealousy to anger. The consequences for the school were sudden and unexpected: wishing to punish her husband for his presumed philandering, Madame Colarossi burned the school archives, leaving only ashes to posterity.[21] To this day, Paris archives are blank about a private school that survived more than one hundred years in its own streets, and the only available records left are the comments written by former students. Regrettably, Camille's observations were not among those recorded, and she never claimed any of Colarossi's teachers as her masters. Instead, she named Alfred Boucher and Paul Dubois, although she does not appear to have studied with Dubois, who was director of the École des Beaux-Arts and Boucher's mentor.

Alfred Boucher intended to help Camille in Paris as he had in Nogent, and he may have advised her to rent her own studio. On the boulevard Montparnasse, Camille had devised a temporary arrangement by turning the maid Eugénie's room into an atelier and sending its dispossessed occupant up to the attic on the next floor. Eugénie, who had loyally followed the Claudels in their twisted odyssey from Villeneuve to Paris, was crushed. She packed her suitcase and left the family.[22] A few months after Eugénie's departure, Camille found a suitable place among the dozens of studios in the quartier Montparnasse, and the Claudel family moved again. At 117, rue Notre-Dame des Champs, the studio's location was ideal: only one street away from the Académie Colarossi and next door to the Claudels' new apartment at number 111. Not far from the Luxembourg Garden, the pleasant rue Notre-Dame des Champs wound its way from the boulevard Raspail toward the boulevard Saint Michel. It held more studios than any other street in Paris, some of them occupied by famous artists: the painters Beaux, Bonheur, Bouguereau, Carolus-Duran, and Whistler all worked at one time or another in rue Notre-Dame des Champs. While the majority of these studios have been destroyed, a few still stand as moving vestiges of a prestigious past.[23]

Other students who found this location appealing became Camille's studio partners. Two of them, the British sculptors Amy Singer and Emily Fawcett, befriended Camille—possibly at Colarossi's—and remained her partners for several years. Sharing the cost of rent and models to cut down on expenses, they also received free lessons from Boucher, who came by the studio once or twice a week. Although Boucher's generosity was commendable, it was by no means unusual in the Parisian art world. In accordance with an old tradition, established artists would regularly visit students' ateliers and charge nothing for their advice. Such opportunity was providential to women, because it allowed them to receive the same free instruction enjoyed only by men at the École des Beaux-Arts. Students of both sexes praised the masters' generosity, conceding that "French artists of eminence are singularly liberal of their time in helping hard-working juniors in their craft."[24] But some women, like May Alcott-Nieriker, concluded that "it is the right thing to be done, and the only way open at present to successfully rectify the injustice of prices charged by Parisian masters for art instruction to women."[25]

In this manner, Boucher became the patron of Camille's atelier. As his weekly visits increased the respect he held for Camille's work, he decided to introduce the young sculptor to his friend Paul Dubois, the director of the École des Beaux-Arts. Thus Camille met Dubois and showed him several clay studies, among them the *David and Goliath* so admired by Mathias Morhardt. Dubois immediately recognized the strength of these early works, a strength he had previously seen elsewhere, and exclaimed: "You took lessons with Monsieur Rodin!" But Camille had not yet met Rodin. She did not even know his name.[26]

The comparison may have been more prophetic than correct, as Morhardt believed: "It was easy to notice that the sculptor who created *L'Age d'Airain* liked beautiful harmonies and avoided violent contrasts of light and dark, while Mademoiselle Claudel's first essays were gnarled, furrowed with deep and dramatic blacks. This did not look like Rodin's art any more than Michaelangelo's art resembled Donatello's."[27]

Boucher's support came to an end when he won the Grand Prix du Salon in 1881 and left for Florence a year later.[28] Before his departure, he asked his friend Rodin to take his place in guiding his protégées. And so, in 1882, Auguste Rodin entered Camille's life.

CHAPTER 3

A CONSTANT CHALLENGE TO COMMON SENSE

"FOR A MAN, being a sculptor is a constant challenge to common sense; for an isolated woman, especially one with my sister's character, it is a pure impossibility."[1] Paul Claudel's words, written in 1951, define in their crushing directness the position of the sculptor. A few reached the top, gaining commissions and honors, but most struggled under very difficult conditions. The nineteenth century is full of stories about penniless sculptors who went on challenging common sense and barely survived. Antoine-Louis Barye, the great animal sculptor, would have starved if he had not taught animal

Auguste Rodin,
c. 1886,
photographed
by Carjat

anatomy at the Jardin des Plantes. Jules Desbois, always in difficult circumstances, constantly turned to his friend Rodin for work and bread. Ernest Hiolle, of the Académie Colarossi, died destitute, and a lottery was organized by fellow artists to assist his family. But it is the fate of Jean-Louis Brian that best illustrates the depth of the drama sometimes played out in the creation of a work of art. Wishing to protect his clay statue of Mercury from freezing temperatures, Brian covered it with his only blanket and froze to death beside it. The art world shook with horror, and the Salon awarded Brian a posthumous medal of honor for his *Mercury*, but the outlook for sculptors remained unchanged.

Rodin knew how merciless sculpting could be. By 1882 he had faced its challenge for a quarter of a century, and he was barely starting to gain recognition. But he had three qualities that made it possible for him to endure the challenge: he had genius, he was stubborn, and he had an enormous capacity for work. The writer Edmond de Goncourt, who visited Rodin in his studio in 1886, described him as "a man with common features, a fleshy nose, clear eyes blinking beneath unhealthy red eyelids, a long yellowish beard, hair cut very short, and a round head, a head suggesting gentle and dogged stubbornness—a man such as I imagine the disciples of Christ."[2]

Rodin was twenty-four years older than Camille. As a child, he had suffered from an undiagnosed myopia and was considered a poor student. Fortunately, he excelled in drawing and went to study art at the École Nationale de Dessin et de Mathématiques in Paris, a trade school nicknamed the Petite École because it became the best preparatory art school for admission to the École des Beaux-Arts, also known as the Grande École. At the Petite École , Rodin became the pupil of an outstanding drawing teacher— Horace Lecoq de Boisbaudran. This unassuming man, who was not himself a great artist, had developed a method that emphasized observation and drawing from memory. Later, Rodin acknowledged his debt to Boisbaudran in glowing terms: "We did not fully appreciate at the time, Legros and I, and the other youngsters, what luck we had in falling in with such a teacher. Most of what he taught me is assuredly in me still."[3] Alphonse Legros, who became well known for his etchings, also remembered that Boisbaudran "set himself to developing in us a memory for pictures; to this end he made us use our powers of observation to the utmost, by accustoming us *to seize upon the essential points of everything.*"[4]

It was in the sculpture class, as he modeled clay, that Rodin found his calling. "I made separate pieces; arms, heads, feet, then attacked the entire figure," he told a visitor. "I understood the ensemble at once; I modeled it with as much ease as I do today. I was in ecstasy."[5] From the very beginning, he conceived the notion of applying to his modeling the same principles he had developed for his drawings, that is, a build-up of profiles. When he drew, he would quickly make sketches of the model from various points of view. When he sculpted, he moved around the model and worked "one profile after another, each separately and all together, turning his work in all directions."[6] The results were vibrant and unacademic and may explain why he failed the entrance to the École des Beaux-Arts three times. With this failure, Rodin lost his only chance to compete for the Prix de Rome. The road for him would therefore be longer and filled with struggles. From this point on, he started leading the double life of decorative sculptor during long working days, and statuary artist during the time he had left: "I knocked off my fourteen hours a day and rested only on Sundays," he said.[7] Working for Carrier-Belleuse, Rodin created countless decorative works, which were signed and sold by his master. But it was through these sometimes tedious commercial works that Rodin perfected his technique and learned two very important things: how to organize a large atelier and how to create numerous variations of a single work.

Rodin spent some of the happiest years of his life in Brussels, where he found work at the end of the Franco-Prussian war of 1870. Although he still labored for others and kept a draconian schedule in order to produce his own sculptures, he was encouraged by the warm welcome he received in Belgium. Its salons were the first to accept his sculptures, especially *L'Homme au nez cassé* (The Man with a Broken Nose), which had been turned down by the French Salon. But even in Belgium he was to face a major disappointment: His *L'Âge d'Airain* (The Age of Bronze) was so realistic that he was accused of having cast it from nature. The same accusation of *surmoulage* was repeated at the French Salon, and Rodin's hope for recognition would have been shattered had he not gained admirers among the younger sculptors. One of them was Boucher, who, working with Rodin in an atelier, saw him complete a pediment at a breathtaking speed: "I took some clay," Rodin said. "For two hours I prepared my *boulettes* [small balls of clay] and then I went to lunch. I came back, put the *boulettes* to work,

Rodin in his atelier working on *The Burghers of Calais,* 1885, photographed by William Elborne. Jessie and Camille can be seen in the background.

and they immediately assumed their desired shape. In five hours I was done."[8] Boucher described this tour de force to Dubois, who immediately came with other sculptors to see Rodin's work; they followed their visit with a strong letter of support. This letter, signed by eight prominent artists, refuted the accusations of *surmoulage* while expressing unreserved admiration for the sculptor's accomplishments.[9] Turquet, the Under-Secretary of Fine Arts and recipient of the letter, immediately commissioned a bronze for *l'Âge d'Airain* and, furthermore, became Rodin's protector. As a result, Rodin received the commission for a door to the Musée des Arts Décoratifs in 1880, a door that would later be called *La Porte de l'Enfer* (the Gates of Hell).[10] He was also given an atelier in the Dépôt des Marbres at 182, rue de l'Université. This place, a sort of warehouse for stone material and stone sculptures, also included ateliers where sculptors could work on official commissions. As one of the occupants, Rodin had finally acquired the recognition he had been seeking for so long. Nevertheless, although recognition and commissions greatly improved his circumstances, several more years would pass before his financial security was finally achieved.

Rodin's long odyssey as a decorative sculptor and mason was not uncommon for male sculptors, and many supported themselves in this manner, even former Prix de Rome winners. Jean-Joseph Perraud, who won the 1847 Prix de Rome, did not have enough money to turn his plaster studies into marble, and he survived only through decorative jobs: "A few architects, needing a number of sculptors to decorate their buildings, gave me a statue here and there," he confessed, "a bas-relief along with everybody else, with the whole brood, work I was glad to do. It was the only thing that allowed me to live, if I was thrifty like a poor woman who sews shoes."[11]

Sculpture is a challenge to common sense by its own nature: it is messy, it is strenuous, and it is expensive. It is messy and strenuous because sculptors work in dust and dirt, spending countless hours doing manual labor. Even the successful Henri Chapu once exclaimed: "I have just finished a laborer's day: twisted metal for my figure's armature, dug out dirt, made clay coils, carried water, cleaned up. . . ."[12] For women it was just as dirty, and probably harder, since women who wished to dress like men had to be issued a special permission by the Prefect of Police. With the hems of their long bustled dresses sweeping the floors, they too climbed up ladders and carried heavy material. Unlike Rodin and Perraud, however, women could not be hired to do a bas-relief "with the whole brood," and the financial aspect of sculpting therefore became even more critical.

Camille would soon learn that a sculptor's atelier may be his least costly item, especially when partners help to share the rent. Materials, foundry costs, and models represent huge expenses that can be absorbed only through the sale of the works created. Clay and plaster are cheap, but they are fragile. With care, small terra-cotta statues can be preserved, but larger ones must be cast into bronze, and this is an onerous process. In addition to the price of the bronze itself, the artist must also pay a founder to do the casting. The task of the founder is to reproduce the original as faithfully as possible. For this, in the nineteenth century, the lost-wax method was preferred by the most meticulous artists. This process, which is still in use, consists of making a negative cast from the original, and then coating this new cast with layers of wax. More plaster is poured over the wax so that it becomes sandwiched between the two plaster molds, which are further held in place with bronze pins. When the forms are heated, the wax melts and escapes through sprues (thin wax cylinders) especially installed for this purpose. The liquid bronze is then poured into the void and takes the place of the "lost wax." In the last step, the sprues and vents are cut off and the visible section joints removed. Polishing the bronze and applying special patina, if desired, finish the work.

The primary advantage of bronze casting is the possibility of making several bronzes from one clay or plaster model so that, if interest in the original work generates private commissions, the artist can make a substantial profit. Unlike bronze, stone carving does not offer the possibility of duplication. The stone, usually marble, has to be bought, installed, and cut each time. Besides being expensive, marble requires a great deal of dexterity and physical endurance from the sculptor, for one slip of the hand can ruin months of work. This is why good *praticiens*—assistants who carved the stone according to the master's maquettes and directives—were of crucial importance to an established nineteenth-century atelier. Financially successful sculptors such as Carrier-Belleuse hired so many assistants that their ateliers looked more like factories than studios. On the other hand, the emerging sculptor could rarely afford this kind of help; he had to carve his own marble and often work as a *praticien* in someone else's atelier at the same time.

Models represented another important expense for artists, considering that one session with a popular model could cost as much as modest food expenses for a whole week.[13] Of course, poor artists and novices tried to convince their friends and relatives to pose for them. For example, Camille's first models were her sister, her brother, and an old servant. However, these amateurs could not be compared to the professional models, who were able to pose for hours, often in awkward positions and without complaining.[14] During the second half of the nineteenth century, new art schools and studios produced an increasing demand for all kinds of models. Consequently, numerous Italians moved to France in response to this demand, and Paris counted five hundred Italian models by the end of the century.[15] Rodin's favorites may have been the two Italian sisters Adèle and Anna Abruzzesi, one brunette and the other blonde, whose beauty never ceased to enrapture him. Adèle posed for one of Rodin's most sexually daring sculptures: *La Femme accroupie* (The Crouching Woman).[16]

Auguste Rodin,
Rose Beuret,
c. 1880. Marble,
1890. Musée
Rodin, Paris

Because art schools chose their new figure models every Monday morning, model markets were held on that day on rue Bonaparte by the École des Beaux-Arts, in Place Pigalle around the fountain, and later, on rue de la Grande Chaumière near the Académie Colarossi. Beautiful women were always in great demand, but the muscular young men and the venerable patriarch who could sit "for every saint in the calendar" were also popular.[17] These men, women, and children created one of the most picturesque features of artists' neighborhoods, and they were, according to one observer, "by no means unconscious of their worth, and very proud of the reputation they have made. . . . Very often a whole family is in the business, and a little boy whom I painted during the winter used to tell me with great pride and satisfaction how his mother was engaged at such an atelier, his father at another, his little brother at a third, and a tiny sister at a fourth."[18]

The relationship between artist and model could be as gratifying or as miserable as any relationship. Some models complained they were cold; others could not sit still. Some arrived late; others disappeared in the middle of a work. This happened to Rodin, who was left with an unfinished *Eve* because his model, Adèle, became pregnant and ran away with her lover.[19] It also happened to Camille, whose Italian male model for her first major work, *Sakuntala,* left for Italy and never returned.[20] But, in general, comments tended to be positive, and everyone appreciated a model who could sit without complaining.

In 1864, when Rodin was twenty-four, he met his own female model. Her name was Rose Beuret, and she was to become his life-long companion. She was then an attractive seamstress whose "slightly masculine features, large bronze-colored eyes which blazed at the least provocation, luxuriant brown hair which she curled in inventive ways" would sometimes appear in Rodin's early sculptures.[21] This simple woman knew how to add a touch of elegance to her humble attire with the addition of large hats, which she wore over her country-fresh face. As she grew older, she lost her charm, but she ever remained "the servant with a simple heart."[22] Rose endured the long years of poverty with Rodin and took care of his studio during his absence. She learned how to keep the clay moist and to protect it from the cold; she watched over the plasters and the marble, making sure they were safely stored. Rodin's letters to her were full of recommendations regarding the sculptures he had left behind in the atelier, and Rose loyally followed his directives. Aside from her job as "keeper of the studio," she sewed garments to help the family survive, and when Rodin's father became senile, she nursed him until his death in 1883.

Rodin and Rose had a son, Auguste, who was given his father's first name but not his last name, for Rodin refused to legally accept paternity. To complicate matters, after a fall from a window, the boy became difficult to handle and somewhat slow-witted. This may explain why Rodin never paid much attention to him. He was more attentive to Rose in the early days, but later he neglected her as well as their son. Occasionally Rodin would ask her to join him on a long Sunday walk, such as they had taken in the past. But he did not want to marry her, and he made sure that she did not meet any of his intellectual and artist friends. Rose could barely write; her lack of education and her limited mental abilities were best kept hidden. Yet her devotion fulfilled Rodin's needs of the moment. Like Delacroix and Courbet, he viewed the "woman's snare" as "the most terrible danger for an artist"[23] and he did not intend to let any woman tie him down. His energy, his passion, his dreams were all given to sculpture.

THE ATELIER RENTED by Camille and her British partners was most likely located on the ground floor, because the heavy weight of stone and clay makes stairways a difficult proposition for sculptors. Photographs show that it consisted of one room, which served both as working studio and sitting-room, since the students could not afford separate areas. But it is evident that Camille and her friends attempted to make the atelier both attractive and comfortable. The photographs reveal a surprisingly neat working space in spite of modeling stands supporting various sculptures in progress. Large Persian-style rugs warm the walls and provide backdrops for models. Paintings, copperware, and even what appears to be a plaster parrot add a decorative touch to the surroundings. The studio also contained a piano, which seems to have been treated as an extra stand for finished pieces. But Camille's sister, Louise, who excelled in music, must have been glad to use it whenever she dropped in for a visit.

"Paris is the realized dream! It's the freedom to work!" Morhardt wrote, echoing Camille's enthusiasm. "It's the possibility of learning a trade, of having a model, of being the artist you want to be, without worrying about the neighbors who stare over the garden walls."[1] The young partners cherished this new-found freedom. Camille was clearly the leader of the group: she usually chose the models and the pose, and she designated everyone's tasks. As a result, she more than once ran into problems with dishonest models who sought to take advantage of the women's inexperience or threatened to leave if they did not have their way. In this regard, Morhardt praised Camille's firmness: "The young artist never gives in. She has acquired of her rights and of her duties, as well as the duties and rights of others, a simple and clear idea on which she does not compromise."[2] Morhardt's observation underlines Camille's pivotal character traits:

assertiveness and determination. Although she was young, she expected respect. Although she was a woman, she would not be bullied. Whatever vision she held of her rights and of her future, she would not alter it under outside pressure.

Recurring irritations, impudent models, and unavoidable accidental breakage did not slow down the artist's productivity. Camille could proudly point to two excellent works when Rodin first came to visit the atelier in 1882: the bust of her brother, *Paul at Thirteen*, and *La vieille Hélène*, the bust of an old Alsatian woman who worked for the Claudel family. Although both pieces belong to the realist tradition, they are quite different in their inspiration. The old woman's gnarled features are exaggerated—her forehead is deeply furrowed, her cheeks bulge out, and her mouth grins in an ironic smile. By contrast, the portrait of Paul is exalted, with his torso draped in the antique style and his head proudly tilted to one side. The impression of pride and heroism that emanates from the bust suggests a candid intention on Camille's part to elevate its model to the status of ancient hero and prompted one critic to call it "Jeune Achille."[3] "The modeling is firm," Morhardt noted. "One finds no weakness, no puffiness. It is solid and flawless. It is also an enthusiastic work, where she successfully insisted upon the characteristics of her brother's face in order to give him this domineering expression, which is truly his."[4]

A third piece, the *Bust of Madame B.*, may have been in its early phase when Rodin first came to the studio; Camille would then have completed it under his guidance. The pensive expression of the model bowing her head, as if contemplating mournful thoughts, reveals a new sensitivity in Camille's realist rendition. Rodin must have been delighted that this bust was accepted for the Salon organized by the Société des Artistes Français in 1883, as were two works by Thérèse Cailloux, another student who briefly shared the Notre-Dame des Champs atelier.[5] In spite of his earlier problems with the Salon, Rodin recognized that it was *the* place where artists could acquire visibility and move toward an eventual recognition.

The Salon took place each year in May. Located on the avenue des Champs-Elysées, it was a marketplace where the award-winning works were bought by the State and where government commissions were granted to the top winners.[6] Although records show that many women artists had sculptures accepted by the Salon, they rarely received awards, and when they did, the awards were minor ones, such as honorable mentions or third-place medals. In 1880 the journalist Jean Alesson sent a letter to Edmond Turquet, the Under-Secretary of State for Fine Arts, and to members of the Salon, pointing out the discrepancy between the number of women who exhibited and the number of awards received by them.[7] His letter, like many others, was overlooked, and the inequitable distribution of awards continued for years, owing in part, to the absence of women among the jury members; with no one to represent them, women had no voice.

At this point in their careers, Rodin's pupils were not particularly concerned about the absence of medal winners in their midst. With two artists in the 1883 Salon and with Rodin as a *patron*, the Notre-Dame des Champs atelier had reasons to celebrate.

By January 1884, Jessie Lipscomb, another British student, joined the promising group and made arrangements to live with the Claudels. She was to play a major part in Camille's life. At twenty-two, Jessie was a serious-looking woman whose ordinary features were adorned by a thick mass of dark hair that tumbled down her back. Later she kept her hair pinned up according to fashion, and the softness of her eyes became more noticeable. But her gentle gaze hid a firmness of character and a forthrightness that were evident in the letters she later sent to Rodin.

Like other British artists of that era, Jessie had crossed the Channel in search of opportunities that had eluded her in England, opportunities for creative independence and individuality of expression, as well as for a way of life liberated from the pressures imposed by a puritanical society.[8] Of course, guardians of Victorian morality frowned at the idea of a young woman crossing the Channel alone. These frowns became outcries when the woman intended to study art in Paris, as Lady Kathleen Kennet Scott found out. "To say that a lass, perhaps not out of her teens, had gone prancing off to Paris to study art," Lady Kennet Scott wrote in her diary, "was to say that she had gone irretrievably to hell."[9]

But Jessie had no concern for Victorian propriety. She had already been on her own as an art student in London, and she liked her newly acquired independence. She therefore had looked to Paris with anticipation rather than trepidation. Jessie was levelheaded and yet, in her own quiet way, she was as passionate about art as the nineteen-year-old tempestuous Camille who welcomed her into her home. It is not surprising that a strong

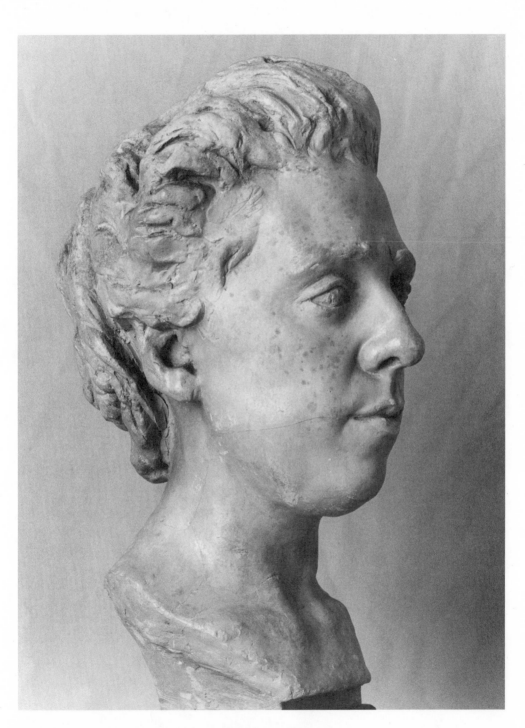

Camille Claudel, *Bust of Jessie Lipscomb.* Terra cotta, 1886. Private collection

attachment quickly grew between these two women who shared the same dream: to gain recognition as sculptors.

Jessie was born in Grantham on 13 June 1861, and she spent the first fourteen years of her life in this ancient borough, which is located about a hundred miles north of London. According to family legend, her mother, Harriet Arnold, had been a barmaid in a Grantham railway hotel, and it is in such a place that she may have met her future husband, Sydney Lipscomb. As a colliery agent, Sydney traveled frequently to Grantham for business purposes. Well aware of the opportunities created by the Industrial Revolution, he successfully invested in the London Coal Exchange, and amassed enough money to provide a comfortable life for his family.[10] Thus Harriet traded her precarious life in the hotel for the sheltered life of a middle-class Victorian woman. From this point on, she became listed in the Peterborough census returns as "wife to colliery agent."[11] What Harriet was like as a woman and as a mother is not known, although when Camille met her in England in 1886, she definitely liked her. All her life, Camille retained the warmest memories of the generous welcome given to her by Jessie's parents.

Information on Sydney Lipscomb is also scant, although he too is remembered as kind-hearted, and family anecdotes reflect favorably on him. A terra-cotta bust made by Jessie when she was twenty portrays him as a well-dressed and dignified gentleman who chose to reveal as little as possible of his generous character. Yet throughout his life, Sydney demonstrated an unusually liberal attitude toward his immediate family, overlooking behavior some viewed as improper and supporting his daughter's choice of a career in the arts. Intriguing evidence of his tolerance is found in his will, where Jessie is named as his "daughter or reputed daughter," shrouding Jessie's true origins in mystery.[12] Sydney may therefore have accepted Jessie as his own child even though doubt as to his paternity existed. But, whatever the word "reputed" meant in his will, Sydney never failed to be the most caring of fathers to Jessie, who remained his only child.

In 1875 Sydney Lipscomb had a large house—called the Wootton House—built at 65 Thorpe Road in Peterborough, and the family moved in the next year. Fourteen-year-old Jessie soon found out that Peterborough had more to offer than Grantham. The city boasted an impressive twelfth-century cathedral and a thriving market. With the arrival of the railway in

1845, the city turned into a major industrial center, and its population grew from around 17,000 in 1876, when the Lipscomb family arrived, to 30,000 in 1901. Culturally, however, Peterborough was depressingly limited because the bulk of its inhabitants were railway workers, many of whom were illiterate, their lives revolving around the thriving public houses.[13]

The prospect for a solid education in this environment, especially for a girl, was unlikely. In Grantham Jessie may have attended one of England's many day schools, which prepared girls to become proper Victorian women and left them, as Dickens would say, "ignorant of the world and its difficulties, and as unprepared to do battle with it at twenty as at ten."[14] In Peterborough a private school would have given Jessie the opportunity to study elementary art, since it was part of the curriculum.[15] Indeed, by the time Jessie reached her twentieth birthday, she had produced a number of excellent drawings and watercolors and had completed the bust of her father.

Impressed by these early works, Jessie's parents decided to support their daughter in her desire for a career in art. At this point, they may have had teaching in mind, for such a career was readily accepted by a society that otherwise took a dim view of women artists. Not far from home, art training could be found at the Nottingham Art School, but in this school, as in most other national art training schools, women received art instruction in separate quarters from their male counterparts and were not allowed access to nude models.

In Nottingham, drawing from plaster casts took the place of life studies and, as late as 1890, a student lamented: "No nude model was then provided for any female student at the Art School. This entailed my having to make endless studies from life-size plaster casts of antique statuary instead. . . . This copying of such stillness I discovered later in life to have been extremely harmful, bringing a woodenness, a dead look, to all my studies."[16] Probably informed of these shortcomings, the Lipscombs decided to choose the distant but most progressive national art school in England, South Kensington, now called the Royal College of Art, where women had access to life studies. South Kensington owed its notoriety to Edward Poynter, the principal since 1875. As a visitor to the École des Beaux-Arts in 1856, he had witnessed the importance the French accorded to life studies and the impressive results achieved by their early implementation. Keenly aware that the most serious flaw of British art schools was the failure to provide regular life studies to all students, Poynter decided to enroll the talents of two well-known French artists, Alphonse Legros and Jules Dalou, both friends of Auguste Rodin.

Legros had moved to England in search of the recognition that kept eluding him in France. He found it in London, where he came to be viewed as the greatest master of printmaking. With characteristic nonchalance, he never took the trouble to learn English, and he reviewed his students' works at South Kensington with the help of an interpreter.[17]

Unlike Legros, Dalou did not move to England by choice. Condemned to life imprisonment in absentia by the French government for his involvement in the uprising of the Paris Commune, he had been forced to flee. Finding himself without any financial means, Dalou enthusiastically welcomed Poynter's offer and joined the South Kensington faculty in 1877.

Right:
Camille Claudel, *Jessie Lipscomb*.
Charcoal and chalk on paper,
1886. Private collection

Opposite:
Jessie Lipscomb working in the
atelier on rue Notre-Dame des
Champs, c. 1886, photographed
by William Elborne. She is
working on a piece similar to
Claudel's *Jeune Fille à la Gerbe*
and Rodin's *Galatèe*.

Dalou did not speak English either, so his teaching methods were rather memorable: "Much waving of the arms and shouting of 'you do so!' as he attacked the clay and tried to explain that sculpture came from *within* the material, not from the surface."[18] But his unusual form of eloquence turned out to be very effective, and single-handedly, Dalou completely rejuvenated the modeling class. After the amnesty given to political offenders by the French government in 1880, Dalou returned to France. When he left, he asked that his work be carried on by his former pupil, Edouard Lantéri. Unlike Dalou, Lantéri stayed in England and "was to become the most respected teacher of sculpture and modelling of his generation."[19] Together, Dalou and Lantéri gave birth to the New Sculpture movement, and many of their students gained recognition for their contributions to British sculpture.

Jessie Lipscomb joined South Kensington too late to meet Dalou, but she was fortunate to receive art instruction from both Legros and Lantéri. Although women in the school did not share the same facilities as their male counterparts, they enjoyed a course of studies that was just as rigorous. Still, when it came to life studies, inequities remained: "The male students work principally from the nude, with occasional poses in costume, each pose continuing about ten days," a woman wrote. "The female classes have a week alternately of draped and undraped figure."[20]

In spite of Poynter's move away from industrial design in order to strengthen training in the fine arts, life studies at South Kensington were still bogged down by too many preparatory classes, and students who left the school for one of the Parisian academies often faced a major readjustment of their approach to the nude. One of them, Alice Green, expressed her confusion over the differences between French and English teaching methods:

> At South Kensington, you have been obliged to put in the very toe-nails of a cast, even when, with all your eyes, you could not see a trace of them. At No. 11, Boulevard de Clichy, if you ventured on much more evident matters, you were sure to hear, *'Ne voyez pas ces petites choses'* [don't see these little things]. The great masses of shadow must be put in broadly and simply, and the lights left untroubled by shadows. *'Clignez les yeux'* [squint] is a very frequent counsel; and 'You must be half blind to be a painter' is quoted to you over and over again by the older students.[21]

After Jessie won the two prizes offered by South Kensington—the Queen's Prize in 1882 and the National Silver Medal in 1883—she knew she wanted to be a sculptor in her own right. The problem was how to do it. As one of the most gifted students of the school, Jessie could have entered the Royal Academy. But since this institution still excluded women from life studies, Legros and Lantéri encouraged her to study in Paris. Other South Kensington female students had crossed the Channel for this purpose, among them, Amy Singer and Emily Fawcett, Camille Claudel's studio partners. As a fellow student from South Kensington, Jessie would be welcome to join them.

It seems that Jessie crossed the Channel to view the situation and was received by the Claudels as a short-term guest. She then decided to return to Paris as a paying guest in the Claudel home and as a partner in Camille's studio. A letter from Camille's mother dated 27 January 1884 provides the details of their contract:

Jessie, Camille, and Louise smoking in the atelier, c. 1886, photographed by William Elborne.

Camille has just informed me of your decision to spend a few months in Paris. I can only be glad for you and for us too because we have a great deal of pleasure to have you as a guest and you will be able to perfect your artistic education. We will be very happy to welcome you in our home and to share our lives with you. I would like to have enough money so that material matters would not need to be raised, unfortunately our financial circumstances, the expenses we have to meet because of the division of our household and the high price of everything in Paris don't allow me to welcome you as I would like, that is to say without financial compensation. I am therefore obliged, dear Miss Lipscomb, to ask you for what I need to spend on your account. Keeping expenses as low as possible, I reach two hundred francs per month.[22]

This arrangement, which placed their daughter into the hands of a respectable French family, must have eased Jessie's parents' concerns regarding the dangers lurking in Paris. It also offered a much more economical approach to art studies overseas. Finally, although the Lipscombs could not know it yet, it would place Jessie under the guidance of the greatest sculptor of the era.

AN INTENSE ARTISTIC period started for both Camille and Jessie, as they set out together to explore the endless treasures of Paris. They made sketches in the Louvre, the Luxembourg Palace, and Versailles, and they worked feverishly in the studio. In late afternoons, they set up a table by the stove and enjoyed a traditional British tea break, spiced up with a cigarette or two. One of William Elborne's photographs shows Jessie, Camille, and Louise dressed in white artist's garb, chatting around a pot of tea and smoking non-chalantly as if it were the most natural thing to do. But it was not, and it would take many years before women would gain the dubious right to smoke in public.

As the *patron* of the atelier, Rodin regularly came to the rue Notre-Dame des Champs and guided the group. A letter of thanks sent by Amy Singer's father shows that, like Boucher, Rodin did not charge for his services.[1] Yet at the time, Rodin was still struggling financially and was therefore very glad to see the same students come to his atelier at rue de l'Université for fee-paying private lessons. For him, paying the rent remained a constant struggle, his correspondence often referring to this problem. Once, Jessie received a note requesting payment for "whatever you think is appropriate for the lessons which, after a fashion, I gave you." Candidly, Rodin added that the rent was due.[2] Jessie kept this note along with all the other letters she received from Rodin and Camille, and this rich correspondence, which took place between 1885 and 1887, provides crucial information about the years Jessie spent in Paris and about the relationship that developed between Camille and Rodin.

The critic Camille Mauclair's portrayal of his friend Rodin points to a blend of shyness and authority, which may have been reassuring to his young pupils: "He looks simple, precise, reserved, courteous, and cordial without playfulness. Little by little, his shyness gives place to a strange and quiet authority. He has no grandiloquence and no awkwardness, and seems more dull than inspired. An immense energy emanates from his sober and measured gestures."[3] But these sober and measured gestures had no mercy for weak or lifeless modeling, as Paul Claudel remembered. Paul, who often visited his sister's atelier, sometimes watched Rodin "with a few blows of his modeling tool, remake his pupils' maquettes from top to bottom."[4]

Rodin wanted to find life in his pupils' maquettes. "We must unfreeze sculpture," he would say. "Life is the thing; everything is in it, and life is movement."[5] Since hands and feet were the foundation of movement, they received his focused attention. "Make hands and feet," answered Rodin to beginners who came to ask for help.[6] One of them, Lady Kathleen Kennet Scott, later remembered the aged Rodin's enthusiasm for studies of hands and feet that had been brought to near perfection:

> He would open small drawers, such as one is used to find birds' eggs in, and show dozens and dozens of exquisitely modelled little hands or feet, tiny things, of a delicious delicacy to compare with the grand rough *Penseur* [Thinker] or his *Bourgeois de Calais* [Burghers of Calais]. He would pick them up tenderly one by one and then turn them about and lay them back. Sometimes he would unwrap from its damp cloth, generally an old shirt, his latest work, and, spreading out his hands to it in uncritical ecstasy, exclaim 'Est-ce beau, ça? Est-ce beau?' Sometimes he would call a model to pose for him, and taking pencil and water-colours would hastily draw. I would watch in amazement to see him draw, never taking his eyes off the model, never looking at all at his paper. Sometimes he signed one and wrote my name on it and gave it to me.[7]

Aside from the study of hands and feet, Rodin constantly emphasized a method based on the observation of the multiple profiles offered by the model. In a conversation with his friend Dujardin-Beaumetz, he insisted upon the value of this method:

> In a human body, the profile is given by the place where the body ends; therefore the body makes its own profile. I place the model so

that the background light outlines the profile. I do it, I turn my stand and my model's stand and, thus, I see another profile. I turn again and, in successive stages, I completely go around the body.

I start again; I bring the profiles closer and closer together and I refine them.

Since the human body has the possibility for infinite profiles, I do as many as I can or as many as I find useful.[8]

Finally, Rodin urged novice sculptors to "exaggerate characteristic features" on beginning their work, aware that "the exaggeration will get toned down fast enough later on."[9] His inspirational teaching may have been best expressed by Gustave Natorp, a German-American who came to Paris to study sculpting in the early 1880s. "I do not believe he has his equal in the ability to give his inferiors the benefit of his vast insight into the great principles of all art by his power of analysis, and by the warmth of his admiration for all that is great in art and in nature."[10] When Natorp left, Rodin told him: "Now I have given you a compass, by means of which, with nature for a professor, you can steer yourself."[11] These words echo his view on the guidance he provided to Camille: "I showed her where to find gold, but the gold she finds is truly hers."[12]

Like Rodin, Morhardt never had any doubt that the gold Camille found was truly hers. Perhaps feeling the need to redress too much injustice, he presented her in his biography not as Rodin's disciple, but rather as his equal: "Right away, [Rodin] recognized Mademoiselle Camille Claudel's prodigious gifts. Right away, he realized that she had in her own nature, an admirable and incomparable artistic temperament. Right away, he became, not a teacher, but rather a brother of the young artist who was later to become his loyal and intelligent young associate."[13]

For her part, Camille instinctively knew that her teacher would become a giant among sculptors. As she listened to his "rapid and luminous suggestions," it was "a new world that revealed itself. . . . And after seeing for so long, in ateliers and exhibits, only lifeless corpses aligned against the walls, it was, at last, the show of life, of passionate life, which was unveiling itself to her in a memorable way."[14]

After working under Rodin's guidance for two years, Camille excelled at modeling, especially hands and feet. Jessie, too, proved to be gifted in modeling, but with her, drapery was the great favorite. The two women seemed to complement each other in art as they did in friendship. In 1885, when Rodin's latest commission for *The Burghers of Calais* created a pressing need for trustworthy assistants, the sculptor asked both Camille and Jessie to join him. With no concern for propriety, twenty-year-old Camille and twenty-three-year-old Jessie joined the previously all-male atelier at rue de l'Université.

By that time, Rodin had several Parisian ateliers to provide space to accommodate an increasing number of assistants and models and to store the multitude of casts produced. The main ateliers were located in the seventh arrondissement, at 182, rue de l'Université—also called Dépôt des Marbres—and in the fifteenth arrondissement, at 117 boulevard Vaugirard. No warm rugs or comforting teapots were to be found in these places! Nothing but bare walls and countless sculptures at various stages of completion. At boulevard Vaugirard, Edmond de Goncourt, who dropped by for a visit, appeared somewhat repelled by "the ordinary sculptor's atelier, with walls spattered with plaster, a wretched cast-iron stove, the cold humidity coming from all these things made of wet clay, wrapped with rags, and with all these casts of heads, arms, legs among which two emaciated cats take the form of fantastic griffin effigies."[15]

At rue de l'Université, there was the same absence of decoration, the same absolute focus upon work: "The air is soaked with work, the work of a lifetime, harsh and relentless work, which never backed away from any effort and never took a moment's respite."[16]

Rodin kept the ateliers given to him at the Dépôt des Marbres until the end of his life, and even though he had many other ateliers in his lifetime, he always gave 182, rue de l'Université as his address. This address became very familiar to Camille and Jessie, who like the other assistants were asked to prepare clay, plaster, and armatures for Rodin's works, to enlarge or reduce his maquettes, and, especially, to make various studies for *The Burghers of Calais* and *The Gates of Hell*. More precisely, Jessie and other assistants received the task of helping "dress" the nude figures of the burghers, which, according to Rodin's preferences, were first created naked. As for Camille, Morhardt recalled that "Rodin trusted her with modeling the hands and feet of many of his figures. To this day, we could still find at rue de l'Université several of these hands, some elegant and svelte, the others

Above:
Auguste Rodin, *Cybèle*. Plaster,
1885. Musée Rodin, Paris

Right:
Camille Claudel, *Jeune Fille à la
Gerbe*. Terra cotta, 1887.
Private collection

knotty and tense, which the master carefully keeps, like pieces of the rarest perfection."[17]

No greater compliment could have been paid to Camille, who quickly became Rodin's most trusted assistant. "He consults her about everything," Morhardt added. "He deliberates each decision with her, and it is only after they are in agreement that he definitely proceeds."[18] The journalist, who had many opportunities to observe Camille in the atelier, was struck by her ability to become totally absorbed in her sculpting:

> Silent and diligent, she remains seated upon her chair. She hardly hears the long chatter of idle people around her. Preoccupied only by her task, she kneads clay and models the foot or the hand of a figurine placed in front of her. Sometimes she raises her head. She looks at the visitor with her big clear eyes, whose gaze is so quizzical and, I should say, so persistent. Then she returns immediately to her interrupted task.[19]

Curiously, Morhardt does not say a word about Jessie's presence in the atelier. Yet as the other female artist in this male environment, Jessie was the crucial reassuring link between Rodin's atelier and the Claudel family. The young women chaperoned each other and, together, they were able to move forward.

At the Dépôt des Marbres, Camille and Jessie had access to all kinds of sculpting materials, especially stone. The place was a sort of warehouse— some said a cemetery—for stone and for finished pieces. Artists like Rodin, who received ateliers at the Dépôt des Marbres from the government, also received blocks of marble as part of their commissions. Although Jessie never worked with stone, Camille, on the other hand, became so proficient in it that she quickly joined the ranks of Rodin's *praticiens*, along with sculptors Jean Baffier and Jules Desbois.

It is well known that Rodin preferred modeling with clay to working with marble. Even when he was poor, he would often have others carve his marble, hiring additional *metteurs-au-point* and *praticiens* as he became more prominent. The *metteur-au-point* would cut and shape the stone according to the general outline of the plaster model. The *praticien*, often a seasoned sculptor himself, would take over and bring the piece to near completion—

an unrewarding task considering that all the glory went to someone else, and that the meager monetary compensations were often erratic. François Pompon, for example, was forced to turn to the law in order to be paid for the 380 hours a month he had spent working for Rodin! And Ernest Nivet moaned that "it is really long to stand on your feet for twelve hours."[20] However, some *praticiens* found Rodin so inspiring that they were happy to spend twelve hours each day in his atelier. The resulting experience was described as both "splendid and atrocious" by his assistant Charles Despiau.[21] "Atrocious" because the exhausting days allowed no time for personal sculptures, and the figures done in the atelier were Rodin's property. "Splendid" because the daily contact with a sculptor of genius brought many opportunities to learn from him.

Much has been made of Rodin's "exploitation" of Camille's work because of the fact that, when she became his assistant, he finished and signed a number of her sculptures. But the road from apprenticeship to mastery in a nineteenth-century atelier was a give-and-take process: assistants worked for a master and learned from him. Whatever they did in the master's atelier belonged to the master. During Rodin's formative years as assistant to Carrier-Belleuse, that master profited from his assistant's genius, and many pieces first attributed to Carrier-Belleuse were later credited to Rodin. Rodin, in turn, used the gifts of his assistants to his own advantage. As a result, confusion in establishing the true authorship of a sculpture often occurred. In Camille's case, the intimacy that developed between her and Rodin and their mutual influence over each other complicated matters even further. Two works in particular, *Jeune Fille à la Gerbe* (Young Woman With a Sheaf), and *Giganti*, point to the subtleties of influence and the difficulties in assigning true authorship when people create together every day and use the same models.

In 1887 Camille completed the figure of a seated young woman, which she called *Jeune Fille à la Gerbe*. The woman bends her right arm over her chest in a typically Claudelian gesture; her legs are slightly folded, her head gently tilted forward. Two years later, Rodin signed a marble version of a similar figure entitled *Galatée*, which appears to have been directly inspired by Camille's. To confuse matters even further, a photograph taken by William Elborne in 1887 shows Jessie Lipscomb working on a clay or plaster figure closely related to the other two pieces. Jessie, however, included a

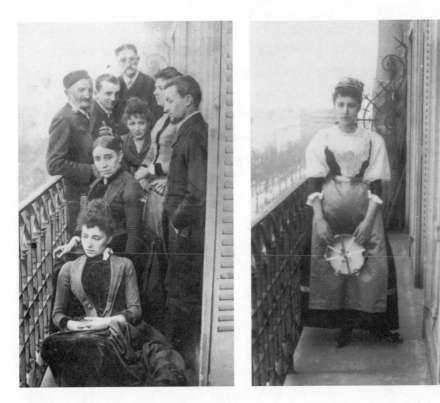

The Claudel family on the balcony of their apartment on the day of Louise's engagement to Ferdinand de Massary in 1886. Camille is in the center.

Camille in costume on the balcony of the family's apartment, c. 1886.

baby on the right side of the figure and twisted the right arm of the female around the infant. While *Jeune Fille à la Gerbe* evoked *Galatée*, Jessie's piece was closer to *La Jeune Mère* (The Young Mother) created about 1885. Unfortunately, Jessie's sculpture no longer exists. Like some of her other plaster or clay works, it was left to fend for itself in an English garden and did not survive the assaults of weather and neglect. But the interpretations of Camille and Jessie established by the photograph are very similar and also recall *Cybèle*, a work started by Rodin for *The Gates of Hell* also about 1885. Camille and Jessie were undoubtedly working on studies for *The Gates of Hell* under Rodin's direction.

Just as intriguing is the case of Giganti, the name given to a colorful Italian model who was used by the three artists and was a long-time favorite of Camille. Camille and Jessie each modeled a bust of Giganti between 1885 and 1887, but with divergent interpretations. Camille, focusing on emotion, exaggerates Giganti's features, flattens the face, emphasizes the mouth and the nose, and lifts the chin. The ensuing impression is one of strength, pride, even arrogance. Unlike Camille, Jessie was interested in visual truth, not in emotional expressivity. In her works, she produced "the same freshness and plasticity" as Camille "but never the same interest in the idea of the correspondence between extreme emotion and the life of the material in the hands of the artist."[22] Consequently, her *Giganti*, although as skillfully executed as Camille's and more faithful to the original, does not have the same impact upon the viewer.

Jessie's *Giganti* was cast in bronze and exhibited at the Royal Academy in London and at the Castle Museum in Nottingham in 1887. To this day, it remains the only known edition. Camille's *Giganti*, also cast in bronze, was first exhibited at the Salon des Artistes Français in 1885, then at the Royal Academy and in Nottingham in 1886. Other casts are now found in the museums of Cherbourg, Lille, and Reims in France and in the Bremen museum in Germany. Unexpectedly, the Bremen *Giganti* bears Rodin's signature.[23] Did Rodin admire this bust so much that he wished to claim it as his own? Or did someone forge his signature in order to increase the value of the piece? The latter explanation seems to be more credible, since Rodin would most likely have signed the original rather than one specific bronze.

Camille and Jessie were at a time in their lives when authorship did not really matter. They worked for Rodin, they learned from him, and they shared models and creations. They also enjoyed other privileges, because the "splendid" side of working in a master's atelier extended beyond learning opportunities. An important artist like Rodin could help his protégées gain access to various Salons, meet possible buyers, and receive recognition in newspapers. While Rodin seems to have done little for Jessie in this regard, numerous notes and letters indicate that he often used his influence on behalf of Camille. But more than pure admiration for his pupil's sculptures motivated him, for by 1885 he was passionately in love with her.

THE ROMANCE THAT bound Camille and Rodin for many years remains surrounded with mystery. Its illicit origins partially explain the reluctance of the partners and their friends to address the matter openly. At the beginning of their relationship, Camille still lived with her parents, and Rodin was with his longtime companion Rose Beuret. Understandably, they were both very careful to avoid being discovered. Their friends, mostly artists who rejected bourgeois values, refrained from making public comments. For example, when Mathias Morhardt wrote Camille's first biography in 1898, the liaison and its painful ending were public knowledge. Yet, although Morhardt knew Camille and Rodin more intimately than anyone else, he persisted in portraying them as spiritual siblings, not as the lovers they truly were.

As late as 1936, Rodin's biographer Judith Cladel chose not to mention Camille's name. Instead, she referred to her as "une grande passion" or "la belle artiste." But "la belle artiste" remained a nameless ghost haunting the pages of a book dedicated to Rodin.[1] And a ghost she was, because even though in 1936 Camille was a patient at the Montdevergues asylum, officially she had been declared dead in 1920.[2]

Events that are denied at the time they occur are often brought back to life through letters or journals discovered later on. Since letters and telegrams were the only means of communication in the nineteenth century, many educated people kept careful records of their correspondence. Although Camille was probably not as fastidious as Jessie in these matters, her letters would have been an invaluable source of information. Unfortunately, her correspondence with her father disappeared after she was confined to the Montdevergues asylum and has probably been destroyed. The same misfortune befell her correspondence with Rodin. According to René Chéruy, Rodin's secretary in the early 1900s, a collection of letters from

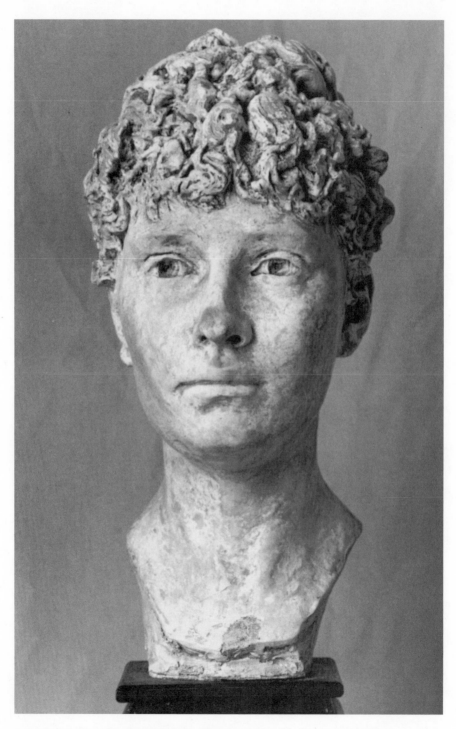

Jessie Lipscomb, *Bust of Camille Claudel*. Plaster, 1886. Private collection

Rodin to Camille was presented to the Musée Rodin by Mathias Morhardt. Their content proved to be sensitive, and René Chéruy became convinced that "out of discretion," the letters would never be published.[3] These letters disappeared from the museum, and a large envelope inscribed in Rodin's handwriting as "Cas Camille Claudel" was left empty. Curiously, some of the missing documents resurfaced a few years ago and are now back in the archives of the Musée Rodin.[4] The first document is an undated letter written by Rodin in a moment of distress after a serious quarrel with Camille. An outpouring of confused feelings, it begins with "Ma féroce amie" and tumbles down like a passionate torrent, omitting the periods, commas, and capital letters that would restrain it:

> My poor head is very sick, and I can't get up any more this morning. Last night, I wandered (for hours) in our favorite places without finding you, how sweet death would be and how long is my agony. Why didn't you wait for me at the atelier? Where are you going? To what suffering have I been destined? During moments of amnesia, I suffer less, but today the relentless pain remains. Camille my beloved in spite of everything, in spite of the madness which I feel impending and which will be your doing, if this continues. Why don't you believe me? I abandon my Salon and sculpture.[5] If I could go anywhere, to a country where I would forget, but there isn't any. Frankly, there are times when I believe I will forget you. But, in an instant, I feel your terrible power. Have pity, cruel girl. I can't go on, I can't spend another day without seeing you. Otherwise the atrocious madness. It is over, I don't work any more, malevolent goddess, and yet I love furiously.
>
> My Camille be assured that I feel love for no other woman, and that my soul belongs to you.
>
> I can't convince you and my arguments are powerless. You don't believe my suffering. I weep and you question it. I have not laughed in so long. I don't sing anymore everything is dull and indifferent to me. I am already a dead man and I don't understand the trouble I went through for things which are now indifferent to me. Let me see you every day; it will be a generous action and maybe I will get better, because you alone can save me through your kindness.

Don't let the slow and hideous disease overtake my intelligence, the burning and ever so pure love I feel for you, at last have mercy my darling and you will be rewarded.

Although Rodin signed the letter at this point, the flow of his emotion was not staunched. He picked up his pen again and added another page:

I kiss your hands, my love, you give me such exalted and ardent enjoyment, near you my soul lives intensely and in its passionate love my respect for you is always above everything, the respect I have for your character, for you my Camille is a cause of my violent passion. Do not treat me mercilessly I ask so little of you.

Don't threaten me and let me see you. Let your soft hand show your kindness for me and sometimes leave it there so that I can kiss it.

I don't regret anything neither the end which appears like a funeral. My life will have fallen into an abyss. But my soul has had its blossoming, late alas. I had to know you. And everything changed into an unknown life, my dull existence burned in a bonfire. Thank you because I owe everything to you, the part of heaven which I had in my life.

Your dear hands leave them on my face, that my flesh be happy that my heart feel again your divine love spreading over me again. I am intoxicated when I am near you. Near you, when I think that I still have this happiness and I complain. And in my cowardice I think that I am done with being unhappy, that I am at the end, no. As long as there is still some hope so little a drop I have to enjoy it at night later at night.

Your hand Camille not the one withdrawing, no happiness in touching it if in the future it does not promise a little tenderness.

Ah! divine beauty, flower who speaks and loves intelligent flower my darling. My dear one I am on my knees facing your beautiful body which I embrace.

"On my knees facing your beautiful body which I embrace," evokes *Éternelle Idole*, one of the *Gates of Hell* figures that Rodin would later reproduce in marble. This work was a revelation to many contemporaries, including the young writer Jules Renard, whose usual irony melted away in front of this piece: "A revelation, an enchantment, these *Gates of Hell*, this little thing, no bigger than my hand, which is called *Éternelle Idole*: a man, his arms behind his back, vanquished, kisses a woman beneath her breasts, glues his lips to her skin, and the woman looks so sad."[6] Camille may have inspired this melancholic woman, stretching above her vanquished lover and lost in her thoughts. She was both "the part of heaven" that came into Rodin's life and the "malevolent goddess" who tormented him with her unpredictable behavior. Confused, disoriented, and in constant need of seeing his rebellious muse, Rodin turned to Jessie for support. Thus started a series of notes and nostalgic letters addressed to "Ma chère Élève," which were barely hidden pretexts to have news of "Mademoiselle Camille."[7]

"Could you give me news of Mademoiselle Camille," he requested in a brief note. Then, like an afterthought: "I hope you are working hard. See you tomorrow." Early in 1886, a telegram reached Jessie: "You did not come last night and were not able to bring our dear stubborn one with you, we love her so much that she is the one who controls us. Thank you for the warm and delicate affection you have for her. I feel optimistic about her stay in England especially with you."[8]

It was Jessie's turn to welcome Camille in her home, and the two were planning a trip to England that would last the entire summer. They left for Peterborough toward the end of May 1886; Camille would not be back home until the middle of September. Coincidentally, Rodin had received an invitation from his friend and former student Gustave Natorp, who lived in London. He seized this opportunity to follow Camille and Jessie to England, and he left for London on May 29, planning to stay for a week. Delighted to hear about his projects, the Lipscombs invited him to Wootton House for a day or two. Rodin could not have been more thrilled. Barely arrived in London, he rushed to the Royal Academy, where Camille was exhibiting a bust that may have been *Giganti*, while Jessie exhibited a bust named *Day Dreams*. He immediately congratulated Jessie on her good work, a gracious gesture, considering that his own piece, *Idylle*, had been rejected by the Royal Academy for the same exhibition. But the rest of his letter reflected his anxiety about Camille: "You were kind enough to send your friendly greetings and also those of Mademoiselle Camille, maybe you were just being merciful; thanks in any case."[9] Camille was omnipresent in his mind.

Jessie Lipscomb, *Day Dreams.* Terra-cotta, 1886. Private collection

He could not help talking about her and about the sadness that plagued him:

> I ask you details about your walks together and if your time is not too precious and your little teacher allows it, you can tell me much.
>
> The sight of beautiful children and beautiful women (and beautiful trees) in the park have changed a little today the crushing sadness which I brought from Paris.
>
> It is cold in London, make sure that your little Parisian does not suffer from it and continue to be precious to her through your true friendship and your angelic kindness.[10]

Perhaps feeling a little guilty toward Rose, Rodin sent her a letter too, and arranged for her to visit their friends in the countryside. "How are you my Darling," he wrote, "I think of you and I am in peace because my work is in your hands. Don't wet it too much and feel with your fingers."[11]

As Rodin was making plans to visit Peterborough, the Lipscombs wrote that they were coming to London. Elated at the idea of having lunch with them, especially with Camille, Rodin told Jessie: "I assure you that London has no more fog for me. . . . All is celebration and all is bright in my mind." Yet he was nervous, wondering how Camille would welcome his unsolicited arrival in England, and he hoped that Jessie could smooth things out for him: "I expect everything from your kindness, to arrange all that could go astray, all that could be troublesome. I am so happy that I am afraid of everything."[12]

Rodin was finally forced to cancel his lunch with the Lipscombs, but he joined them on June 4 in Peterborough and stayed through the next morning. This brief visit did nothing to ease the tension between the lovers because, while the Lipscombs welcomed him warmly, Camille remained distant and spoiled his joy. Her behavior when Jessie sang a Scottish ballad seemed especially disturbing to Rodin: "The melody of your ballad," he wrote to Jessie the next day, "came fluttering around my poor head, the whole morning. At the very moment when I discovered you were a musician and I enjoyed hearing you sing, our dear princess had enough. I am wrong, but you saw what power she has over everyone who approaches her and over you too." Trying his newly acquired English, he signed: "God bay" in large letters.[13]

A short and mysterious letter belongs to the group sent from 70 Ennismore Gardens, Natorp's address. Like the others, it is addressed to Jessie: "Always plead my case although it is hopeless. If you get a 'yes' send me a telegram." It does not appear that Rodin got his desired "yes," because he left England soon afterward.[14] A letter from his friend the art critic Octave Mirbeau had called him back to Paris, where he was to participate in a special exhibition of painting and sculpture at the Georges Petit Gallery. With much regret, he turned down an invitation to return to Peterborough on June 13, and he crossed the Channel back to Paris without seeing Camille a second time.

Although Camille may have seemed to be acting like a spoiled adolescent, she was too focused on her artistic career to risk losing her teacher and mentor out of sheer capriciousness. In reality, she seems to have been motivated by a need to improve her increasingly difficult artistic and emotional circumstances.

No one knows exactly when Camille and Rodin became lovers, but by 1886 their relationship was at least a year old. Camille's parents were totally unaware of the romance that had developed between their daughter and her teacher. They assumed that Rodin was married to Rose Beuret and accordingly addressed them as man and wife. On one occasion, Madame Claudel sent a gracious invitation to Rodin and his "wife": "Could you come and join us for dinner tomorrow night, you would make us very happy. . . . Please present our compliments to Madame Rodin and allow us to cordially shake your hand." The invitation was repeated when Rodin claimed Rose was ill: "We are expecting your visit and Madame Rodin's, as soon as she is feeling better. We are all very happy to welcome you, everyone charges me to insist that you come; the day that suits you will suit us too, any day."[15] Thirty years later, Louise Claudel, still livid at the thought of this invitation, wrote tersely to Camille: "I, naive enough to invite the 'great man' to Villeneuve, with Madame Rodin, his concubine! And you, you and your sugary manners, were living with him like a kept woman."[16]

In her private life, Camille was risking more than Rodin, and she justly feared the consequences of discovery. In her professional life, doubt and frustration were surfacing. She gave much to Rodin: her energy, talent, even her beauty, since she posed for several portraits he made of her between 1884 and 1886. Her contribution as a model may also have extended to some of the nudes Rodin created during this period. In exchange, she expected his strong support in the art world for exhibitions, articles in newspapers, and introduction to possible buyers. Camille also expected his focused attention, without interference from the ever-present Rose, ever-familiar female models, and ever-soliciting students. She had proved earlier that her determination could prevail over her father's hesitations, and she put this same determination to work on Rodin.

The letters exchanged in England indicate that Rodin showed more concern for his assistant's success than she was willing to admit. In spite of all his engagements in London, Rodin found the time to serve as an intermediary between Camille and Gauchez, director of the magazine *l'Art*. Prompted by Rodin, Gauchez agreed to publish a drawing of the bust Camille had made of her brother Paul, along with a short article. As a reward, Rodin received one of the few letters Camille sent him that summer, a girlish note requesting her friend's enlightened help:

Camille with members of the Singer family in front of North Hill Cottage, Frome, England, 1886. John Webb Singer is surrounded by his wife, granddaughter, son, and daughter-in-law.

Monsieur Rodin,

I have started a note for Mr. Gauchez and I got completely tied up in it and it is certainly the most stupid thing in the world. Could you correct it please and write me a great tirade on the movement and research of nature, etc. I did not manage to pull it off. Return the corrected note as soon as possible otherwise Mr. Gauchez will be mad at me again.

Camille[17]

The difference of tone between Camille's carefree writing and Rodin's nostalgic letters to Jessie is striking. Camille was obviously not impressed with Rodin's efforts to earn her good will. She was enjoying herself in England, and she intended to keep her distance from the confusions of Paris.

In July Camille and Jessie left Peterborough to visit their studio partner Amy Singer in Frome, a picturesque town in Somerset, built on the steep hills of the riverbanks. The winding, cobbled streets took them to North

Hill Cottage, the home of the Singer family. Almost everyone in the Singer family was immersed in artistic pursuits, and Camille must have quickly felt at home in this environment. Amy's father, John Webb Singer, a watch- and clockmaker by trade, founded the Frome Art Metal Works and, later, the local statue foundry. Because he wanted his workers to be artists as well as craftsmen, he also founded the Frome Art School, where local youths received an education modeled after the South Kensington curriculum. Not surprisingly, John Webb Singer sent three of his four children to South Kensington. His two sons, intending to take over their father's business, became successful silversmiths, while Amy, his older daughter, chose to focus on sculpting.[18]

Camille, therefore, had the opportunity to learn much about the business aspect of her art, as Mr. Singer led her through his foundry and his school. But she especially enjoyed walking with Amy and Jessie along the river Frome or crossing the old bridge to join the long, winding streets beyond the Market Square. Other discoveries awaited her when the Singers decided to take their guests to the spa town of Bath, famous for its waters since Roman times, and to the busy port of Bristol.

When Jessie had to return to Peterborough, Camille chose to remain a little longer in Frome. On a rainy day, she wrote a playful letter to Jessie. "Today it is raining and I am in a bad mood, and so is Amy," she abruptly started. "Therefore we decided to write to you." Jessie had sent photographs of the trips they had taken together, so Camille requested the glass plate negatives to make duplicates. The unseasoned traveler was very proud of her recent adventures and wanted to impress her relatives with the souvenir photographs. After profusely thanking the Lipscombs for their hospitality, Camille mentioned the delicious jam pudding she had so often eaten in their home and humorously added: "I will always have a tear of regret when I think of the delicious roly-polys."[19] But sculpting was never far from her mind, and she was making plans to present one or two busts at the Nottingham exhibition in September.

Other exciting travels lay ahead, as Camille was soon to accompany the Lipscombs to the Isle of Wight. There they would visit their other partner, Emily Fawcett, and Florence Jeans, a friend of Jessie's. Their plans also included Paul Claudel, who had been invited to join them on the island. On August 12, the Lipscombs met Camille in Portsmouth and they all took a ferry to Shanklin, on the Isle of Wight. Camille spent nearly a month on the green and peaceful island, "in a small house at the bottom of a cliff, so close to the sea that strong tides sometimes wet the hedges of fuchsias in the garden."[20] She also developed a close friendship with Florence, whom she addressed with a joyful and familiar voice. It is interesting to note that, while Camille's letters to Florence started with "Chère Florence,"[21] Jessie was greeted with the more formal "Chère Miss Lipscomb." Oddly enough, the same formality affected her letters to Rodin. The few that survive open with "Monsieur Rodin," a greeting reflecting their difference in age, but also the unavoidable distance created by the constant necessity to repress signs of affection in public.

It was at Florence Jeans's house that Camille left a delightfully candid document which displayed much of her sardonic wit. It came out of one of those albums, common at the time, entitled "An Album of Confessions to Record Thoughts, Feelings, etc."[22] The flyleaf included a series of questions written in English and blanks to fill in. Although the album belonged to Florence, the answers were in French and in Camille's hand:

Your favourite virtue.
I *don't have any: they are all boring.*

Your favourite qualities in man.
To obey his wife

Your favourite qualities in woman.
To make her husband fret.

Your favourite occupation.
To do nothing.

Your chief characteristic.
Caprice and inconstancy.

Your idea of happiness.
To marry general Boulanger [a very popular minister of war].

Your idea of misery.
To be the mother of many children.

Your favourite colour and flower.
The most changing colour and the flower which does not change.

If not yourself, who would you be?
A hackney horse in Paris.

Where would you like to live?
In the heart of monsieur Wilson [son-in-law of French president Jules Grévy].

Your favourite prose authors.
Monsieur Pellerin author of the famous pictures [of Épinal].

Your favourite poets.
One who does not write verses.

Your favourite painters and composers.
Myself.

Your favourite heroes in real life.
Pranzini or Trupmann (choose).

Your favourite heroines in real life.
Louise Michel [one of the leaders of the French Commune].

Your favourite heroes in fiction.
Richard III.

Your favourite heroines in fiction.
Lady Macbeth.

Your favourite food and drink.
De la cuisine de Merlatti (love and fresh water).

Your favourite names.
Abdonide, Joséphyr, Alphée, Boulang [very unusual names].

Your pet aversion.
Maids, hackney drivers, and models.

What characters in history do you most dislike?
They are all disagreeable.

What is your present state of mind?
It is too difficult to tell.

For what faults have you most tolerance?
I tolerate all my faults but not at <u>all other people's.</u>

Your favourite motto.
A bird <u>in the hand</u> is worth two <u>in the bush.</u>
Camille Claudel 16 May 1888

Through these amusing answers emerges the portrait of an assertive woman who diverged completely from the meek Victorian ideal. Here, Camille obviously enjoyed poking fun at the standard bland questions found in this sort of album. It is therefore difficult to ascertain when her answers were serious and when they were merely facetious. The provocative choices of Richard III and Lady Macbeth as fictional heroes may simply confirm her admiration for ambitious and willful characters. But the choice of Louise Michel, one of the leaders of the Commune, as a real-life heroine, underlines her affinity with women who threw off the Victorian yoke. Louise Michel, also called "the Red Virgin," chose to dress like a soldier during the Commune and to fight with the men rather than spend her time in organized committees with other women. Educated and fearless, she could move entire crowds with her fiery speeches. Although Michel's far left political views did not match Camille's conservative political beliefs, her stand as an equal to the men around her was matched by Camille's sentiments.

Yet Camille was swayed like everyone else by the dashing but rather spineless General Boulanger, the new young minister of war, whose power of seduction would have been a real threat to the Republic had he been more like Richard III. Fortunately for the French people, he was not, and his popularity eventually waned as fast as it had arisen.

While Camille was enjoying the company of her British friends, Rodin was sinking into a depressed mood. Fearing that he had been forgotten, he confessed to Jessie: "I often look at my mailbox, sometimes I return suddenly from far away, from the countryside, from everywhere thinking about a letter from England. Don't let me be hurt like this by waiting too long and try to get your friend to be less lazy."[23] Yet, professionally, good news was not lacking. The show at the Georges Petit Gallery had been a huge success, and Rodin was reaping general applause. At last widely recognized for the great sculptor he truly was, he could share clippings of the glowing articles written about him. But Camille's behavior had made him so insecure that he feared her reactions to his good fortune: "I am afraid of having been pedantic when I sent you newspapers," he writes again to Jessie, "but it was not out of vanity. I thought I would acquire more of your esteem and friendship. Maybe it will be the reverse, and what I thought good will end in derision. I know that with a certain laugh *young women can singularly shrink success* and turn it into ridicule. Moreover, they are right."[24]

The master had fallen on the mercy of his students' whims. When Jessie announced the approaching trip to the Isle of Wight, Rodin begged:

"Try to arrange my coming for a few days. You know that I have great trust in the pleasure of these charming walks which give flora and gaiety to work in my atelier later in the winter."[25]

Although he was not invited to the Isle of Wight, Rodin could look forward to August 25, the date he believed Camille would return, and he offered his services as a guide:

> If it was possible that toward the twenty-fifth of the month I came and met you in Calais, you could go on a tour before going to Villeneuve, a nice tour to see cities of France or Belgium.
>
> I know that this depends upon your plans and upon Mademoiselle Camille's caprice. . . . Try to do what you can and I will, as usual, be most grateful. Yes do this and I will be happy especially that your teacher will be useful to you, even to our dear and great artist.[26]

This hope also fell through because Camille remained in England in order to present her *Giganti* at the Autumn Exhibition in Nottingham. After the exhibition, Camille rewarded Rodin's constancy with a friendly letter expressing concern for his health, but scolding him like a child:

> I am really sorry to hear you are sick again. I am sure that you have again eaten too much in your accursed dinners, with the accursed people I hate and who take your time and your health and return nothing.
>
> But I don't want to say anything because I know I am unable to protect you from the harm that I see. . . .
>
> You can believe that I am not very happy here; it seems that I am so far away from you! And that I am a complete stranger to you! There is always something missing tormenting me.[27]

Here again, Camille sounds more like Rodin's older sister than his much younger lover; and in spite of her claim that she was not very happy away from him, she seemed in no hurry to return home. There is no doubt that her love for Rodin was not rooted in passion. It sprang from her admiration for his genius and from her tendency to view him as a godlike figure who could open the doors of success for her.

Camille returned to France around the middle of September. Instead of being happy to be home, she lamented in a letter to Jessie: "I am constantly thinking about Shanklin, Frome, Peterborough, and you all. I cried during the whole return trip."[28] A nostalgic letter to Florence Jeans is even more revealing and proves that Camille could write very affectionate letters—the type of letters Rodin would have been so happy to receive during her long absence that summer:

> When you left on Saturday, I felt a horrible void, I saw you everywhere, on the beach, in your room, in the garden: impossible for me to get used to the idea that you had left. . . .
>
> I will never forget my beautiful days with you in Shanklin, they are certainly the most pleasant ones of my life. Look, I have tears in my eyes just to think about it. I am furious to be here, it is the end of happiness for a whole year.
>
> I hope that you will think of me, as we agreed, on the first of each month at 8 p.m. We will remember our little evening walk with the moon and the little boats so dark on the sea.[29]

When the first of October arrived, Camille hoped that "a beneficial magnetic current"[30] would lead them toward each other. Camille did not say a word about Rodin, either to Jessie or to Florence. Yet the war of nerves between the two lovers was about to end. On October 12, Rodin bowed to her wishes and offered her an astonishing contract:

> In the future and starting from today 12 October 1886, I will have for a student only Mademoiselle Camille Claudel and I will protect her alone through all the means I have at my disposal through my friends who will be hers especially through my influential friends.
>
> I will accept no other students so that no other rival talent could be produced by chance, although I suppose that one rarely meets artists as naturally gifted.
>
> At the exhibition, I will do everything I can for the placement and the newspapers.
>
> Under no pretext will I go to Mme. . . to whom I will not teach sculpture anymore. After the exhibition in May we will go to Italy and will live there communally for at least six months of an indissoluble

liaison after which Mademoiselle Camille will be my wife. I will be very happy to offer a marble figurine if Mademoiselle Camille wishes to accept it within four or five months.

From now to May I will have no other woman otherwise the conditions of this contract are broken.

If my Chilean commission comes through, we will go to Chile instead of Italy.

I will take none of the models I have known.

We will have a photograph taken by Carjat in the outfit worn by Mademoiselle Camille at the Académie, day clothes and possibly evening clothes.

Mademoiselle Camille will stay in Paris until May.

Mademoiselle Camille promises to welcome me to her atelier four times a month until May.

Rodin[31]

Although jumbled in its presentation, and mixing trivial concerns with serious ones, this contract addresses two different issues, a professional one and a private one. Professionally, it sets the foundations for a privileged association with the most important sculptor of the period: exclusive tutoring, introduction to influential people and possible buyers, help in the placement of Camille's works in exhibitions, assistance with newspaper reviews. Personally, it yields to Camille's bouts of jealousy regarding other students and former models. But, most of all, it clearly promises marriage— in writing—after a six-month trial period of communal living in Italy. Marriage with Rodin, which Rose had never managed in all her years with him, may have appeared to Camille as the only true sign of victory over her rival. Camille's persistence on this matter of marriage also suggests that her break with the moral values of the bourgeoisie was not complete and that she still viewed marriage as a social and emotional necessity.

We can only conjecture what Camille intended to do with this private contract. While the moral codes of the nineteenth century would have allowed her to use this document as a legal tool, there is no indication that she ever attempted to do so. For the moment, the informal contract seemed to soothe her need to be recognized both as an artist and as a woman by the man she loved, and by a society that controlled too much of her future.

CHAPTER 7 | **JESSIE'S LAST DAYS IN PARIS**

JESSIE'S CALM NATURE was seriously challenged during the crisis between Camille and Rodin. Much to her discomfort, she found herself caught between her art master and her studio partner and forced to act both as confidante and as emissary, since Rodin's letters to her usually included messages for Camille. In spite of the awkwardness of the situation, Jessie managed to please everyone for a while. Although Rodin was primarily focused on Camille, he appreciated Jessie's attempts to keep him informed, and he gave her one of his sculptures, a small group of two children, which Jessie treasured for the rest of her life. He also repeatedly thanked her with

Camille Claudel, photographed by Carjat, c. 1886

warm comments scattered throughout his letters. "I don't know how to show my appreciation for your kindness," he confessed. "You don't know how much good you bring to me." And again: "Your letter is alive for me, and beneath your discretion, I feel your compassion." As for Camille, her sojourn in England remained a constant source of enchanting memories, and she wrote to Jessie soon after arriving in Paris: "I never had so much fun in my life."[1]

Jessie must have breathed a sigh of relief when Rodin stopped inundating her with his letters. By October 1886, she could congratulate herself on the diplomatic skills that had allowed her to remain on friendly terms with both of the love adversaries. But so far as Jessie was concerned, the war of nerves between Camille and Rodin was overshadowed by a more important event when she became engaged to her childhood friend William Elborne. The engagement was celebrated on 13 June 1886, and Rodin sent a letter to Mr. and Mrs. Lipscomb, lamenting the fact that he could not join them: "I was looking forward to participating in the celebration next Sunday and to raise a toast to the happiness of your dear daughter, with all my heart joining in the love you feel for her and I would have liked to salute Monsieur Osborne [Elborne] and to thank him for his photograph."[2] Instead, Rodin reluctantly returned to Paris to prepare his show at the Georges Petit Gallery.

Jessie was, of course, disappointed by Rodin's absence, but this disappointment did not mar her happiness. William Elborne had been part of her life for so long that her engagement to him seemed completely natural in the course of events. As an only child, Jessie had found in the large Elborne family the brothers and sisters she had never had. She was particularly close to Mary Anne, also known as Polly, and to Elizabeth, also known as Lizzie; the two sisters and Jessie were about the same age. Besides Polly and Lizzie, William had three other sisters and two brothers, all but one born in the small village of Barkstone-le-Vale, near Grantham. Although the Elbornes belonged to the landed gentry, the family was somewhat impoverished and probably unable to provide large dowries. This might explain why out of eight children, only the two oldest married.

William was three years older than Jessie. In the photographs taken in Camille's studio, he has the appearance of the perfect Victorian gentleman, with a thick mustache, a well-tailored suit, a white vest, and a carnation in the buttonhole of his jacket. His serious pose seems out of place in the odd set-up of the studio, where Camille mockingly plays the queen bee among her brood. But William enjoyed the company of artists, and he liked to photograph them at work. Never traveling without his camera, he photographed his friends in their studio when he went to France at the beginning of 1886, and he surprised Jessie with an appreciative note written on the back of one print: "Miss Lipscomb goes in very strongly for art—This is a proof of her at work in her private studio in Paris."[3] When William returned to Paris the following year, he also photographed Rodin in his atelier. Occasionally Jessie would use William's camera and take a candid shot of her teacher. She was especially proud of Rodin's reflection in a mirror, which she had managed to capture at the right moment, and she wrote to him in September 1887: "Everyone loves your photograph in the mirror—only you look a little tired—that's all."[4]

In the summer of 1886, Rodin was particularly hungry for photographs that included Camille, and he repeatedly begged Jessie to send him the most recent ones: "You will forgive me for speaking so often of Monsieur Elborne and of the photographs," he wrote in August. "I know that Monsieur Elborne is a distinguished scholar who has a great future ahead of him, part of which has already been achieved. When I remind you of the prints he takes to please you and your friends, I don't intend to give too much importance to this favorite pastime."[5]

Ironically this favorite pastime was probably William's most important contribution to posterity. At the time, he had studied chemistry and pharmacy at Trinity College in Cambridge, but he had not yet earned an advanced degree. On the other hand, the photographs he took of Camille and Jessie in the studio at rue Notre-Dame des Champs are the only visual records left of their lives during this period and are therefore extremely valuable. One in particular, which shows Camille perched on a scaffolding at work on the large version of *Sakuntala* while Jessie finishes a smaller female figure, is a classic illustration of women's art and social history.[6]

It is difficult to assess whether William and Jessie intended to marry in the near future or whether they had knowingly embarked upon one of those long engagements that were then so common. Certainly William's professional status was far from being resolved, and Jessie did not show any intention of abandoning her art studies in Paris. On the contrary, she was very pleased with her recent successes at the Royal Academy in London and at the Midland Counties Art Museum in Nottingham, and she planned to present other pieces the next year.

In the year preceding her engagement, Jessie had exhibited her first sculpture at the Royal Academy: a terra-cotta *Portrait Study*, which was also shown in autumn in Nottingham. Two other terra-cotta busts, one of her father and one of her fiancé, were shown only in Nottingham. In 1886, Jessie exhibited a remarkable terra-cotta bust named *Day Dreams*, which received Rodin's praise when he viewed it at the Royal Academy. "I saw your bust which is well placed and deserves it," he wrote to her, underlining the compliment. It is again through Rodin's letters that we learn about the repeated success of *Day Dreams* at the Nottingham autumn exhibition: "I am proud that Mademoiselle Camille and you, Mademoiselle, had success in Nottingham," he commented.[7] Camille had indeed followed in Jessie's footsteps and showed her *Giganti* both in Nottingham and at the Royal Academy.

Day Dreams departs from Jessie's preceding works by its emotional expressivity. William's sister Polly was the model whose exquisite beauty inspired the artist to produce what may be her most stirring work. While a certain stiffness emanates from the more conventional busts of Jessie's father and of her fiancé, *Day Dreams*, on the contrary, reflects the intimate ties between the artist and her model. In this portrait, Polly's vulnerability is revealed through her pensive expression and the inclination of her head. With her eyes cast downward, she appears to be lost in a melancholy dream. The delicate modeling of her dress enhances the sensitive contour of her face, and she turns away from the viewer as if to retire within herself.

The year 1887 marked the last of Jessie's exhibitions. In Nottingham, she showed another terra-cotta piece inspired by Polly: a graceful statuette named *Sans Souci* (Without Worries) for the carefree feeling that emanates from it. She also exhibited a portrait study of Camille in plaster, *Mademoiselle Camille Claudel*, which she had made the previous summer when the artists worked on each other's busts. This portrait captures Camille's willful expression in a manner that recalls her earlier photograph by César. Finally, Jessie's third and last piece for 1887, the bust of *Giganti*, was shown both in Nottingham and at the Royal Academy. As for Jessie's unadorned portrait by Camille, it seems to have been left behind in Peterborough and was never

Jessie Lipscomb, *Giganti*.
Bronze, 1887. Private collection

Camille Claudel, *Giganti*. Bronze, c. 1886.
Museums of Cherbourg, Lille, and Reims

Jessie Lipscomb, *Sans Soucis*.
Plaster, 1887. Private collection

exhibited. Unlike Camille, Jessie does not appear to have exhibited in France. She was, above all, a portraitist in the Victorian tradition, and her work appealed especially to the British public. She never ventured into large-scale works, and she avoided imaginary subjects or allegorical interpretations, all of which appealed to the French public.

After her long diplomatic summer, Jessie made plans to return to Paris in January 1887 to resume her classes with Rodin. However, Mr. Claudel's job transfer to Compiègne and the ensuing upheaval it created when his family helped him move, forced Jessie to delay her arrival until the middle of February. At that point, she was welcomed to the Claudels' home by a rather unenthusiastic Camille, who had accumulated a number of grudges against her. Camille's first signs of annoyance appeared in the letters she had sent to her friend Florence Jeans in December: "I have little news of the Lipscombs and never things that are easy to understand in the

Jessie Lipscomb, *Woman Stretching*.
Plaster, 1886. Private collection

letters Jessie sends me, I assure you." By the time Jessie announced her arrival, Camille's irritation had reached new dimensions:

> Jessie arrives on Tuesday evening. I think she must have bought many dresses this year because she asked for a large reduction in the fees of my atelier. You surprise me when you say their house is for rent: What! this dear Wootton House!
>
> Jessie will be a lodger in our house and will work with me all day long. I hope like you that she won't leave her memory in Manchester and again tell me imaginary things.[8]

There is no doubt that Camille was angry with Jessie's request for a reduction in studio fees, and this prompted her natural sarcasm. Yet, the news that Wootton House was for rent raises the possibility of financial setbacks in the Lipscomb family, which would have forced Jessie to be more careful with her own finances. In a previous letter, Jessie had voiced her concerns over what she viewed as an inflated bill for the casting of a bust, and Camille, who disagreed, had lashed out at her with an overblown and sarcastic offer.

> But, my dear, I am very happy that you wish for me to pay something for you! What happiness if my money can be useful to you! I will therefore pay the bill for the casting of this bust, and the one for baking this same bust and some studies of yours. Also, if you don't mind, I will send to Peterborough your *Narcisse*, your studies, and the busts because I don't have much room in my atelier and you will allow me as well to pay for the shipping, won't you? Since all of this concerns me. You talk to me of 16 shillings, which I can't possibly remember, but undoubtedly I owe them to you; tell me if I can send them right away?
>
> All I am asking is for your parents to cease to be angry with you because you pay for what you owe. And I would love my money if it could save you trouble. It is so little for me: all I have to do is to stop taking [my model] Jasmina for this month, and all will be done.[9]

In spite of these differences, Jessie settled in Paris and looked forward to joining her friend Emily Fawcett as they resumed their lessons with Rodin. Unaware of the October "contract" agreed upon between Camille and Rodin, the two women were dumbfounded by Rodin's aloofness. In a letter dated 15 March 1887, Jessie very directly expressed her frustrations to him:

> Dear Monsieur Rodin,
>
> We intend to go and work in your atelier next Saturday—if this does not bother you. You know I come to tell you honestly that we came especially from England in order to receive your advice, and that you promised to give it to us. We don't care to stay with Miss Claudel if it annoys you, and the disagreements you have with her do not concern us. I hope we will have your lessons as in the past and we are ready to do what you wish. Tell us honestly what you intend to do

with us so that we know whether to stay here in Paris or return to England. Would you please, dear Sir, give us an answer as soon as possible.

Yours truly,

Your student, Jessie Lipscomb[10]

Rodin reacted with indifference to Jessie's scolding but with his usual concern for Camille: "Yes if it pleases Mademoiselle Claudel, come on Saturday, the whole day (and Mademoiselle Fawcett too). Most of all, I pray you <u>to give me her news by return mail</u>, which you did not do." Scribbled above "her news by return mail" were the words "and yours too," but this can't have fooled Jessie.[11] Once more, Rodin was attaching a special price to his lessons: Jessie was again to act as emissary. Unfortunately, she had become sick of it, and this would further strain her relationship with Camille.

Nevertheless, Jessie remained in Paris for about three months, and William joined her for a week in April. Although Camille remarked that "since his arrival, Jessie has been in a constant fret and lets no one rest for a moment," she enjoyed William's visit and described it to Florence:

We recently went for a very pleasant excursion to Versailles with Jessie, William, and Mr. Rodin. First we visited the palaces and the gardens, then we walked through the woods to a very picturesque village where we dined at seven p.m. From there, we came back with the help of the stars and the moon, still in the woods, and we took the train two kilometers away. It was a lot of fun, but how tired Will was![12]

These temporary good feelings did not last. Two months later, Camille wrote to Florence that she had had a falling out with Jessie and that their relationship was "broken forever." In Camille's view, Jessie was obviously all wrong, and she lamented: "During her last stay in Paris, she had the most shameful conduct toward me, I could not give you all the details because it would take too long; suffice it to say that before her departure I had it out with her and I told her I would not receive her in my atelier in the future."[13]

Later, yielding to Florence's curiosity, Camille gave her a more elaborate explanation:

For reasons unclear to me, she demonstrated a constant hostility toward me which she expressed through gross indelicacies. With her confused and indiscreet character, she caused me constant trouble and hurt me in my interests and my friendships. If I told you that she gave sculpting lessons during the three months she was in Paris, you would be surprised, wouldn't you? Well! I was as surprised as you are when I learned it two days before her departure, and even more so when I was told that <u>her students!!!</u> were British women who came to my studio with the intention of joining in, and that she told them she could give lessons just as well as Mr. Rodin and for a lower price, and that I asked too much for my studio.[14]

Unfortunately, Jessie's version of the dispute did not survive. Camille burned much of her personal correspondence during this period, and consequently both Jessie's and Florence's letters vanished. "Don't fear anything for your letters," she wrote to Florence in February. "They are burnt one by one and I hope you do the same with mine."[15] One may wonder whether Camille's first signs of paranoia came to the fore at this time, or whether Jessie really gave her cause for anger. But, in spite of what Camille said of her "indiscreet character," Jessie kept her grievances to herself.

Everything from Jessie's request for a lower rent to the necessity of her earning a living indicates that she was running out of money. Her fight with Camille could not have been more poorly timed. Because of it, she had lost Rodin's protection and Camille's atelier, and her career had reached an impasse. She therefore returned to England with a heavy heart and remained silent for some time. Finally, a letter written from New Barnet and dated 15 September 1887, reached Rodin:

Dear Monsieur Rodin,

I have been exceedingly sick since July—and even now I am not very strong—I regret, dear Sir, that you did not receive the photographs sooner—but I was forbidden to do a single thing.

You will see that the large photographs are not absolutely clear—but it was my mistake when I made the exposures in your atelier—the others are much better, don't you think? Everyone loves your photograph in the mirror—only you look a little tired—that's all.

You can put all the photographs you have in the same album—
with a little glue.

And now my dear teacher—I have news for you—I am soon
to be married to Mr. Elborne—in December I think—And you know
how happy we will be to see you one day in our home in Manchester.
You will always be welcome as a friend.

Affectionately yours.

Your student, Jessie Lipscomb[16]

Jessie had made her choice. Although she may still have harbored the
dream of continuing with her sculpting after William's career was launched,
she knew that motherhood did not go hand-in-hand with artistic pursuits. At
this point, however, she valued marriage and motherhood more than sculpting, and there is no reason to believe that she ever regretted her choice. "I
wish you much happiness," Rodin wrote back to Jessie, "because all of life
is here in the man or the woman we love."[17] A rather curious remark in view
of Rodin's own tangled relationships.

Jessie also sent an announcement and several photographs to the
Claudels. It was Camille's mother who wrote back to thank her and to send
wishes of happiness to the future couple: "You will, both Mr. Elborne and
you, be much happier than to be separated for such long periods."[18] Madame
Claudel could relate to separation, since her own husband was still living
away from home and came to visit the family only on Sundays.

Jessie Lipscomb married William Elborne on 26 December 1887 at
Great Saint Helen's Church, Bishopsgate, in London. Jessie's father
was listed as "colliery agent" and William's father as "gentleman." William was
already living in Manchester, where he held the position of lecturer at
Owen's College, so Manchester became Jessie's home for a while. But Jessie
did not forget Rodin and, after her marriage, she sent him a piece of the
wedding cake. As the years passed, she kept in touch with him, writing him
occasional letters to announce the birth of her children and other important
events and sometimes mentioning Camille with kindly words. But Camille
had turned her back on Jessie; she focused all her attention on two subjects:
her art and Rodin.

THE LATE 1880s proved to be years of change, hope, and productivity for Camille. Appeased by Rodin's promises, she behaved more supportively toward him and allowed temporary compromises into their relationship. In some ways, Rodin's family circumstances were more complicated than hers, owing to the presence of Rose and their son, Auguste. Only close friends of Rodin's, such as the writer Octave Mirbeau, got to meet either Rose or Auguste, and their comments were short but rather alarming: "He has a son," said Mirbeau, "a strange son, with an extraordinary eye and a murderer's head, who never says a word and spends his whole life in the fortifications, drawing *soldiers' backs*, backs where his father sometimes finds genius. . . . This son, we only get to see him at supper, then he disappears."[1] Auguste joined the army in 1886 and disappeared completely for many years. But Rose stayed, faithful as ever, still unaware of what was going on. "A little washerwoman," as Mirbeau mockingly described her, "not in the least able to communicate with [Rodin] and left in complete ignorance of what he does."[2] With Camille, on the other hand, Rodin had found "the happiness of being always understood, of being exceeded in his expectations. It was one of the great joys of his artistic life."[3]

Not surprisingly, Camille inspired some of the masterpieces Rodin produced during these happy years. In 1884 he completed two small busts of Camille, including one with a Phrygian cap. He kept these for himself, but he created new ones, which he turned into *L'Aurore* (Dawn), and *La Pensée* (Thought). *La Pensée*, Camille's best-known portrait by Rodin, freezes her in time and place. It is a disquieting piece where the mind—unlike *The Thinker*—is cut off from the body. Camille's chin is still partially immersed in the block of marble, and a peasant bridal cap hides her hair. Only the large contemplating eyes and the expressionless mouth remain exposed. But

Camille and Jessie sculpting in the Notre-Dame des Champs atelier, 1886. Camille is
working on *Sakuntala*, and Jessie is working on *Woman Stretching*

Camille Claudel, *Vertumne et Pomone*. Marble version of *Sakuntala*, 1905. Musée Rodin, Paris

Camille's body is said to be more visible in another work, the beautiful nude *La Danaïde*, for which she may have posed in moments of privacy.[4] And it is her spirit and the passionate feelings she inspired in Rodin that animate *The Kiss* (or *Paolo and Francesca)* and *Éernelle Idole*.

Thus Camille was the muse and the artist companion of Rodin's dreams. She was also a moving echo of his own past. With her, Rodin had found again the tough but supportive partner of his youth, his beloved sister Maria, who died at only twenty-four. Camille had the same determination, the same strength of character, and the same understanding of Rodin's genius. He could not bring himself to give her up any more than he could face the idea of abandoning Rose. He therefore left things as they were and turned his attention toward the other promises he had written out in October.

The easiest one, the photograph by Carjat (see page 73), was soon undertaken, and Camille's loveliness, enhanced by an elegant costume, was recorded for posterity by the famous photographer. Rodin used this opportunity to have his own portrait done, later sending a signed print to his "student Miss Lipscomb" back in Peterborough.

Professionally, Rodin proved to be very helpful to his assistant, and his timely words to his friends of the Parisian magazine *L'Art* brought

Auguste Rodin, *Éternelle Idole.* Marble, 1889. Musée Rodin, Paris

encouraging results: critic Paul Leroi wrote an article praising Camille for the bust of her sister, Louise, and for her charcoal drawings. Leroi's article was illustrated by three of her drawings: two portraits of women from the Vosges mountains and a nude study. Eventually, Paul Leroi became one of Camille's admirers, but he warned her from the beginning against Rodin's powerful influence. "We only need to express, in the case of Mademoiselle Claudel, a reserve inspired by an interest for her future," he wrote. "Monsieur Rodin is such a powerful personality, his mastery of such a superior order, that one must beware of being absorbed by his fascinating influence; in a word, the young artist must be Mademoiselle Claudel exclusively, not just a reflection."[5]

One year later, Leroi supported Camille wholeheartedly, when he viewed her latest piece at the Salon—the bust of Paul at eighteen. Satisfied that Camille was following her own voice, Leroi called her an "inspired young woman who is passionate about her work and who imparts so much character to everything she undertakes."[6] Included in his article were four of the charcoal drawings done by Camille when she was in England: three studies of old women and the portrait of Dr. Jeans, Florence's father.

Coming from the hands of such a respected art critic as Paul Leroi, these praises must have bolstered Camille's confidence in her own work. At the time, she had given herself the challenge of creating her first large-scale sculpture, and she needed all the confidence she could muster. Her animated letters to Florence Jeans often refer to the intense schedule she kept after her return from England, and she wrote in November 1886:

> I am now working on my two large figures larger than life-size and I have two models each day: a woman in the morning and a man in the evening. You can imagine how tired I am; I regularly work twelve hours a day, from 7 a.m. to 7 p.m., and when I come back I can hardly stand on my feet and I go to bed right away. I have all sorts of problems and I feel discouraged and I often think of the Shanklin walks.[7]

She worked steadily on this group all through the next year until an unforeseeable event gave her much anxiety: "I have had the problem of seeing my male model go to Italy and . . . stay there," she lamented to Florence on Christmas Day. "I am therefore obliged to make many changes which are long and costly."[8] Camille knew this model well because she had completed several pieces with him, including *Giganti*. Replacing him can't have been easy. Fortunately, Jasmina, the female model, did not cause any problems, at least for the moment.

The plaster of this group was finished in time for the 1888 Salon and was so successful that it won an honorable mention. Camille gave it the name of the heroine of a fifth-century Hindu drama, *Sakuntala*.[9] This drama had recently been adapted as a ballet in France, and Camille may have had the opportunity to see it. It tells the legend of King Duchmanta, who fell in love with Sakuntala, a Brahmin girl, and gave her a wedding ring. When a curse wiped out the king's memory, Sakuntala was not recognized as his wife and was forced to hide in the forest, where she bore a child. Only the ring could have restored the king's memory, but it had been lost in the lake. Years later, a fisherman found it and the lovers were reunited. Camille chose the moment of reunion when the king, on his knees, with his head lifted toward Sakuntala, receives the graceful woman who abandons herself to his caress. His left arm encircles his beloved while his right arm supports her, for she appears to be almost fainting under the force of her emotion. The eroticism of the naked bodies reaching out to each other is transcended by the delicately modest posture of the woman, whose hand hides her breast while her head rests upon her husband's forehead.

The critic André Michel appropriately noted "a profound feeling of tenderness both chaste and passionate, an impression of quivering, of restrained ardor. . . ."[10] Many critics were unsparing in their praise of *Sakuntala*; Paul Leroi called it "the most extraordinary new work in the Salon" and found it "a remarkable achievement that such a young woman was able to conceive and create so successfully a group of this importance."[11]

Paul Leroi's readiness to acknowledge Camille's original talent did not necessarily represent a general point of view. More and more, Camille would be confronted with the harsh reality of being branded as Rodin's pupil. In her work, many would look for Rodin's influence rather than for the originality of her interpretation. *Sakuntala* was often compared to *The Kiss*, which angered Camille's brother, Paul, to no end, for he viewed his sister's work as immensely superior to Rodin's: "In the first," he said, referring to *The Kiss*, "the man is, so to speak, seated to dine at the woman. He sits down to better enjoy her. He uses both hands, and she does her best, as they say in American English, to *deliver the goods*. In my sister's group, the spiritual is everything, the man on his knees is pure desire; his face lifted, he embraces this marvelous being, this sacred flesh given to him from above, before he even dares to seize it. . . . It is impossible to see anything at the same time more passionate and more chaste."[12]

Sakuntala seems to be closer to *Éternelle Idole,* where the man, on his knees, is facing the woman. But the feeling conveyed in Rodin's work is one of imbalance resulting from the man's passionate gesture and the woman's melancholic distance. Not so with Camille's group. *Sakuntala* is a careful blend of the sensual and the emotional, as well as a careful balance of the masculine and the feminine: even though the man is on his knees, he supports his overwhelmed companion.

The legend of Sakuntala attracted Camille for personal as well as artistic reasons. The young artist could certainly relate to the innocent Sakuntala, who trusted the king and was left in a difficult position. Like Sakuntala, Camille was forced to hide one aspect of her life and to hope that she would eventually be recognized. The year 1887 had not been an easy one. Camille's letters to Florence Jeans indicate that the long working hours had taken their toll, and at times she appeared drained both physically and mentally. Although the agreement with Rodin placed May as the date for their "indissoluble liaison," this deadline went by unnoticed: Rodin's Chilean commission fell through, and the promised trip to Italy did not materialize. Consequently, the issue of marriage was also postponed. It is therefore not surprising that Jessie found Camille in an especially sensitive mood and ready for a fight when May came.

After Jessie's departure, instead of going to Italy with Rodin, Camille resumed her Paris routine of hard work interrupted by a dull summer break in Compiègne, her father's new abode (he had been transferred again). Nothing exciting seemed to be happening, so Camille was truly delighted to accept Florence's invitation to join her on the Isle of Wight in September. Two weeks later, Camille abruptly canceled the trip, claiming financial difficulties. Although she professed to be quite distressed by this turn of events, in reality her cancellation was the result of an unexpected opportunity to spend a week or two alone with Rodin in the Loire Valley. Possibly feeling guilty about the cancelled trip to Italy, Rodin tried to make it up to Camille with a few days of peace at the château of Islette in Azay-le-Rideau, where he let several rooms. It was the two artists' first interlude in this idyllic refuge, but not the last, for they came back in subsequent years, sometimes separately. Camille sent to Rodin one of her few surviving letters from this romantic hideaway. Like the others, it bears no date:

Monsieur Rodin,

Since I have nothing to do, I am writing to you again. You can't imagine how good life is at Islette.

Today I ate in the large middle room (which is used as a conservatory), where you can see the garden on both sides. Madame Courcelles suggested (without my saying anything) that, if you wished, you could eat there once in a while and even all the time (I think she would really like it) and it is so pretty there!

I walked about the park. Everything has been cut, hay, wheat, oats. One can stroll around everywhere. It is charming. If you are nice, and keep your promise, we will be in paradise.

You will have the room you want to work in. The old woman will be at your feet, I think.

She told me I could bathe in the river, where her daughter and the maid bathe without any danger.

With your permission, I will do the same because it is great fun and it will spare me the trouble of going to the hot baths in Azay. Would you be so kind to buy me a little bathing costume dark blue with white trimming, in two pieces, blouse and pantaloons (medium size) at the Louvre or Bon Marché or in Tours?

I sleep completely naked to make me believe you are here, but when I wake up it is not the same thing.

Many kisses.

Camille

Most of all, don't deceive me with other women any more.[13]

This letter indicates a definite shift in their relationship. Only a few months earlier, Rodin had played the desperate pursuer and Camille the elusive partner; but after the "contract," the tables were turned, and Camille became the one who had to wait. The impatient and strong-willed woman had placed her fate in the hands of her lover, and she was learning the subtleties practiced by dependent women. "If you are nice, and keep your promise, we will be in paradise," she reminds him. Surprisingly submissive, she asks his permission to go swimming. Then, in a tentative gesture toward communal living, she wonders if he could buy her one of those bathing costumes that had become the rage in Paris. At Islette Rose was far away, and Camille could maintain the illusion that Rodin was hers or would soon be hers alone. But the illusion was not so easy to sustain, and the small voice of vulnerability crept into the postscript in an appeal for sexual honesty.

In October, back in Paris, a disenchanted Camille sent an unusually brief note to her British friend:

> Dear Florence,
>
> I have been back in Paris for two weeks. Nothing new. Life is still bitter.
>
> Affectionate kisses.
>
> Camille[14]

Camille seemed to turn to Florence during the late 1880s, whenever something went wrong. Her liaison with Rodin cut her off from women her own age, and she had no close female friends in Paris. On the other hand, Florence was far enough away to ensure that she would remain ignorant of Camille's private life. She was also too discreet to ask why "life was still bitter."

Camille's trip to Islette proved to be no more than a brief escape. Yet it had disastrous repercussions on her relationship with her family, for the Claudels—or at least Paul—seem to have discovered the truth at this time. The upheaval caused by this revelation forced Camille to move out of the family apartment at 31, boulevard de Port-Royal and to rent a place at 113, boulevard d'Italie, on the southeastern edge of the city. On the first day of January 1888, Rodin paid Camille's annual rent.[15]

Paul's emotion can be appraised by the remains of a play he wrote in 1888. Although he destroyed it to spare his parents, he later published part of it as *Fragment d'un drame*. The lead character is a fallen woman, a carnal sinner, a betrayer, one who must be left behind by those who loved her. "I allowed excess against my body," she confesses. "I committed a crime that excludes forgiveness . . . a man lay over me." Her brother turns his back to her: "I break away from you, sister whom I called impious in the past!" Her husband (or her fiancé) leaves her: "Adieu! Thus we must part, and I never to return . . . and you! What long, painful and underground roads shall we take? Upon what path shall I meet you again?"[16]

Camille was already "impious" in the eyes of her young brother who, at eighteen, had converted to Catholicism on Christmas day in 1886. His conversion had been sudden and, like so many religious conversions, it was total. Since then, "all the books, all the arguments, all the fortunes of a busy life," he wrote, "were unable to shake my faith or, to tell the truth, touch it."[17] Although his conversion was powerful and final, Paul kept it a secret for five years. He did not dare confront his "pagan" family, especially the domineering Camille, who had brought Renan's blasphemous *Life of Jesus* into the Claudel household, exclaiming: "All we learned in matters of religion is a joke; here is the proof!"[18] Paul himself had revered Renan until his conversion, and he shuddered at the mere thought of this reverence. Camille's agnosticism pained him all the more because he loved his impossible sister. But in recent years, the paths they had taken drove them further and further apart. Camille's artistic pursuits, her budding success, left the younger sibling behind. He felt lonely and cast aside. Camille's affair with Rodin was therefore a catastrophe for Paul, who took it as a complete betrayal. It sparked in him a profound hatred for Rodin and a permanent mistrust of his sister's conduct. The same can be said of the reactions of Madame Claudel and of her younger daughter, who dreaded the possibility of scandal and never forgave Camille.

Work and emotional drama took their toll on Camille, so she needed to escape for a while. In March 1888, she wrote to Florence a curious letter that raised many questions in the mind of the reader. The letter was mailed from a hotel in Southampton, England, where Camille claimed she was staying "all alone, with [her] box of colors, like a boy." She had spent two days in Shanklin, on the Isle of Wight, she said, and was heading for Brighton, after which she would return to France via Belgium. She knew that Florence was not in Shanklin at this time of year, but she undertook the trip anyway. "Presently it was absolutely necessary for me to leave," she confided, "because I was tired and discouraged, otherwise I would have waited for the warm days."[19]

Given Rodin's ties with Belgium and England, it is probable that he

Auguste Rodin, *L'Aurore*. Marble, 1885.
Musée Rodin, Paris

Auguste Rodin, *La Pensée*. Marble, 1893–95.
Musée Rodin, Paris

accompanied Camille, if not to Shanklin, where she was too well known, then for the rest of the trip. Camille's move out of her family apartment had freed her from the constraints of the past, and the two were able to travel together more often.

In Paris they could see each other daily in the fascinating new atelier Rodin had discovered at 68, boulevard d'Italie, a few feet away from Camille's residence and a long distance from the apartment he shared with Rose on rue de Bourgogne. It was an eighteenth-century mansion, hidden by the overgrown vegetation of a dilapidated property. Named Folie Payen after the land surrounding it, or Folie Le Prestre, after its first owner Le Prestre de Neufbourg, the crumbling residence presented a facade richly decorated with six columns supporting a terrace. Statues of Pomona, Flora, and other garden goddesses nestling in wall recesses earned it the nickname of "château des bergères"—the castle of the shepherdesses. Partially in ruins, it still offered usable rooms on the ground floor. Mysterious and romantic, it was said to have sheltered the poet Alfred de Musset's rendez-vous with George Sand.[20] This eighteenth-century wreck of a building became

Rodin's favorite atelier and the place where he and Camille could meet away from inquisitive eyes. He kept it for ten years and managed to rescue broken pieces of its sculptured walls when crews came later to demolish the beloved old residence.

Soon after the 1888 Salon, Camille started working on two new sculptures: a group of waltzers and a bust of Charles Lhermitte, child of the painter Léon Lhermitte. The waltzers were still barely more than a rough shape, but the bust would be ready in time for the Salon to be held at the 1889 Universal Exhibition. Although a more modest achievement than *Sakuntala*, the bust was well received by the critics, and we can read in *La Gazette des Beaux-Arts:* "A little boy's head, by Camille Claudel, has the most exquisite delicacy, a charming softness, a breath of childlike innocence. Nature has been caught truthfully and interpreted with love."[21]

For his part, Rodin was working ceaselessly in the hope of showing his *Gates of Hell* at the Universal Exhibition. As the time came nearer, Rodin realized he would not meet his deadline, so he accepted Monet's proposal for a major retrospective of both their works at the Georges Petit Gallery in June. Rodin and Monet were good friends, and Monet was enthusiastic about the retrospective. Rodin, probably disappointed by his inability to finish the *Gates*, dragged his feet and proved rather uncooperative. Goncourt commented in his *Journal* that "terrible scenes took place in which gentle Rodin, suddenly showing a Rodin unknown to his friends, shouted 'I don't give a damn about Monet, I don't give a damn about anyone, I only care about myself.'"[22] But the show was a huge success for both men, and the public was able to admire for the first time 145 paintings by Monet and 36 sculptures by Rodin, including the final version of *The Burghers of Calais*.

Exhausted after the retrospective, Rodin decided he needed a vacation. As usual, he left Paris without telling any of his friends where he was going, and chances are that Rose was not told either. Artists who knew him joked about it. "Rodin, the sculptor, sometimes disappears for days and no one knows where he goes," wrote Goncourt, "and when he returns and is asked where he went, he says 'I just saw cathedrals.'"[23]

In this case, he was planning not to see cathedrals but to go to Spain, stopping in southern France along the way. On August 9, after he had been traveling for three weeks, he sent a brief note to Rose from Toulouse advising her to stay a little longer at the home of their friend Dr. Vivier, where

La Folie Le Prestre in 1901. This atelier was shared by Claudel and Rodin from the late 1880s to the early 1890s.

Rodin often sent Rose when he wanted to have peace in his household.[24] The preceding day, another letter was mailed from Toulouse, but this one was not from Rodin. It had been sent by Camille to her friend Florence. Although Camille appeared very happy with her discovery of the Pyrenees and Spain, she had some explaining to do because, earlier, she had turned down an invitation to England on the pretext that the trip would be too expensive. So, once again, to hide the fact that she was traveling with Rodin, Camille made up a plausible story. This time, she said she was serving as a sort of art governess to a British family and that she was accompanying them on their journey.[25]

After stopping in Toulouse, Camille and Rodin returned to Paris via the Auvergne and Switzerland. Their trip had lasted two months. During their absence, many people came to call on Rodin, among whom may have been Mrs. Jessie Elborne, who traveled to Paris with her husband to view the International Exhibition. "Remember me to Mademoiselle Camille and tell her we have a little girl," Jessie had written to Rodin earlier in January. "She is nine weeks old, and she is very pretty—with her dark blue eyes." Jessie was now living in Manchester, where she sometimes gave private art lessons. Her letters to Rodin were short but always full of nostalgia for the happy days she had lived in Paris.

WHEN JESSIE ELBORNE crossed the Channel in 1889 to visit the Universal Exhibition in Paris, she joined millions of tourists who had come from as far away as China to participate in the festivities. Conceived to commemorate the centennial of the French Revolution, the exhibition exploded into a huge celebration luring dazzled visitors to its endless displays. People marveled at the replicas of African bazaars and villages, cheered at the live performances of Asian theater and dance, and wallowed in the unfamiliar musical sounds, pungent smells, and shimmering colors of the exhibition. Edmond de Goncourt, smitten like everyone else by the festivities, described in his *Journal* the huge crowds, the countless footsteps creating the effect of rushing water, the excitement of women, and "the Place de la Concorde, an apotheosis of white light in the middle of which the obelisk appeared with the rosy color of a champagne sorbet—the Eiffel Tower looking like a beacon left behind by a vanished generation, a generation of men ten cubits tall."[1]

Everyone gawked at Eiffel's new creation, but conservative Parisians were outraged by what they viewed as a metal horror three hundred meters high. "Paris is now stabbed by this iron blade," wrote an angry journalist who rejoiced that the tower could not be seen from the Pont des Arts. Alas! It could be seen at every street corner in the form of souvenirs, bottles, nougats, or handkerchiefs. It was a "nouveau-riche" takeover that "crushed the old aristocracy of genius."[2] Yet the same prophets of doom did not seem to mind the alluring twenty-foot plaster siren who welcomed them at the main gate. With her hourglass shape and her fashionable clothes, she struck every Frenchman as the quintessential *fin de siècle Parisienne*.

The few pieces Rodin presented at the Universal Exhibition were viewed as an extension of his major retrospective with Monet, and many visitors headed for the Georges Petit Gallery to admire the works by Rodin and Monet on display there. Unquestionably, this retrospective marked the beginning of fame for both.

As for Camille, her bust of Charles Lhermitte was noticed by only a few critics. In spite of its charm, it was a more modest undertaking than *Sakuntala*, and was meant as a gift to her friend Léon Lhermitte, a painter and the model's father. For months, Camille's attention had been focused on other pieces that remained unfinished by the time of the exhibition, and she intended to resume her spartan schedule in September, after returning from her journey with Rodin. In fact, her most urgent project was due as early as October and held a special significance, since it was her first commission. "My countrymen have commissioned a bust of the Republic," she wrote to Florence in August, "It will be placed on the fountain of my native town and I have to deliver it on the first of October."[3] The idea had come from Étienne Moreau-Nélaton, a historian from Fère, the village where Camille had been born. The centennial was the appropriate time to honor the Republic, he thought, and what better way to do it than to invite Fère's most gifted child to execute the bust of "a woman of the people" who, traditionally, symbolizes the Republic? But Étienne Moreau-Nélaton did not take into account the conservative tendencies of his village. The audacity of his proposal—a commission offered to a woman—stunned the City Council members, who quickly rejected the project.[4]

Camille did not seem overly disappointed by this turn of events. Happy and rested after her long vacation, she eagerly returned to her atelier on the boulevard d'Italie and to two unfinished sculptures: a group of waltzers and a bust of Rodin. Although she never mentioned Rodin in her letters to Florence, Camille had been working on his bust since 1888, and she was experiencing a great deal of frustration because Rodin could never rest long enough to pose as a model. Hence, her work had to be abandoned and resumed several times. The clay dried and the piece started to fall apart. It was saved at the last minute when a fresh mold was taken from the original.[5] Camille was then able to finish the bust, which was cast into bronze at Rodin's expense and exhibited at the 1892 Salon.

As far as Rodin was concerned, this piece was "the finest sculptured head since Donatello,"[6] and he wanted to secure a good place for it in the Salon. His determination created a comical dance with the Minister of Fine

Camille Claudel,
*Bust of Auguste
Rodin.* Bronze,
1892. Musée
Rodin, Paris

Arts who, fortunately, was his friend. When Rodin first viewed his bust before the opening of the Salon, he did not like its placement and asked that it be moved. Alas, the new location proved to be even worse, and Rodin, embarrassed, asked to have it returned to its original spot. "If it had been one of my works, I would not have gone back on this matter," he tried to explain, "but it is my duty to defend the interests of a young artist whose real talent rightly deserves the greatest solicitude."[7] Rodin had no need to fret, for Camille's piece was extremely well received by the critics. Yet not everyone agreed, and this time, Camille lost the support of Paul Leroi, who objected to the Rodinesque manner of the execution. "Her *Bust of the Sculptor Rodin* would justify more eloquent praise if she had not determined, to my great chagrin, to pastiche her master instead of being herself."[8] But Paul Leroi missed the point. In creating a Rodinesque bust of Rodin, Camille was, in fact, honoring her master and offering him a perfect example of the excellence of his method. Morhardt justly noted that "from whatever angle it is observed, its profiles are always exact, without any weakness, alteration or hesitation."[9] Others viewed it as a "superb bust, screaming with underlying life"[10] and "a powerful interpretation, full of eloquence."[11]

Paul Leroi's ill humor may have been partly directed against the Salon where the bust was exhibited. He hated the new Salon located on the Champ de Mars, and he cursed every artist who joined it. Disgruntled by Jules Dalou's participation in the new Salon, Leroi proclaimed: "I'll be damned if I understand why he left the Salon [of the Champs Elysées] for this mediocre Champ de Mars!" And he was annoyed that Jules Desbois also "had left for the Champ de Mars without rhyme or reason, only by pure imitation, absolutely like lemmings."[12]

Dalou and Desbois were not lemmings. To them, it had been a simple matter of integrity. The split occurred because a special International Committee was created to oversee the art works presented at the Universal Exhibition. More open to new visions, this committee granted its awards quite differently from committees in the preceding years: routinely favored artists were abandoned, while newcomers and foreign artists were rewarded. Offended, the old guard of the Société des Artistes Français refused to grant the traditional privileges accorded to the winners, and a confrontation took place with the members of the International Committee. Finally, the most important members of the committee, among whom were Meissonier, Dalou, and Rodin, simply walked out and created the Société Nationale des Beaux-Arts, whose first Salon was organized on the Champ de Mars in 1890. Wisely, the committee members decided to include no medals or awards of any kind. From this point on, both Auguste Rodin and Camille Claudel exhibited at the Champ de Mars.

The *Bust of Auguste Rodin* was the first work presented by Camille at the Champ de Mars. It proved quite successful, probably the most successful of all her sculptures, thanks to the fame of its model. Mathias Morhardt even managed to convince the editor of the newspaper *Mercure de France* to order the casting of fifteen bronzes of the *Bust of Auguste Rodin*.[13]

Like Morhardt, Rodin was looking for ways to help Camille. Soon after the opening of the Salon, he sent a letter to the director of *le Courrier de l'Aisne*, the local newspaper of Camille's birthplace: "Allow me to call to your attention my pupil Mademoiselle Camille Claudel who is from your *département* and who is currently enjoying a great success with her well-placed bust of me at the Salon," he wrote. "Parisian newspapers are regarding her highly. I would personally be flattered if you gave recognition to her talent, and if you mentioned, in your 'Courrier de l'Aisne,' the name, already quite well known, of Mademoiselle Camille Claudel."[14] Three days later, Rodin thanked the newspaper for including Camille among a listing of local artists who were doing well at the Salon.

Rodin's desire to help and to earn some sense of gratitude from his beloved pupil occasionally took on farcical overtones, as when he wrote a letter on behalf of Paul Claudel. By 1889, Paul had decided to embark on a diplomatic career, and he was ready to present his candidacy to the Foreign Ministry. Although his hatred for Rodin was already full-blown, Paul was not above accepting his assistance in this matter. Eventually, probably yielding to Camille's wishes, Rodin penned a note whose evident clumsiness reflected his discomfort with the awkward circumstances:

> My dear Minister,
>
> Please allow me to seek your support on behalf of a young man from a good republican family (he is very intelligent), who completed his studies at Louis-le-Grand and is now studying law. He wishes to present himself to the January 15 entrance examination for consulate diplomatic careers, and his name must be entered on the list of the candidates. . . .[15]

Whether or not Rodin's letter had anything to do with the outcome is not known, but soon after, Paul began his career at the Foreign Ministry in Paris. Three years later, in February 1893, he received his first official position as vice consul in New York.

The same year, Camille finally exhibited her group of waltzers, entitled *La Valse* (The Waltz). Behind the stunning sensuality of *La Valse* is a background story repeated time and again whenever the artist turned to the French government for a commission. Camille wanted a marble commission for *La Valse* because, in her eyes, a sculpture was not fully realized without being created in marble. She was an outstanding marble sculptor, cutting the stone herself and fine-polishing it with the bone of a lamb's leg. Earlier, in 1889, she had already made an attempt to receive a commission for a marble version of *Sakuntala*. "I know," she had written to the Minister of Fine Arts, "that it is difficult to be given a block of marble before the State decides to acquire the work, but I still hope that you will help me to complete this group, which will truly be finished only when it is done in marble."[16] Her request had not been granted.

On 8 February 1892, Camille decided to draw the attention of the Ministry of Fine Arts to her group of waltzers: "I have recently finished a small group, half life-size, called "The Waltzers" which was found good by several artists, including Monsieur Rodin. It is for this group, Monsieur le Ministre, that I am requesting a marble commission."[17] The Minister of Fine Arts responded by sending Inspector Armand Dayot to her studio in order to evaluate the group. Since Dayot was a friend of Rodin, it can be assumed that he was positively disposed toward Camille, and yet he did not escape the prejudices of the time, which locked women out of certain subjects. Confronted with a composition representing a couple waltzing in the nude, Dayot felt quite uncomfortable. His long report to the Minister of Fine Arts indicates that he was torn between his admiration for the execution of the work and his distaste for its obvious sexuality.

> In her group "La Valse" Mademoiselle Claudel presents two people in complete nudity who, in an apparent *heaviness* of movement which can be explained by the *lightness* of their clothing, are waltzing and entwined. I want to state that all the details of this group represent a virtuoso performance and that Rodin himself could not have studied with more artistic finesse and consciousness the quivering life of muscles and skin.
>
> But, for two reasons, this work cannot be accepted as presented to me. First, the realistic and violent accent that emanates from it, forbids placing it in a public space, in spite of its unquestionable value. The closeness of the sexual organs is rendered with a surprising sensuality, which is considerably reinforced by the absolute nudity of all the human details.
>
> Second, the idea of the subject is too imperfectly expressed. . . . The nude waltzers are heavy and don't twirl. And, as I was saying above, the heaviness of their allure is mostly due to the lightness of their clothing. What characterizes the lightness of the waltz, is the rapid twirling of veils, the rhythmic spinning of draperies, which give wings to the dancers.[18]

Dayot advised Camille to dress her figures and to choose the type of clothing that would allow her to reveal as much of the bodies as she saw fit. Exasperated to receive this kind of advice from the inspector, Camille complained to Rodin. The next day, Rodin tried to come to her rescue by writing to Dayot a letter supporting Camille's original project: "Mademoiselle Claudel asks to do only the nude, in this case please let her have the nude because it is good, and as long as she does not want to do drapery, she would not do it well."[19] Either Rodin missed the point or he sidestepped the issue. For Dayot, it was not a matter of quality but a matter of propriety. The nudity of the figures did not bother him so much as "the closeness of the sexual organs" and the "surprising sensuality" emanating from a sculpture coming from the hands of a woman. As a result, Dayot would not budge. Therefore, Camille would either have to give up the marble interpretation or alter her composition. She altered her composition. On December 21, she wrote to the Director of Fine Arts: "During the whole summer I did studies of draperies on the same group, and they are completed. I am now ready to submit them again to Monsieur l'Inspecteur. . . ."[20]

This time Dayot supported Camille's request wholeheartedly. He noted that the sculptor had spent six months trying to add pointed touches to the symbolism of the piece, and that the draperies, although thin, fulfilled their purpose, which was to hide "too visibly realistic details." According to him, "this beautiful group, showing striking originality and powerful execution will gain a great deal when transcribed into marble."[21] Dayot's verdict was heeded, and the Minister of Fine Arts immediately sent an order that granted Camille a block of marble and a six-thousand-franc payment to complete the work. A letter was also drafted to announce the good news to the artist. Unfortunately, it was never sent to Camille because Henry Roujon, the Director of Fine Arts, put everything on hold.[22] Apparently, Roujon was not convinced that propriety had prevailed.

As late as 1895, the poet Marcel Schwob, a good friend of Paul and Camille, still hoped to reverse the negative decision on *La Valse*. Invited to dinner at Mirbeau's house along with Rodin and Roujon, he jumped on the opportunity to manipulate the obstinate Director of Fine Arts and proposed a scheme to Mirbeau: "Since you invited Roujon for dinner, you would do a good thing if you got him to approve the state purchase of *La Valse* by Mademoiselle Claudel. You know that it had almost been commissioned—

and Roujon has adopted toward her an ill will that is hard to understand. He certainly could do this. Will you? We would be three against him, with you and Monsieur Rodin."[23]

Unfortunately, Marcel Schwob's plan did not take into account Roujon's conventional views. As the Director of Fine Arts, Roujon defended the official art limitations imposed upon women artists. "Ah! if Camille Claudel had stooped to sculpting elegant dancers, of a socialite elegance," Louis Vauxelles said later, "her success would have been sudden and fabulous; the artist, scornful of this type of success, chose to symbolize rhythm, melody, and intoxication."[24] But when Camille chose to symbolize sexual intoxication, she stepped into an area long off-limits to women. As such, her piece was unacceptable. The promised commission never materialized, and, therefore, the marble version was never realized.[25]

The objections of the Ministry of Fine Arts did not prevent *La Valse* from earning a chorus of critical acclaim at the Salon. For Mirbeau, "Mademoiselle Camille Claudel daringly took on what may be the most difficult to convey for a sculptor: a dance movement. So that it does not become crude, so that it does not remain frozen in stone, infinite art is required. Mademoiselle Claudel had this art."[26] The imbalance created by the oblique stance of the embracing figures, accentuated by the long flowing train of the woman, captures both the movement of the dance and the blend of spirituality and sensuality so characteristic of Camille's sculptures. More openly sensual than *Sakuntala*, it retains a compelling feeling of tenderness, abandon, and guidance. While Jules Renard claimed that "the couple wants to go to bed and finish the dance with love-making,"[27] Mirbeau more pointedly wondered "I don't know where they are going, to love or to death. . . ."[28]

The success of this sculpture led to the creation in reduced size of several versions without the veil that first enveloped the dancers. One of these ended up on Claude Debussy's fireplace mantel and thus induced unfounded speculations regarding a love affair between the composer and Camille. Debussy was then going through an unstable period in his private life and once confided his distress to his friend Robert Godet. "I am still very confused," he wrote after a painful break-up. "The sadly expected ending of this story I told you about; banal ending with anecdotes, words which should never have been said. . . ."[29] But he never named the woman, and she has not yet been identified. As for Camille, in 1891 she was enjoying a stable

Camille Claudel, *La Valse*. Bronze, 1905. Private collection

Camille Claudel,
Clotho. Plaster, 1893.
Musée Rodin, Paris

and hopeful relationship with Rodin. It would have been out of character for her to be involved in a love affair that could have ruined her artistic and personal expectations.

It is certain, however, that Camille and Debussy were friends. They met during the period when Camille was free from her family and more socially visible. Rodin, who never took Rose anywhere, did not have the same reservations about being seen with the attractive and gifted Camille. On the contrary, he introduced her to his friends and to anyone who might be helpful to her career. It is during this period that she met her most devoted admirers in the arena of art criticism—Morhardt, Geffroy, Marx, and Mirbeau—as well as writers and visual artists. She also sometimes accompanied her brother, Paul, to literary evenings, and she was seen more than once at the poet Stéphane Mallarmé's Tuesdays, where she probably met Debussy, a strong admirer of Mallarmé's poetry. The friendship between Camille and Debussy blossomed at Robert Godet's house, where Camille learned to savor music that conveyed the emotions she was trying to express in her sculpture.

The attraction was mutual, and Debussy discovered in Camille's works "a deep feeling of intimacy, like an echo of secret or familiar emotions coming from within. . . ."[30] Both artists were enthusiastic about Asian art, Debussy about Javanese music and Camille about Japanese art. Robert Godet remembered seeing them bent over Japanese prints in silent excitement during the period when "*La Mangwa* from Hokusai became their exotic Bible."[31] *La Valse* "left [Debussy's] study only when he did," wrote Godet. "The languor and the passion of this piece, joined in one single rhythm that slows down only to take off again, seduced our Claude till the end, and brought him much consolation."[32]

Debussy was touched very differently by *Clotho*, a second sculpture exhibited by Camille at the 1893 Salon. He feared it, and with good reason, since Clotho, according to Greek mythology, was one of the three sisters who wove the fate of man. To underline Clotho's frightening appearance, Camille represented her as a shriveled old woman tangled in the threads of the lives she was weaving. Like a spider caught in her own web, she unsuccessfully pulled on the skeins that fell around her and covered part of her wrinkled head. Both Morhardt and Mirbeau admired this piece tremendously. To Morhardt, it was a masterpiece, a jewel, which "recalled ancient ivory" and had been "revised, rubbed, and softened."[33] To Mirbeau, it was a horrifying vision of death "with her flesh hanging like rags against her sides, her shriveled breasts . . . nimble and nervous legs whose strides cut human lives, she laughs in her death mask."[34]

La Valse and *Clotho* had their share of detractors, as vehement in their ferocity as Camille's friends were in their enthusiasm. In the *Gazette des Beaux-Arts,* for example, Henri Bouchot referred to the "two inexpressible rags signed by Mademoiselle Claudel."[35] Others refused to see her as a sculptor in her own right. To them, she was good because she imitated

Rodin, a frequent opinion of the less enlightened critics. "M. Auguste Rodin," we read in *La Plume*, "evoked rather slavishly by Mademoiselle Camille Claudel, whose two groups nevertheless demonstrate some ingenuity."[36]

This sort of criticism is neither unusual nor surprising. What is more disconcerting to a woman sculptor and to women in general are the expressions of incredulity scattered among the most glowing reviews of Camille's works. A woman like Camille was generally viewed as a phenomenon and a source of constant amazement. "Mademoiselle Camille Claudel," said Mirbeau, "brings us works that, by their invention and the power of their execution, go well beyond what can be expected of a woman."[37] And, after raving about *La Valse* and *Clotho*, Mirbeau felt obliged to add that Camille's works conveyed "so profound a poetry and so male a conception that we pause quite surprised in front of this artistic beauty coming from a woman."[38] Robert Godet, more succinct in his appraisal, was just as blunt. He called Camille "the only woman genius in the art in which she created."[39]

This lack of understanding on the part of such well-intentioned men as Mirbeau and Godet testifies to the prejudices of the time. A woman could not be expected to have genius; if she did, she was perceived as sexually ambiguous. We only need to read some of the entries from the diary of the respected but misogynist writer Edmond de Goncourt to understand the extent and the weight of such prejudices. "I am convinced that if we had performed an autopsy on talented women like Madame Sand, Madame Viardot, etc.," he asserted, "we would find in them genital parts close to those of men, clitoris related to our penises."[40]

Goncourt had met Camille at Léon Daudet's house, but his paternalistic commentary was limited to her looks. To him, she was Rodin's student and nothing more: "Tonight, at Daudet's, little Claudel, Rodin's student, in a blouse embroidered with large Japanese flowers, with her childlike face, her beautiful eyes, her inventive language, and her provincial accent."[41] Although the description might be viewed by some as rather flattering, it is doubtful that "little Claudel" would have appreciated it. In fact, "little Claudel" was tired of being told that she was a woman, that she was Rodin's student, and that her work was Rodinesque. As Rodin's fame soared, her own visibility remained low and generally attached to Rodin's name. It was becoming increasingly clear that she needed to come out from under his shadow.

ALTHOUGH CAMILLE SAW the necessity of distancing herself from Rodin in order to be accepted as an artist in her own right, she could not deny that he had been immensely supportive of her work. Rodin did not share the sexual prejudices of his contemporaries. He opened the doors of his ateliers to Camille and Jessie, and he kept them open to other women as well. To him, Camille was *une femme de génie*—a woman of genius—and he never felt compelled to resort to the usual derogatory comments others reserved for women in general. As an artist, Rodin found his inspiration in the female body which in his eyes incarnated the most exalting side of creation. "What a dazzling sight: a woman who undresses," he once wrote. "It is like the sun piercing the clouds. . . . Each model embodies Nature in its entirety."[1] As he saw his models undress in his cold atelier and keep their poses for hours, he developed a profound respect for their endurance, along with feelings of affectionate friendship, which sometimes belied his reputation as a satyr.

One of Rodin's models liked to tell the story of what happened to a woman friend of hers. This woman had no job and no money, and Rodin hired her. "He paid her well and, will you believe it, he set her up in her own place. . . . And what did he ask in exchange? . . . Nothing," the model said, punctuating her words with a lively gesture. "He kept her as a model for a long time and he remained very correct with her. . . . We learned this story. . . . So it is a real pleasure for us to pose in his atelier."[2]

On the other hand, Octave Mirbeau, who knew Rodin very well, claimed that he "could do anything, even a crime, for a woman." Mirbeau added that, when he and Rodin were guests at Monet's house for dinner, Rodin stared so insistently at Monet's four beautiful daughters that one after another, they all got up and left the table.[3]

Rodin's own casual point of view on his relationship with women may be best illustrated by an answer he gave one day to Rose Beuret, as they observed a cat in their garden. "Look," Rose exclaimed, "the cat is the same color as your beard was when you were young. I wonder if he is as big a lady-killer as you were?" "I behaved as a man does," Rodin retorted.[4]

There is no doubt that Camille viewed Rodin's many models as potential troublemakers. She feared Rodin's infidelities, and she let him know about it. But what threatened her most of all was his prolonged relationship with Rose Beuret. Although the two sculptors worked together in the dilapidated mansion on the boulevard d'Italie, Rodin returned every night to the house on rue des Grands-Augustins, where Rose waited for him. By 1892 these circumstances still had not changed, and Camille could not delude herself any longer. Her dream of two great artists inspired by the same vision and creating side by side had turned into the daily humiliation of having to share her lover with another woman. With the arrogance of youth, Camille viewed Rose as old, stupid, and decrepit, and she expressed her antipathy in a series of scathing cartoons. In the first one, entitled *Le Reveil, Douce remonstrance par Beuret* (Waking up, Mild Reprimand by Beuret), a middle-aged, naked Rodin wraps his arm around Rose's wrinkled body while she pokes him in the chest in a gesture of remonstrance. In the second one, *Le Système cellulaire* (The Jail System), Rose, as a naked old hag, paces up and down while guarding a prisoner in chains, who is, of course, none other than Rodin. Rose's weapon is a broom, the tool of her housekeeping trade. The third one, *Le Collage* (Glued Together), portrays the couple on all fours and stuck together like dogs in sexual congress. Under the title Camille wrote: "Ah! it's true! That does hold?" Besides its general meaning of *gluing*, the French word *collage* refers to unmarried couples living together, and this "collage" was obviously much stronger than Camille had anticipated. It was clear that Rodin would never leave Rose. The cruelty of the cartoons reveals the intensity of Camille's anger and her need to retaliate by humiliating the man who was failing her.

Rose too was suffering. She had become aware of Rodin's relationship with Camille, and she was terrified that he would leave her for the younger and talented rival. Many years later, Rose still shed tears when she remembered the "New Year's Days she had spent all alone, while Rodin was squandering money and flowers on that 'odious C.'"[5] Roses's pain had not been silent, for she abused her companion with endless violent scenes. Since

Camille Claudel,
*Le réveil—Douce
remonstrance par
Beuret.* Pen and ink
on paper, c. 1892.
Musée Rodin, Paris

Camille Claudel,
Le Système cellulaire.
Pen and ink on
paper, c. 1892.
Musée Rodin, Paris

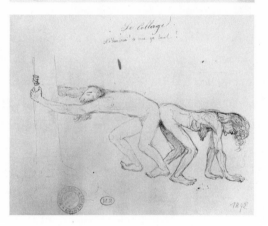

Camille Claudel,
Le Collage. Pen and
ink on paper, c. 1892.
Musée Rodin, Paris

Rose had a weak heart and had once suffered a heart attack, Rodin feared the consequences of these scenes. Fortunately for both, their good friend Dr. Vivier took care of Rose, welcoming her to his home in a small town south of Paris whenever Rodin took off on one of his travels.[6] Although Rodin did not want to give up the pleasure of spending his summers in the Loire Valley with Camille, he often expressed his anxiety about the health of his companion. In an ironic way, he tried to be fair to both women by giving them an equal share of his time and attention, even an equal share of the gifts offered to him. For example, when Edmond Bigand-Kaire, a sea captain and a generous friend, once wished to send him a barrel of wine, Rodin requested that it be sent to Camille "whose health is still delicate." But another time the barrels were sent to Rodin's home, because Camille "still had some."[7]

It is doubtful that the two women understood this twisted sense of fair play, for both became distressed and confrontational. In the boulevard d'Italie, Rodin faced Camille's growing sarcasm, while at rue des Grands-Augustins, Rose treated him with increasing fury. The ideal arrangement he had tried to build for himself—security with his older companion, love and creativity with the younger one—was falling apart. Camille asked him directly to leave Rose. "She wanted Rodin to leave his poor old Rose, who had been his companion during his days of poverty and who had shared his long misery," Morhardt remembered. "He could not bring himself to do it, although as a man and an artist, he passionately loved Camille Claudel." Rodin told Morhardt one day: "She is unfair and—forgive me if I add—like all women."[8]

Since Rodin remained unable to come to a decision, it was Camille who took the first step. Early in 1892, she moved out of the old mansion they shared on the boulevard d'Italie and rented an apartment near the Eiffel Tower, at 11, avenue de La Bourdonnais. She also kept her studio at 113, boulevard d'Italie, and Rodin, for the time being, paid the rent for both places.[9]

It was not yet a complete break-up, but a move for space, for clearer thinking, and an affirmation of personal and artistic independence. But Rodin panicked. He knew Camille was drifting away from him, and he could not accept it. A friend, the critic Roger Marx, remembered Rodin's coming to his home in tears and confiding that he had no power left over her.[10] Because Camille had renewed her ties with her relatives, Rodin's visits to her new atelier were more difficult and not always welcome, as indicated by a letter sent by her mother around this period, to which Camille added a quick note:

My dear Camille,

I was very surprised to hear that you are still in Paris; I thought you had left a month ago. I will therefore come and see you tomorrow Thursday. I will leave from here at 9:00 and I will be at your place around 11:30. We will have lunch together and I will return here tonight.

Try to be free around noon and at home at avenue de la Bourdonnais.

Good bye. Love,
Louise Claudel

On the back of the same letter, Camille wrote:

Monsieur Rodin,
Don't come here because this is the letter I just received.
Let us avoid trouble.
Anyway I am feeling better.
Camille[11]

Camille and Rodin maintained distant ties for a few more months, but when summer came, Camille went to Islette alone, and the letter she sent to Rodin upon her return to Paris bears the ominous marks of a dying relationship.

Monsieur,
I am back in Paris. I was not able to take all my belongings from Islette because it would have been too expensive. We agreed that I would return next year. I had delusions. I had to pay as much as 300 francs to Madame Courcelles and 100 francs to the molder; 60 francs for the trip and excess luggage, pieces, etc. I have 20 francs left and I only brought back one group and one bronze, my linen, my books, my drawings, etc. I had lunch with the Vaissiers, who were very gracious and reassured me.
Camille[12]

Camille was obviously moving out of Islette. Her letter is impersonal, from the dry "monsieur" to the material details. She had been alone at Islette and had paid her own expenses. If the Vaissiers were there to reassure her, Rodin was not. Camille returned to Islette the next year, but before leaving, she sent a troubling letter to Rodin on 25 June 1893.[13]

I was absent when you came. Because my father arrived yesterday, I went to dine and sleep at my parents'. As for my health, I am not feeling any better because I cannot stay in bed, having constant cause for walking. I will probably not leave until Thursday. In fact, Mademoiselle Vaissier came to serve me and told me all sorts of fables concerning me at Islette. They say I leave at night by the window of my tower, hanging from a red umbrella with which I set fire to the forest!!!

It is certainly true that people in small, isolated villages were capable of concocting very strange stories. Yet one wonders if the difficult preceding year had left its mark upon Camille's imagination. Furthermore, it was not the first time that she referred to her poor health. It was probably during this period that the tension between her and Rodin was exacerbated by an unwanted pregnancy.[14] Again, mystery shrouds what really happened, but Lucien Descaves, a contemporary of Camille and a highly respected man, remembered seeing the artist at one of Goncourt's Sunday meetings, and wrote in his memoirs: "Brief apparition, one evening, of Mademoiselle Claudel, the writer's sister and Rodin's student, perhaps even his victim. . . . Her misfortune was revealed to me through an intimate and distressing correspondence. . . . I don't have the right to say any more."[15]

But not everyone was as discreet as Descaves, and soon "rumor had it that she had at least two children (males) and it is known through a reliable source that one of Rodin's closest collaborators sometimes was sent by Rodin himself to pay for the pension of two children, who could have been those two."[16] The rumor must have crossed the Channel, because Jessie once told her family that Camille had had two children by Rodin. But it must be remembered that Jessie had left Paris long before these events and did not remain in touch with Camille. She therefore could not have had firsthand knowledge of what was happening in France.

By the time Judith Cladel was writing Rodin's biography, Camille's supposed two children had grown to four. "It is rumored . . . that you and she have . . . four children," Cladel said to Rodin one day, to which he answered: "If that were true, my duty would have been only too clear."[17]

One thing is now certain: Camille had at least one abortion. A 1939 letter from Paul Claudel to his friend Marie Romain-Rolland, who had admitted a past abortion, lifts all doubts regarding this painful experience:[18]

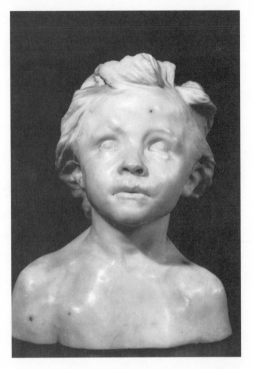

Auguste Rodin, *L'Adieu*. Plaster, 1892

Camille Claudel, *La Petite de l'Islette*. Marble, 1895. Musée Rodin, Paris

Note that a person who is very close to me committed the same crime and that she has been paying for it in a house for the insane for *26 years*. To kill a child, to kill an immortal soul, it is horrible! It is awful! How can you live and breathe with such a crime upon your conscience (maybe I did not understand you?). . . . Anyway I do not speak to you with the indignation of a Pharisee, but with the compassion of a brother.

It is probable that Camille went to Islette to regain her strength after the abortion. The combination of humiliation, sorrow, and remorse must have weighed heavily upon her and may explain the story she told Rodin in which she was seen as a woman flying out of the window carrying a red umbrella and setting fire to the forest. After the abortion, she may have unconsciously viewed herself as a witch destroying life, and some of her delusions probably started at that time. These delusions increased Rodin's anguish. Judith Cladel saw him frequently in those days, because she lived very close to the home he shared with Rose Beuret; Cladel noticed his absent-mindedness, his tired look, and physical traits betraying anxiety and lack of sleep. "He was clearly going through a most distressing experience of some sort," she wrote.[19]

In 1892 Rodin tried to exorcise his obsessions by sculpting a last private portrait of his lost love, *La Convalescente* or *L'Adieu*. In the marble version, Camille's head and hands barely emerge from the stone, as if a storm is about to engulf her. She seems to float away with her hands to her lips in a gesture of final good-bye.

One morning in 1893, Rodin moved out of the old house at rue des Grands-Augustins, and out of Paris altogether. He told Judith Cladel that Rose's health and his own required a move to the country, and he settled down in Bellevue, near Sèvres, where the boat service made it easy for him to reach his ateliers.[20] The break-up with Camille was complete. Rodin was fifty-three and Camille twenty-nine.

In spite of this last tragic episode, Camille remained focused upon her work. In 1892 she exhibited her bust of Rodin, and in 1893 *La Valse* and

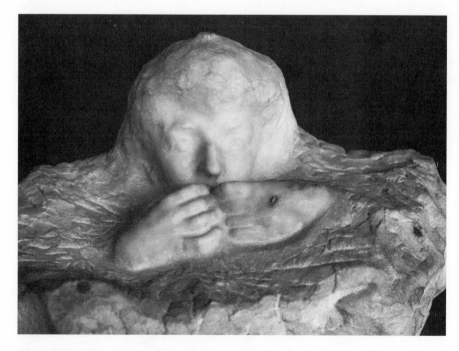

Auguste Rodin, *La Convalescente*. Marble, 1892. Musée Rodin, Paris

Clotho. At Islette, she had started to work on the bust of a child (*La Petite de l'Islette* or *La petite Châtelaine*). The six-year-old granddaughter of Madame Courcelles, owner of the castle, posed for this bust, and because the child often became tired, the clay model required sixty-two sittings, spread over two summers, in order to be completed.[21] Although it is the portrait of a girl with a braid tumbling down her back, it does not convey the expected characteristics of innocence. Instead, the intensity of the child's expression radiates a surprising blend of knowledge and fragility. The critic Gustave Geffroy greatly admired "this child head with feverish eyes, a new expression for a naive and anxious being who wants to know."[22] Roger Marx noted in *La Revue encyclopédique* that "Mademoiselle Camille Claudel's bust is endowed with the intense and inspired radiance of young life."[23]

Once more Camille hoped to attract the support of the French government, and she asked the Ministry of Fine Arts to acquire this piece. "If I believe the encouragement I received regarding this work, I don't think I am being too forward in my soliciting," she wrote.[24] But the state turned down her offer. The bronze was later bought by the Baron de Rothschild, and the plaster was purchased by Morhardt for the Société Populaire des Beaux-Arts.[25]

Camille made four marble versions of this bust. One of them, with a thick braid, was exhibited at the 1895 Salon with the title *Jeanne enfant* (Joan as a Child) in honor of Joan of Arc, and another, with flowing hair, was exhibited a year later. Camille's extraordinary skill in carving marble astonished everyone. The latter bust especially was a technical feat: the child's hair was rendered entirely with open strands, and the bust itself hollowed out to let the light play on the face and increase its mystery. Morhardt later remembered Rodin saying that this bust gave him "the impetus for competition."[26] Indeed, according to Morhardt, Camille had become a worthy rival of Rodin. Yet, he said, their styles could be contrasted so easily that even a child could see the differences. Rodin's modeling is delicate; it "avoids clashes, sudden solutions, and the lack of transition from shadow to light or light to shadow." On the other hand, Camille "especially likes vigorous contrasts, sudden and dramatic passages without any transition from shadow to light."[27] Ironically, the same could be said of the choices they made in life, for Rodin fled from drama and clashes as much as Camille seemed drawn to them.

CAMILLE WAS DEEPLY wounded and vulnerable when she walked out of Rodin's atelier, but she was also determined to make a name for herself and to find her own distinctive voice. Living only for her art, she worked relentlessly, and the decade following her break-up with Rodin encompasses the most prolific years of her career. Later, her brother gave his own version of this period when he wrote: "The divorce was a necessity for the man, for my sister it was a total, profound and definitive catastrophe. . . . She had bet everything on Rodin, she lost everything with him. The beautiful vessel, for a while tossed upon bitter waves, was finally engulfed."[1]

But Paul did not acknowledge that it took ten years for the vessel to be engulfed and that during this time many ill winds added their share of destruction to the weakened hull. In 1892, as bitterly disappointed as she may have been, Camille did not sink. She was forced to alter considerably her vision of the future and to face the art world without the help of a powerful mentor, but she continued to create on her own. It must also be noted that Rodin still intervened on her behalf, as he did in the case of *La Valse*, whenever his opinion could influence journalists or politicians. In fact, he would have liked to maintain some form of friendship with Camille, and as late as 1893 he still came to her atelier for an occasional visit. But his visits were no longer welcome. Camille worried that he would see her unfinished works, and she fretted about people's gossip. Finally, she appealed to Morhardt's loyalty and asked him to contact Rodin:

Dear Sir,

Please, do whatever you can to prevent Monsieur Rodin from coming to see me on Tuesday. I don't like to show unfinished things and budding studies; we have time to see them when they are completely finished, so why make all my ideas known before they are ripe?

If you could, at the same time, delicately and shrewdly instill in Monsieur Rodin the idea of not coming to see me any more, you would give me the greatest pleasure that I have ever felt. Monsieur Rodin is not unaware that many nasty people have said he made my sculpture; therefore why do everything possible to give credence to such calumny?

If Monsieur Rodin really wishes me well, he can do it without having people believe that I owe the success of the sculptures on which I work to his advice and his inspiration.

Please, excuse me, Monsieur, for speaking to you frankly, and acknowledge my sincere friendship.

Camille Claudel[2]

Camille's request was heeded, and Rodin would not try to contact her for two years. During this period, Camille enjoyed satisfactory relations with her family, especially with Paul, and in August 1893 she accepted an invitation to join Florence Jeans on the Isle of Wight. Five years had elapsed since the friends had last seen each other, and Florence had become Mrs. Back in the interval. Never oblivious to her art, Camille planned to sculpt the bust of her host, and she brought with her to Shanklin a package of sculpting clay—a rather unusual piece of luggage, which was sure to be closely investigated at the border. "I hope they won't put me in jail at the customs thinking the clay is a dynamite bomb," she joked.[3]

But this was not a joking matter, because several bombs had already exploded in Paris, and the population was becoming edgy. Although French political life had not been particularly calm during the 1880s it became a real storm in the 1890s, after the expectations placed on General Boulanger had collapsed. The inefficiency and the callousness of politicians, combined with the misery of the common people exploited by the Industrial Revolution, gave impetus to the anarchist movement. Within this movement, a group of extremists embarked on a series of bombings, targeting judges and politicians, whose homes they blew up. Although Ravachol, the author of some of the bombings was executed in 1893, acts of terrorism spread to cafés and restaurants, killing ordinary people and frightening everyone.

Finally, after President Sadi Carnot was stabbed to death, the French government passed severe laws aimed at stripping anarchists of their access to propaganda, and the anarchist movement disintegrated.

Fortunately for Camille, no one at the border took her for a terrorist, and she spent a pleasant vacation with her friends. A photograph confirms that she put her clay to good use when she made a bust of Florence's husband, but up to now, the piece has not been located. This visit was Camille's last stay with Florence and their last contact. Although Camille undertook a short trip to the island of Guernsey the following summer, she did not return to the Isle of Wight.

In Paris Camille's social life centered around her brother and his friends. But Paul was given a temporary position as consul in Boston and left for the United States in April 1893. After his departure, Camille found herself totally alone. The remote location of her atelier discouraged potential visitors and further contributed to her isolation. At times she was overcome by the weight of this new solitary life, and Morhardt remembered her words when he wrote: "Her feeling of solitude is such that she sometimes has the strange fear of having forgotten the use of speech."[4] To compensate, Camille spoke aloud to herself or visited the concierge, who never ran out of gossip. She also took long walks on the boulevard d'Italie which, as a working-class neighborhood, offered scenes fit to stimulate the imagination of an artist. A worker coming home; an old, blind violinist; a couple in a loving embrace; or a group of children playing provided the rough material she needed. Upon returning to her atelier, Camille immediately modeled the street scenes she had just witnessed, and ideas for new projects soon formed in her mind. They were new, very different from what her contemporaries were doing, and she was eager to share them with Paul. Her excitement is visible in a letter she sent him in December 1893.[5]

I have many new ideas that would really please you, really thrill you. They agree with your thoughts. Here is a sketch of the last one (*La Confidence*):

Three people behind a screen listen to a fourth.

———

Graces

Very small people around a large table listen to prayer before a meal.

Sundays

Three men in new outfits perched upon a very high cart leave for Mass.

The Sin

A young woman crouched upon a bench cries; her surprised parents stare at her.

Camille drew quick sketches to illustrate each project. She explained that she intended to make small terra cottas of these scenes and to dress her figures. Her reason became obvious when she added: "You see that it is not at all like Rodin, and it is dressed." Since Rodin worked on the grand scale, she would work small; since he dealt with the nude, she would dress her figures. Her head was working feverishly, so feverishly that she crossed the line of paranoia. "I share these findings only with you, don't show them," she urged Paul, underlining her words. For the first time, Camille expressed her anxiety that someone might steal her ideas. Inexorably, this anxiety would become increasingly worse. For the moment, however, she found "great pleasure in [her] work." Her enthusiasm was bolstered by the invitation she had received to exhibit at the 1894 Salon in Brussels, where she planned to show four pieces: *Sakuntala,* the bust of a woman with a hood, *La Valse,* and "the Islette girl." She did not realize that she owed this invitation to Rodin's request of four years earlier, a fact that might have dampened her enthusiasm.

In her letter to Paul, Camille twice referred to a three-figure group that had been the focus of her attention since the unraveling of her relationship with Rodin. It was *Le Chemin de la vie* (The Path of Life), or *L'Age mûr* (The Age of Maturity), and it represented a middle-aged man drawn forward by Old Age and reluctantly turning his back on Youth. "I will add a leaning tree to express Destiny," she explained. As she made another sketch, she added: "Here is how it will be, in full width." She hoped to show it at the 1894 Salon, but the group was so ambitious a project that it could not be completed for several years. Instead, she chose to finish the figure of Youth separately from the others and to exhibit it as *Le Dieu envolé* (The God Has Flown Away), or *L'Implorante* (The Supplicant).

Youth is a beautiful and fragile-looking woman on her knees, naked, her whole body stretched toward the god who has just left her, her arms reaching out imploringly. Morhardt justly pointed to the importance of the curve of the arms, which "record in space the idea of the one who is absent."[6] The reference to the myth of Psyche hid a more personal story, for the god who had flown away was both Cupid and Rodin. Rodin understood it immediately when he saw the piece at the Champ de Mars Salon, and his emotion prompted him to request a review from a journalist friend:

> Dear Mr. Bouyer,
>
> Thank you for your friendly note. I would like to ask you since I am absent from the Champ de Mars to transfer your study upon my student Mademoiselle Camille Claudel, who has been successful with her bust of a child; and for me preferably with a woman on her knees, *le Dieu envolé*.
>
> Rodin[7]

Rodin did not know yet that two more figures were in the works: a middle-aged man and an old woman. Had he known, he might have been more cautious.

Although Rodin could no longer see Camille, Morhardt kept him informed of her circumstances, and these had become worrisome. Without her steady income from Rodin's atelier, Camille had run out of money. Her financial difficulties became apparent as early as December 1893, when she wrote in her letter to Paul: "I thank you for the offer you make to lend me some money. This time I don't refuse because I ran out of Mother's 600 francs and time for the rent has come, I pray you, if it does not cause you any problem, to send me 150 to 200 francs."[8] In April 1894, she unsuccessfully asked the Ministry to purchase her bronze of the Islette girl, and in December of the same year, she was denied a block of marble for *Sakuntala*. When Rodin tried to intercede in her favor, he was told that blocks of marble were exclusively reserved for commissions.[9] By January 1895, Camille was so impoverished that she approached the art dealer Durand-Ruel in the attempt to sell one of her possessions, a painting by Alexander Harrison called *The Wave*. But Durand-Ruel had troubles of his own and could not help her.

Fortunately for Camille, Rodin and Morhardt were determined to do

Camille Claudel, *L'Implorante.* Bronze, 1894–1905. Musée Rodin, Paris

something for her, and they came up with an idea for a commission. Both were in charge of a huge banquet held on 16 January 1895 to celebrate the seventieth birthday of the great painter Puvis de Chavannes. Rodin presided over the organizing committee, and Morhardt was its secretary. The banquet, held at the Hôtel Continental, was to be a grand affair involving some six hundred luminaries, all men. Although Rodin expressed his interest in inviting women artists, the idea was rejected by the other members. "We did not dare invite them!" Morhardt wrote later. "At that time, the presence of women at a banquet of this importance would have been viewed as almost revolutionary. It did not bother us, but it would have detracted from the sense of prestige and the solemnity of the occasion."[10] However, Camille's work was honored by the committee, even though she was not allowed to attend. Her presence was felt through a special gesture attached to the banquet: in honor of Puvis de Chavannes, the committee had decided to donate a sculpture to the Musée du Luxembourg, and this sculpture, thanks to

Rodin and Morhardt, was to be created by Camille Claudel. With a gift of one thousand francs, almost half the sum required for the commission, Rodin launched the subscription that allowed Camille to carve the marble version of *Clotho*. The guests must have been especially generous, because Morhardt informed Rodin in March that he had just bought the plaster of "the Islette girl" with the remaining funds.[11]

With her financial plight temporarily eased, Camille could focus on her work. Of the street and home scenes she had described in her letter to Paul, *The Sin* held special interest because it was a direct reference to her life. Unfortunately, the project was never undertaken. In fact, of all the small projects she had described, only *La Confidence* was completed. The idea for this work originated after Camille observed four women sharing stories during a train ride. The artist huddled her figures behind a screen and skillfully reproduced the tension of the bodies, the mesmerized faces of the listeners, and the seductive gesture of the storyteller. According to Morhardt, the work was "a prodigious masterpiece," and he was enthralled by the life given to the small figures. In spite of its simplicity, the piece was a drama, and Morhardt thought it was a poem. "It is a poem where blood flows, where something palpitates, where shoulders are lifted by an inner emotion, where chests are breathing, where the prodigious richness of life is manifested."[12] Roger Marx echoed his feelings when he wrote: "Eloquent poses, arched backs, crossed arms, translate in a minuscule and admirable group, the human being totally transfixed by the act of listening."[13]

The plaster of *La Confidence*, better known as *Les Causeuses* (The Gossips), was exhibited at the Champ de Mars in 1895. It was a huge success and led to the creation of other editions of this work, some with a screen, others without it, some in plaster, others in bronze, marble, and even onyx. Several plaster casts were made from the marble version and sold to various collectors, including Rodin. The most spectacular version, the one in green onyx—a very hard stone to carve—was exhibited in 1897 with great success.

Octave Mirbeau, stunned by the beauty and the originality of *Les Causeuses*, seized the opportunity to draw attention to Camille's work. On 12 May 1895, he honored her with an enthusiastic article, which Morhardt called "her first beam of fame."[14] Presented as a dialogue between the writer and his imaginary friend Kariste, it salutes Camille as "a wonderful and great artist . . . something unique, a revolt of nature: a woman of genius."[15]

In the dialogue, Kariste plays the role of the naive admirer who wonders why "the state is not on its knees in front of her to ask her for such master-pieces." Mirbeau plays the more realistic character, ironically answering: "Go and say this in the offices [of the Ministry]! You will be welcome!" Calling attention to Camille's financial difficulties, he voices his fear that she might stop sculpting. "Can you give her bread?" he asks Kariste, who revolts against this idea, "Can you pay her models, her molders, her casting, her marble?" In Mirbeau's eyes, recognition and help from the Ministry of Public Instruction and Fine Arts would solve these problems, so he ends his article with an appeal to the good will of the minister, asking him to provide financial relief to the artist so that she may create in peace.[16]

Mirbeau's glowing article and his appeal to the Ministry were the "beam of sunshine" Camille needed at that time.[17] The effort was also warmly welcomed by Rodin, who sent a long letter of appreciation to Mir-beau, a letter that shows his love for Camille was still very much alive:

> As for Mademoiselle Claudel who has the talent at the Champ de Mars, she is almost unappreciated. You have a project for her, you

Camille Claudel, *Les Causeuses*. Onyx and bronze, 1897. Musée Rodin, Paris

made her known, in spite of this time of lies, you made sacrifices for her, for me, for your conviction. It is your heart, Mirbeau, that is an obstacle; it is your generosity that disturbs.

I don't know if Mademoiselle Claudel will agree to come to your house on the same day as me. We have not seen each other for two years and I have not written her, I am therefore not in a position to let her know, you must do everything. If I must be there, Mademoiselle Claudel will decide it. I feel better sometimes when I am happy, but our lives are so cruel.

[Puvis de] Chavannes is supposed to write a letter to the minister; it will be signed by a few friends, but I don't have any trust in this: all seem to believe that Mademoiselle Claudel is my protégée anyway, even though she is a misunderstood artist; she can boast that she had against her my friends the sculptors and the others too who have always paralyzed me at the Ministry because, there, we are not knowledgeable. Let us not become discouraged, dear friend, because I am certain of her final success, but the poor artist will be sad, sadder then, knowing life, regretting and crying, being possibly aware that she succeeded too late, victim of the pride of the artist who works honestly, having the regret of the strength she left behind in this fight and in this late glory, which gives one only sickness in exchange.

My regards to Madame Mirbeau.

Rodin

My letter is too depressing. Don't let Mademoiselle Claudel see it.

I think Mademoiselle Claudel's address is still 113, boulevard d'Italie.[18]

Rodin was evidently thinking of his own lifelong struggles when he wrote his letter. He knew exactly what sort of daily frustrations Camille was enduring, and he dreaded the powerful French bureaucracy. Like Morhardt and Mirbeau, he was unfaltering in his determination to get a government commission for Camille, enrolling the help of artists and critics to maintain the pressure upon the Ministry. In May 1895, he wrote art critic Gabriel Mourey on her behalf:

My dear Mourey,

Although you don't agree with Mirbeau on Burne-Jones, you have the same opinion regarding Mademoiselle Claudel. We have been friends for more than two years, so do something for this woman of genius (the word is not too strong) whom I love so much, for her art, and for whom you have been so kind.

True artists, my dear friend, are being dispossessed of exhibitions and pushed away by organized amateurs; may true writers come to the rescue of one of them. . . .

Rodin[19]

Mourey responded to Rodin's pleas with two laudatory articles, one in *Le Nouveau Monde* and the other in *Le Studio*. The articles from Mirbeau and Mourey, the letter from Puvis de Chavannes, and the support of fellow artists finally caught the attention of Raymond Poincaré, the new Minister of Public Instruction and Fine Arts. Encouraged by Poincaré's apparent good will, Morhardt and Rodin started plotting to organize a chance encounter between Camille and the minister. They knew it would not be easy, considering that Camille stubbornly refused to meet anyone, but Rodin thought he could arrange for a carriage to pick up Camille and bring her to his atelier when the minister was there. However, would she agree to come? For a while, Morhardt played the emissary between the two artists, altering the plans to make them more appealing. Finally, Rodin decided to break his long silence and to write to Camille:

As for the minister, it is exceptional. He comes to pick me up on Monday at the atelier to go to your atelier, and I think that your interest and politeness require that I be with him, so that we don't look ridiculous, he and I. In any case there is a plan that I want to be successful, and I must have the freedom to bring either now or later, one by one, Mr. Leygues, Mr. Poincaré, and Mr. Bourgeois.

This way, I will get some results.

It will be the last step for your glory and your position.

It is your strict interest so that you don't waste your future.

Mr. Leygues praised your Waltz to Mr. Bourgeois yesterday.

As for me I will see you only as much as will be strictly necessary. The sight of you, I assure you, scares me and would probably throw me into bigger suffering. . . . and although I am sick, I wanted to do what I could and I hope to see my efforts crowned, probably by a commission, which would be an affirmation to the world and which would send you art lovers.

You must know that I am unhappy to see your plight.

I don't come for myself but I am forced to accompany Mr. Leygues. . . .

Therefore make this sacrifice for your future, and soon you will be strong and you will not need any servant anymore.

I send you my wishes, not for your glory which is already accomplished, but so that your peace of mind and your serenity at work are assured.

Your devoted servant

Rodin

Only hope one day at a time and if time seems long, remain confident because it is the last effort and your position will be so beautiful later, like mine but happier, as you deserve.[20]

It is not known whether Camille was swayed by Rodin's arguments, but shortly after these events, in June 1895, art inspector Armand Silvestre came to her atelier with the intention of offering her a state commission for a bust. However, Camille convinced Armand Silvestre that it was a better idea to help her finish her three-figure group. On July 5, Silvestre wrote to the minister:

Mademoiselle Claudel submitted the maquette of a group of a very interesting composition, and its studies are already quite advanced. It represents Middle Age embodied by a man attracted by Old Age while Youth tries to hold him back. The movement is really lyrical and the preoccupation with Rodin obvious. The artist prefers that the state commission this work which she says she can make in marble for 5,000 francs. Without giving her any specific hope on this subject, I promised to let you know her wishes. It really is, from a woman, a very noble and well thought-out work.[21]

On July 25, Raymond Poincaré signed an official decree directing Camille to create the plaster of *L'Age mûr* for the sum of 2,500 francs. A letter was immediately sent to inform Camille of the good news, and another was drafted for Rodin. But the draft prepared for Rodin was crossed out, with a note adding: "Don't write Rodin. Strike from the record."[22] It appears that someone in the ministry was nervous about a work that reflected Camille's "preoccupation with Rodin," as Silvestre put it in his report, and judged it preferable to keep things quiet. The piece, they may have realized, was not inspired just by man's fate, but also by Rodin's life. Thus, circumstances resulted in an ostensible irony: Camille's first state commission, received after so much effort from her friends, including Rodin, carried the risk of offending Rodin in what he viewed as most important: the secrecy of his private life.

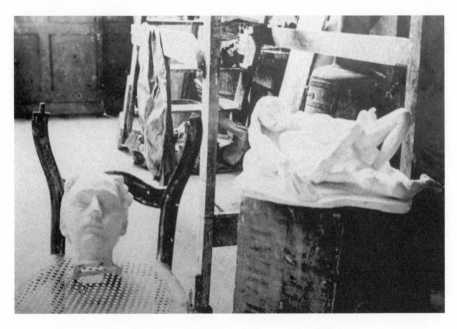

Rodin's atelier with the bust of Camille Claudel visible in the foreground, c. 1885

CAMILLE WAS DELIGHTED to see her brother return from Boston in March 1895. Paul would stay in France for four months before leaving again, this time for the consulate of Shanghai, China. Meanwhile, he renewed old ties with his friends Maurice Pottecher, Marcel Schwob, and Jules Renard, and sometimes he joined their lunch gatherings at the Café d'Harcourt to discuss the latest events. Jules Renard, a journalist and author of successful comedies, recorded his impressions of these encounters in his now famous *Journal*.

Paul Claudel and Jules Renard could not have been more different. Unlike Paul, Renard was not religious. Although he hid a heart of gold behind a mask of permanent irony, his wit was feared by many, including Camille, who told him once: "You scare me, Monsieur Renard. You will ridicule me in one of your books."[1] By 1895 Paul had become an important playwright, but unlike Renard, his plays were not popular comedies. *Tête d'Or*, *La Jeune fille Violaine*, and *L'Echange* were dramas greatly admired by intellectuals, who regarded Paul as a genius. Renard too admired his genius, but not his character. He was obviously irritated by Paul's stiff mannerisms and by his dogmatic tendencies. Paul's voice reminded him of "a speaking machine" pouring out convictions that were not to be trusted. "He admires and detests like a child," Renard complained.[2]

Jules Renard has provided us the description of a very strange dinner in Camille's atelier. "Ghostly evening," he called it. The atelier had been decorated in unusual ways:

Atelier crossed by beams, with lanterns hanging from strings. We light them. Armoire doors, which Mademoiselle Claudel stuck against the wall. Chandeliers where a candle goes on an iron point and which can be used as daggers, and rough studies sleeping under some cloth. And this waltzing group where the couple seems to want to go to bed and finish the dance with lovemaking.[3]

Camille was wearing heavy makeup, which accentuated the general eeriness of the place. "Her powdered face comes alive only through her eyes and her mouth. Sometimes it looks dead," Renard noted. He spent the evening observing the uneasy comportment of his three hosts, Camille, Paul, and Madame Claudel. A violinist friend of Paul's, Christian de Lara-pidie, was also present, but his music annoyed Camille, and as usual, she voiced her irritation in not-so-subtle terms: "She hates music, she says it aloud, as she thinks it, and her brother rages with his nose in his plate, and one can feel his hands tense with anger and his legs shake under the table." As for Madame Claudel, "I did not hear a word of what the mother said," Renard quipped. "Yet she answered every one of our words, added her little commentary to herself alone, or heaved a sigh."

When the conversation lingered over literature and music, Renard was particularly disgruntled: "These people want us to believe that their emotions are more complete than ours," he fumed while observing Paul and his musician friend. "We feel everything you feel, plus . . . plus what? A small sensual pleasure, the exhilaration given by a glass of alcohol. I can hardly believe that this little man, barely alive, can go further in his enjoyment of art than Victor Hugo or Lamartine, who did not like music."[4]

Surprisingly, Paul Claudel's friendship with Jules Renard lasted another five years, probably because Paul was away from home more often than not. He left in July, this time for China, and Camille was alone again. But success made solitude easier to handle. In September, more unexpected good news reached Camille: the Châteauroux museum was interested in buying her painting by Harrison. When she had failed to sell it to the art dealer Durand-Ruel in January, the sculptor Ernest Nivet had offered to help her. Nivet was from Châteauroux where he had studied sculpting until he decided to move to Paris. He joined Rodin's atelier in 1891, but he hated the working conditions, and his disillusions brought him closer to Camille. Like her, he was disappointed by Rodin, and he often voiced his frustrations in the letters he sent to his former art teacher in Châteauroux:

You would need to do what Mademoiselle Claudel said: work at Rodin's for several years, that is to say spend a good part of your youth in his atelier, and then when you leave it, you have done nothing and learned nothing. At least, when you work alone, the least you can do is be yourself, and not be a mixture of one and the other, like many of Monsieur Rodin's *praticiens* who exhibit each year at the Salon.[5]

Nivet's ties with Châteauroux proved to be useful to Camille, who was finally able to sell her Harrison painting. Delighted with the sale, she decided to give her large plaster of *Sakuntala* to the Châteauroux museum, which was announced in the local newspaper on 10 October 1895. "[The sculpture] will take its place among the best works of art of the Châteauroux museum," the journalist rejoiced.[6] A few days later, preparations were made to receive the group and move it to the second floor. In the ensuing commotion of moving the plaster upstairs, one foot was broken. Nevertheless, the sculpture was placed in the main hall, in spite of the objections voiced by two councilmen.

On November 18, Camille came to Châteauroux to view the results. She was warmly welcomed by the members of the art committee, and another laudatory article appeared in the newspaper. This was enough to stir the ill feelings of several conservative bourgeois of the city, who retaliated with virulent epithets thrown at Camille's work and at those who had accepted it. They made sexual jokes of the Hindu legend, howled over the choice of location, computed the real cost of the piece to the city of Châteauroux, and finally turned their wrath on Camille's work. It was unfinished, the proportions were all wrong, the heads were hard to find, and no one could tell which was the male and which was the female. One member of the Châteauroux commission even suggested the acquisition of a curtain to hide the group from public sight.[7]

Camille's friends did not leave this outrage unanswered. Several of her champions reacted promptly and sharply, including the well-known critic Gustave Geffroy: "Those who saw [*Sakuntala*] at the Salon retain in their memory the anatomical science and the passionate expression of these two figures . . . and those who became, in the Indre, the defenders of this proud and passionate artist, have honored themselves and deserve to receive the salute of their companions from Paris and everywhere."[8]

Rodin immediately acknowledged his gratitude to Geffroy with a note of thanks. "You came to Mademoiselle Claudel's rescue with your authority," he wrote, "with your concern for art, with praise, courageously, because those who have respect for talent and for the use to make of it are rare."[9] Rodin's unfailing support of Camille during these years was all the more commendable in that he was already immersed in the most harrowing art experience of his life: the Balzac affair. Wishing to honor Honoré de Balzac, the Société des Gens de Lettres had commissioned Rodin to create a statue of the great writer. Although Rodin had accepted the commission four years earlier, with a promised delivery in 1893, the finished product was nowhere in sight. Made and unmade time and again, never to the satisfaction of the sculptor, who wanted a work of genius for a writer of genius, the statue remained unfinished, and Rodin was now facing the fury of the most conservative members of the Société, who wanted their finished product or their money back. At times Rodin appeared drained of energy and in poor health, yet he did not forget Camille's needs.

It is hard to tell how much Camille was aware of Rodin's constant solicitude. Because he was afraid of hurting her pride, Rodin preferred to keep a low profile and to hide his interventions behind an intermediary. Most of the time, the intermediary was Mathias Morhardt, because Camille had become a friend of his family. Frequently included in the list of dinner guests, she seemed to appreciate Madame Morhardt's risotto as much as the convivial ambiance that reigned at these dinners.

Camille owed her first real client, Maurice Fenaille, to the constant "plotting" that took place between Morhardt and Rodin. "I would like to see you as soon as possible," Morhardt wrote to Rodin in October 1896. "It is absolutely necessary that we agree on the subject of Mademoiselle Claudel. She authorized me to contact Monsieur Fenaille, but I would not want to do it without consulting you and even without asking you to do it with me. Are you ready for it?"[10] Camille needed an advance to cover her expenses for a bust she was making for Fenaille, and the matter may have been slightly sensitive. But Fenaille proved to be very understanding when he wrote back to Rodin: "I will go next week to Mademoiselle Claudel's atelier to give her what you tell me and see her works, on Wednesday or Thursday, and to your atelier next Saturday."[11] Shortly thereafter, Camille wrote a note of thanks to Morhardt. She did not seem to be aware that Rodin was behind it all.

As an editor for *Le Temps*, Morhardt had connections to some of the most important people in Paris; his friendship therefore was invaluable. One year after the commission in honor of Puvis de Chavannes, Morhardt, who was Swiss, included Camille in another event. In January 1896, he organized a special exhibition in Geneva that focused on the work of Pierre-Cécile Puvis de Chavannes, Auguste Rodin, and Eugène Carrière. Camille was invited to present one of her plasters of *La Confidence* (*Les Causeuses*), and this plaster was later bought by the Geneva museum.

Although Camille could not know the extent of Rodin's actions on her behalf, she was aware that he had been one of her allies in her ongoing battle with the art world. When she unexpectedly ran into him at an art opening, she was unusually convivial and gracious with him. She had every reason to be; her finances were healthy, her visibility higher than ever, and she owed part of her new happiness to Rodin. Their differences appeared forgotten, and Rodin could not believe his good luck. Overjoyed, he wrote Camille a letter even more difficult to decipher than usual:

> My Supreme friend,
>
> I am still sick and yet, if I must be cured, I will be cured, because the art opening where I saw you is for me the beginning of a consolation which will bring my health back to me. My very dear friend, how kind you were and how I like your intelligence. . . . How much pain I must receive and how great was my sin; but I knew when I saw you that there was a fatality from which I could not escape.
>
> Ah! my divine friend, you will be happy, be patient, everything has its price here.
>
> I was paid for my work, I pay for my sins, and my enduring pain is a striking example of justice.
>
> Thaulow came to see me. He told me that your small figures are admirable. He may have seen the breaks, but he probably does not mind. In any case, your group will be taken. Morhardt . . . too, and we always talk about you, about what you do.
>
> Only, you have the gift to reign over everyone.
>
> I send my respectful adoration.
>
> Your Rodin, happy to receive your kindness[12]

Camille's letters to Rodin were more businesslike. In March she warned him of the impending visit of Léon Maillard, who was writing a book on Rodin and wanted to publish two sketches of him made by Camille. "Since he is being difficult in paying me," she wrote, "I said that you did not wish to see these sketches published. (Don't contradict me too much.)"[13] Camille had recovered the voice she had used with Rodin in England: assertive, practical, and reserved. The reconciliation would be friendly but distant, and it would remain largely epistolary.

Camille was preparing for the 1896 Salon, and Rodin returned to his previous idea of introducing her to high-placed politicians. This time he aimed even higher, for he had the president of the Republic in mind. But Camille showed little interest in politicians. Was it ill will, discomfort, or real complications? In any case, she turned down his offer:

Monsieur Rodin,

I thank you for your kind invitation to introduce me to the president of the Republic. Unfortunately, since I have not been out of my atelier for two months, I have no appropriate costume for this circumstance. I will have my dress only tomorrow for the art opening. Furthermore, I am determined to finish my little women in marble. There was some breakage, which will take the whole day for me to repair, but I hope they will be ready tomorrow for the opening (if there is still time to place them there).

Please, excuse me and don't believe it is ill will.

With all my thanks.

Camille Claudel[14]

The "little women " were the marble version of *Les Causeuses*, which Camille was making for the Danish painter Fritz Thaulow. It was not finished on time for the 1896 Salon, in which she showed only one piece —*La petite Châtelaine* in marble, with hair flowing down her back. Some months later, Camille was still working on *Les Causeuses* in marble, hoping to show it at the next Salon. "You and Monsieur Rodin know how long and difficult marble is and how much delay was caused by my assistants," she wrote to Morhardt.[15] She needed to find someone intelligent to help her finish the screen while she polished the figures. But the onyx version was finished first and exhibited in 1897 with tremendous success, while the marble version was bought by Thaulow in 1898, apparently without being shown at the Salon. "We stop, surprised and delighted," the critic Jeanniot wrote of the onyx version, "in front of this strange work, skillfully executed and of uncommon size."[16]

Camille also presented two other pieces at the 1897 Salon: *The Bust of Madame D.*, directly cut in marble, and another small work, a plaster called *La Vague* (The Wave) which, like *Les Causeuses*, would later be made in onyx and bronze. Although *La Vague* belongs to the same inspiration as *Les Causeuses*, with small female figures at the center of the piece, the large wave towering above the women points to the influence of the Japanese artist Hokusai, who was much admired by Camille. The plaster of *La Vague* was bought in June by Morhardt but paid for by Rodin.[17]

Camille's new prominence in the art world brought her the attention of journalists who wanted to write about her life. At the end of 1896, an anonymous article that appeared in *Revue encyclopédique Larousse*, painted her as "the modern woman."[18] One year later, Henry de Braisne published a more serious article in the *Revue idéaliste*. According to him, Camille led the way for a more enlightened treatment of women in the art world after she was chosen to be part of the jury at the Champ de Mars. "Mademoiselle Claudel is without rival when it comes to her will power, her hard work, her incredible integrity, her faith in truth, which to her is Beauty," he wrote. He defended her against those who accused her of imitating Rodin, and stressed, on the contrary, the originality of her work.[19]

Meanwhile, in 1897, Rodin had finally found the shape of *Balzac* that was to shake the art world. Morhardt remembered seeing him "dress" six identical plaster casts of Balzac with equal length of fabric. "The last figure had something imperious and grandiose," he decided.[20] More dramatic, more massive than the others, it was Rodin's choice. He turned the cloth into a robe with sleeves thrown over the shoulders. Then he charged his *praticien* Le Bossé to enlarge the piece for the 1898 Salon. After all the sound and fury he had endured from his detractors, Rodin yearned to hear Camille's appraisal of his *Balzac*, so he asked Le Bossé to find out. Camille's answer proves that she and Rodin still agreed in matters of art:

Camille Claudel, *La Vague*. Plaster, 1897. Lost.

You ask me by the intermediary of Le Bossé, to write what I think of your statue of Balzac: I find it very great and very beautiful and the best among your studies on the same subject. Especially the accentuated effect of the head, which contrasts with the simplicity of the drapery, is well-chosen and absolutely striking.

I also like very much the idea of floating sleeves, which express well the heedless spirit of Balzac. All in all I think that you must expect a huge success, especially among the real connoisseurs who cannot find any comparison between this statue and all the ones that, until now, have decorated the city of Paris.[21]

The rest of her letter is worrisome. In fact, Camille indicates that she has been sick for some time. But her physical sickness does not explain the irrationality of her argumentation when she turns against the devoted Morhardt. As usual, Morhardt had come to her aid when he secured a commission from the *Mercure de France* for ten casts of the bust of Rodin. Yet when Camille realized that the cost of casting and finishing might exceed the money she had received for the commission, she became irrational. She declared Morhardt insincere and began to question his intentions. The long article he was writing about her had to be stopped, she said. "It was meant to bring anger and revenge upon [her]." Actually, according to Camille, the whole Morhardt family could not be trusted: "They just pretend but I think that, in reality, their whole clan takes a dim view of their efforts to obtain commissions for me and to bring attention upon me." Madame Morhardt, as a woman, was especially suspect. "Anyway," Camille insisted, "you know what black hatred women feel toward me as soon as they see me, until I return inside my shell, they use every possible weapon; and, furthermore, as soon as a generous man tries to help me out, a woman is here to hold his arm and prevent him from acting. So I run the risk of never harvesting the fruits of my efforts and to die in the shadow of calumnies and suspicions." Again, a call for secrecy concluded her long diatribe: "What I tell you is completely secret and so that you can really judge the situation for yourself."

Suspicion, irrationality, call for secrecy, all evidence of the paranoia that was quickly taking hold of her. In a letter sent to Paul Claudel after the 1897 Salon, Morhardt tactfully expressed his concerns regarding the pressure Camille was enduring at the moment: "Unfortunately, there are still so many difficulties connected to the very essence of her genius! She has just had a very painful week with two assistants she had to fire and who persecuted her with incredible malice: we had them arrested by the police. Let us hope they have learned their lesson."[22] Morhardt may also have noticed Camille's nervous distress resulting from this incident and her frustration at the time wasted when she had to appear in front of the judge.

Henry de Braisne also made disquieting comments in his article on Camille: "If you manage to earn the confidence of Mademoiselle Claudel— and it is not easily achieved: this artist, introverted and extremely reserved with unwelcome visitors, is talkative only with her friends." Further down the page, he added: "She may have bitter hours of discouragement, mad despair, but she remains what she is, an incomparable artist."[23]

Rodin was shaken by Camille's letter. "You have against you the difficulties of life and of your imagination," he observed sadly in his answer on December 2. He insisted upon Morhardt's devotion and urged Camille to remain loyal to her friends. The article Morhardt wrote about her, he added, was "beautiful, very beautiful, and should be published." Adopting the voice of the older friend, Rodin attempted to show her the path of reason:

> I am sorry to see you nervous and embarking on a path I know, alas, too well. I am certain you have a gift for sculpting. You have a heroic perseverance, you are an honest man, a brave man in the struggle you have been waging, and which draws admiration from all. Ignore the gossips, and especially, <u>don't lose your friends through capricious discontent</u>. Everyone will be under your command, if you wish. <u>Don't speak</u> and keep on working. Your reputation is almost achieved. But how ironic is this illusionary thing when one is not happy. What terrible years I have spent. I barely start to recognize myself. These days and the kindness with which you judged my Balzac reassure me somewhat, because I would have needed your advice in the black abandon in which I was left, for dead I think. . . .
>
> Believe me, my friend, abandon your female tendency to dismiss persons of good will. Show your admirable works. There is a justice, believe me. One is punished and one is rewarded. A genius like you is rare.[24]

In the margin of the letter, Rodin sketched Jacob wrestling with the Angel, a symbol of Camille's "great struggle with the terrible angel keeping the miserable world away from geniuses like you." "Gentleness and patience," he finally cautioned his restless friend. Rodin's letter points to the most tragic aspect of his relationship with Camille—an early awareness of her mental instability. He had had plenty of opportunities to witness sudden fits of anger, unexplained distrust of well-intentioned people, and delusions that made her, at times, lose all sense of reason. These characteristics came to light during the period preceding their break-up, when she tore Rose to pieces in her cartoons and became more violent with him. The writer Paul Morand remembered seeing Rodin coming to his home during these days of anguish, and a particular scene stuck in his mind:

> I was very young when, one morning, Rodin came to lunch. "He comes here to run away from his admirer!" my father said. The idea that a big and fat giant like Rodin could be afraid of a woman amused me. My father corrected me. "This is not a laughing matter," he said. "It is a very sad story. This young woman is his best student, she has genius, she is very beautiful and she loves him; but she is mad. Her name is Camille Claudel."[25]

Madness is a word too often misused. Camille was not mad. She created, she exhibited, and she interacted socially. But she had moments of irrationality that scared the people who loved her, especially Rodin, and this fear may have done as much to separate him from Camille as did the presence of Rose in his life.

The shift in Camille's works from large pieces to small scenes may also have meant more than a mere attempt to separate her art from Rodin's. As innocent as they may appear, these small scenes harbor disturbing elements; squeezed into a corner or dwarfed by their environment, the small characters reflect the shrinking world of Camille as she increasingly withdrew, soon to live in complete isolation. In *La Vague*, three women hold hands as they are playing in the water. But they are suddenly surprised by an immense wave which towers and curls and threatens to swallow them. Crouching and looking up, there is nothing they can do to prevent the catastrophe from happening. The wave holds them up like toys in a huge hand ready to close.

RODIN WAS GRATEFUL for Camille's warm appreciation of his *Balzac*, but he feared the public might not understand it as well as she did. He was right. When the piece was exhibited in the Salon du Champ de Mars in 1898, the success predicted by Camille was instead an upheaval, with Rodin in the middle of an artistic controversy he would have preferred to avoid. His visionary creation became the target of most unsavory comments from a large part of the public who flocked to the show. Even worse, the members of the Société des Gens de Lettres declared they "had the duty and the regret to protest against the sketch exhibited by Monsieur Rodin at the Salon and in which they refuse to recognize the statue of Balzac."[1] With his masterpiece reduced to the rank of "sketch" and declared unworthy of Balzac, Rodin was left with the dubious choice of either refunding the 10,000 francs he had received in advance or suing the society. Because he valued his peace of mind most of all, he chose to refund the money. This offense to Rodin outraged his enlightened friends, who immediately mounted a counterattack in the form of a letter of protest. Almost every artist of any worth signed it. Then they started a 30,000-franc subscription in order to purchase the statue and set it in a public place. All would have gone well if not for the Dreyfus affair.

While the Balzac affair caused trepidation in the art world, the Dreyfus affair turned French society upside down for years. Barely noticed by anyone when it started in 1894, it eventually developed into a dishonorable saga of spies, false documents, manipulation of justice, and anti-Semitism, and it involved some of the highest authorities in the French army.

Alfred Dreyfus, a French captain of Jewish background, was arrested in October 1894 on the charge of spying for the Germans. Court-martialed for high treason even though there was not a shred of evidence against him, he was deported for life to French Guiana. He would have rotted away on Devil's Island for the rest of his life had it not been for his loyal wife and his endlessly devoted brother, who fought for his freedom and his rehabilitation. Slowly, they uncovered the facts and rounded up sympathizers. By November 1897, they had proof that the incriminating documents had been written not by Dreyfus but by officer Esterhazy, a debt-ridden and shady character. Esterhazy was tried, yet against all common sense and against all decency, he was acquitted. This launched the Dreyfus affair, like a bomb thrown at the very heart of the Republic. On 13 January 1898, the novelist Émile Zola showed himself to be the most courageous of all Dreyfus's supporters when, on the front page of the newspaper *l'Aurore*, he signed his name at the end of a passionate letter to the president of the French Republic. This letter, now as famous as the affair itself, was entitled "J'accuse." In it Zola proclaimed the innocence of Dreyfus, attacked the French army, and denounced anti-Semitism. The government retaliated by trying Zola in court, which ended with the sentence of a heavy fine and a year of imprisonment. Zola chose exile to England instead. But truth had been spoken, and it could not be suppressed again. In spite of the avalanche of hateful articles in much of the press, Dreyfus was eventually pardoned by the new French president in 1899 and cleared of all accusations in 1906.

These twelve years literally split France into two camps—the Dreyfusards and the anti-Dreyfusards. While the former spoke in the name of justice, the latter cited reasons of state, grounded in the still-sensitive loss of the 1870 war against the Prussians. Anti-Semitism, stirred by extreme-right newspapers, sprouted everywhere. Riots erupted in the cities, Jewish stores were burned, and neighbors turned against neighbors. In Rennes, where Dreyfus's second trial took place, no hotel would receive Madame Dreyfus, who had to accept the hospitality of a compassionate local woman. Within families, things were sometimes just as bad, as fathers turned against sons, brothers against sisters, simply because they held different views on the affair. Witness a famous cartoon of a family dinner where the host wisely declares: "Most of all! Let us not speak about the Dreyfus affair!" But the next drawing shows the table overturned, dishes scattered, people jumping at one another's throats, and even the dog running away with a fork stuck in his backside. The caption underneath notes: "They spoke about it."[2]

Completed in this climate, Rodin's *Balzac* had long been defended by

Zola, who was president of the Société des Gens de Lettres when the commission was granted to the sculptor. This was something of an embarrassment to Rodin, who was quietly anti-Dreyfusard and who refused to sign a manifesto on Zola's behalf. But when the subscription sponsors, with the exception of Renoir and Forain, turned out to be all Dreyfusards, Rodin panicked. To the dismay of his friends, he declined the subscription and kept the *Balzac*. Among those who battled for Rodin, Lucien Descaves was the most appalled: "So, it is true, Rodin, you fear to be compromised, classified, regimented, by signatures which are alas! the same on your subscription as on the manifesto in favor of Zola! . . . However, think. If these did not defend you, if these had not taken, with their usual generosity, the initiative of the subscription, oh! Rodin, I ask you, who would support you?"[3] Yet, *Balzac* had found the best home it would ever have: the garden of the Villa des Brillants in Meudon, Rodin's new residence after 1894. There, *Balzac* rose, mysterious and ghostlike, a spirit guarding its secret in an expanse of lush vegetation.

Like Rodin, the Claudels were against Dreyfus. This caused a rupture with several of their friends, including Jules Renard, who had become a passionate advocate for Zola and Dreyfus. Paul Claudel and Jules Renard met one last time after Paul's return from China in 1900. Their encounter again took place in Camille's atelier, where Renard noticed a portrait of the anti-Semitic journalist Rochefort. On a table was lying a copy of the right-wing publication *La Libre Parole*, which claimed the motto "France for the French."[4] Renard appraised Paul mercilessly in his journal:

> He speaks about the harm the Dreyfus affair caused us abroad. This intelligent man, this poet, smells like a raging priest with acrid blood.
> —But what about tolerance? I said.
> —There are houses for this, he answered.

Paul was making a pun on the French expression *maison de tolérance*, which refers to a house of prostitution. His rejection of tolerance, compounded with his strong religious convictions explain his belief in Dreyfus's guilt. As for Camille, although she broke away from her family on personal issues, she shared the same conservative political views. Like most bourgeois families in France, the Claudels formed a clan that presented itself as a solid

Camille Claudel, *L'Age mûr*. Bronze, 1902. Musée d'Orsay, Paris

block to the world, even when they tore at one another in private. Camille remained very much part of this clan, and although she had broken away from Catholicism, she viewed Jews and Protestants as outsiders, as different, and therefore not to be trusted. When she complained to Rodin about Morhardt, who was Swiss and Protestant, she underlined their differences of birth and religion: "It would be better if Morhardt devoted his efforts to Raymond Vernet and those who share the same country and the same religion,"[5] she told him. Morhardt's support of Dreyfus made him all the more suspect to Camille and threatened a friendship that, until then, appeared secure. Yet, while Camille agreed with Rodin on the Dreyfus affair, she refused to sign the subscription presented by Edmond Bigand Kaire on the sculptor's behalf, declaring, "Monsieur Rodin's glory did not need any subscription and his talent is above all this furor."[6]

The journalist Judith Cladel also got a taste of Camille's inflexible beliefs when she came to her atelier with the idea of writing an article about her sculpture. This article was meant for *La Fronde*, a feminist review that supported Dreyfus. "Shortly after my visit," Judith Cladel wrote, "I received a letter asking that my article be published only in a paper or magazine whose political opinions were similar to her own."[7] Years later, Morhardt wrote to Cladel: "[Camille] had long been the cherished child of our home. The Dreyfus affair determined her to leave us with bitter violence."[8] But Morhardt's assessment of the break-up between them was only partly correct. Something much more serious happened on a personal level, something that touched Camille to the core of her being and unleashed all the demons that were still kept at bay within her: the crucial conflict over her most recent work, *Le Chemin de la vie* (The Path of Life), more often called *L'Age mûr* (The Age of Maturity).

Camille worked ceaselessly on *L'Age mûr* after she received the commission from the Ministry of Fine Arts in July 1895. Six months later, with her private funds depleted, she requested a monetary advance, and art inspector Armand Silvestre was dispatched to her atelier. Satisfied with her progress, Silvestre supported her request. In July Camille received an advance of 1,000 francs, and she continued working on her piece for many long months. Finally, in October 1898, she informed Henry Roujon, the conservative Director of Fine Arts, that her plaster was finished; the following month, Armand Silvestre returned to view the group. His new report supports Camille for a commission:

In a past report, I described this composition, which includes three figures representing Man at the end of his maturity, breathtakingly led by Age while he stretches a useless hand toward Youth who wants in vain to follow him. The artist made a few modifications to her maquette. Mademoiselle Claudel separated the hand of her main character from the figure of Youth to better express its distance. Furthermore, she enveloped the figure of Old Age with floating draperies, which accentuate the speed of her walk. These three figures are well studied from nature and include beautiful anatomical pieces. As it is, the group is interesting and of a very modern technique. It deserves the commission for the bronze which is requested by the artist, and I can only give a favorable recommendation to her wish.

The impression of Rodin is striking in this work, but the subject is treated with infinite conscience. We can say it is through its quality of invention and movement that it takes after the technique of the master and not because of deliberate negligence.[9]

As he did once before when he referred to Camille's "preoccupation with Rodin," Silvestre used an ambiguous word to introduce the same idea in his report: "the impression" of Rodin rather than "the influence." Silvestre may have understood that beyond the general allegory, this work was the most personal statement Camille had yet created: Rodin abandons Camille to follow Rose. In this second version, the man's hand no longer touches the young woman's, and she remains alone, on her knees, her whole body stretched toward the man who is leaving her. The composition is unbalanced, as if the pull of Old Age, whose arms are gripping the man on both sides, is so powerful that it carries everything with it. "This young naked woman, that's my sister! My sister Camille," Paul wrote, overwhelmed by emotion. "Imploring, humiliated, on her knees, this magnificent, proud girl, she saw herself like this. Imploring, humiliated, on her knees and naked!"[10]

With *L'Age mûr*, Camille tried to redeem what she had invested in Rodin. It was a way to reaffirm the fundamental significance of what had taken place between them, to reaffirm it and to make it public. At the same time, she feared Rodin's reaction to such a personal work, so she carefully kept it away from his sight. When the state failed to pay her on time, she did not turn to Morhardt for help as she had always done; rather, she turned to her father. Therefore, on 14 November 1898, Monsieur Claudel took his pen and did his best to put some sense into the heads of the uncaring politicians who controlled the fate of his daughter's work. "But Monsieur," he wrote in shocked disbelief to the Director of Fine Arts, "you must know that for such an important work as Mademoiselle Claudel's group, she had to endure numerous monetary advances, cost of models, castings, etc. Artists are generally not rich, and making them wait for the payment of their works is a terrible inconvenience."[11] Although someone in the ministry wrote on Monsieur Claudel's letter "Is it possible! In any case, immediately answer with a very polite letter," nothing reached the Claudels. This time, Camille, furious, took the matter into her own hands:

Monsieur,

You honored me, four years ago, with a commission for the group "L'Age mûr" for which you gave me 1,000 francs, with 1,500 francs left to receive and which I was supposed to get with the completion of the work. Upon a first refusal on your part, my father wrote you a letter but you did not deign to answer. (It is highly probable that if my request had been supported by some of your friends like Monsieur Rodin, for example, Monsieur Morhardt or someone else, you would not hesitate to give what you owe me.) I will content myself with noting that I had 2,000 francs of advanced expenses for this group and that, whether or not it pleases Rodin or Morhardt, I must be paid, otherwise I will deal with them directly. I wish to let you know that I am in no mood to be kept waiting, even by you.

Sincerely,
Camille Claudel[12]

Henry Roujon, who was probably not used to receiving such threatening requests, nevertheless obliged, and Camille was paid on 5 January 1899. Although she appeared to implicate Rodin and Morhardt in some obscure plot against her, neither of them knew of the existence of *L'Age mûr* and therefore could not have acted against her at this point. In any case, the ministry proceeded with the next step: a commission for the bronze. In June 1899, an order was drafted by the Ministry of Fine Arts entrusting Camille Claudel with the bronze casting of the group. The amount she was to receive was left blank, as well as the date. But on June 24, for unknown reasons, a note from Henry Roujon canceled the commission.

Six years later, in April 1905, a communication from the Head of Works to the Under-Secretary of Fine Arts, confided that "the translation of this work in marble or in bronze has been abandoned by the administration of Fine Arts since 1899. The commission had been prepared and submitted to Monsieur Roujon, then Director of Fine Arts who, on June 24, gave the order to cancel the commission, for reasons which do not appear in the dossier, and which must be related to the nature of the work."[13] But the work had already been approved, considering that the state had financed the plaster. Roujon's action can only be explained in terms of outside pressure, and this pressure must have come from Rodin.

In May 1899, Camille had exhibited *L'Age mûr* at the Salon along with three other works, the marble of *Clotho*, the bust of comtesse de Maigret, and the plaster of *Persée*. For the first time, Rodin had the opportunity to view *L'Age mûr*, and what he saw was his private life made public. Shocked, hurt, and angry, he probably used his power to make sure it would never happen again: the commission for the bronze was canceled. Worse, the next year, when Camille tried to exhibit *L'Age mûr* at the 1900 Universal Exhibition, it was rejected. In disgust, she withdrew all her works from the exhibition.[14] Her resentment was exacerbated by Rodin's symbolic triumph at the same exhibition; allowed to build his own pavilion on Place de l'Alma, Rodin showed 136 sculptures, including *Balzac* and the still unfinished *Gates of Hell*, and museums from all over the world came to buy his works. Fame and fortune were embracing him at the very moment when Camille saw *L'Age mûr* pushed into oblivion.

The conflict between Camille and Rodin over *L'Age mûr* put an abrupt end to their renewed friendship. From this point on, Rodin stopped supporting Camille's work, and she, for her part, started to view him as a villain intent on destroying her. The consequences of this bitter and definitive break-up were enormous for Camille, and they would become more apparent with time. One of these consequences surfaced in 1903, when she left the Société Nationale and returned to the Société des Artistes Français, where she had not exhibited since 1889. In a letter to the painter Henri Lerolle, she confided: "Monsieur Rodin (whom you know) found much fun this year in cutting off my livelihood everywhere, after forcing me to leave the Salon of the Nationale because of the malicious things he did to me."[15]

Camille did not give up on *L'Age mûr* or on the promise made by the Ministry of Fine Arts. Her pathetic battle against the French government for more than a decade embodies the type of ordeal she had to go through as a female artist during this period. Her appeals to the ministry fell on deaf ears in spite of the intervention of various male friends, among them Eugène Blot, Camille's art dealer. As the treasurer of the Friends of the Luxembourg Museum, Blot attempted to refresh the memory of Dujardin-Beaumetz, the Under-Secretary of Fine Arts:

In a few words, we asked that the state follow up on a promise formerly made by Armand Silvestre to purchase her bronze group *La*

Jeunesse et l'Age mûr. The price had been set for 8,000 or 10,000 francs, and the beginning of its execution took place because she received 2,000 francs for the purchase of the plaster and she was told the commission for a bronze would follow.

It never came. It is the rest of this commission, Monsieur the Under-Secretary of State, that I solicit for Mademoiselle C. Claudel, in the name of the artistic interest she inspires and because of her situation as an unfortunate woman whose talent is envied by many, but who is forgotten by everyone.

There would be here, for you, an action of kindness and justice, a beautiful compensation for a regrettable oversight considering that C. Claudel has never received any commission from the state. You will be generally applauded and, among us, Friends of the Luxembourg Museum, sincerely and deeply thanked.[16]

Each letter sent to the ministry received the same laconic answer: no promise for a commission had ever been made. Unfortunately, art inspector Armand Silvestre, who had appraised Camille's work and informed her of the forthcoming commission, had died in the interval, and support for Camille's claim had thus vanished. She therefore added this humiliation to her long list of misfortunes, never forgetting that Rodin had, by his actions, ruined her chance of getting an important state commission that could have helped her become financially secure.

L'Age mûr was saved by Captain Louis Tissier, an art amateur who had admired Camille's group when it was exhibited at the Salon in 1899. At that time, he had asked Camille to sell him a plaster of the kneeling figure, but he let her convince him to have a bronze made of the figure instead. As an officer in the French army, Tissier was constantly on the move, but he returned to Camille's atelier in 1901 and viewed her group again. She told him she had defied the state's request that she deliver the plaster to the Dépôt des Marbres because she feared it would be left to rot in such a place. Moved by her plight, Louis Tissier decided to help her. In a letter to Paul Claudel written in 1943, he related what happened:

A desire seized me to save her work from destruction by having it cast; I already had one of the figures. Unfortunately, the base especially modeled for it did not fit with the other part. Your sister convinced me to have the whole work cast. But, as I was still an officer at the mercy of numerous peregrinations, how could I take a three-figure group half life size to my future garrisons? We looked for a solution.

Camille Claudel proposed to separate the piece in three parts to ease its transportation. One, the drapery, fixed upon the back of Old Age by a mortise and tenon joint and a screw, and the two figures that you call in your article of *L'Art décoratif*, one "L'Age mûr" and the other "L'Imploration." This explains why you can see two visible tenons in the base: they fit in two corresponding sockets of the part *L'Age mûr* and, once fit, re-create the whole work, which has been put back together.

I accepted her offer. We had to find an appropriate foundry. Rudier first proposed by your sister gave an estimate, which my modest financial means prohibited. We agreed with the Thiébaut Frères foundry and the artist, herself, would make the necessary cuts in the plaster and personally supervise all the work done in the atelier des Ternes where I went to see it: the casting was perfect.[17]

This bronze marks Camille's return to the Salon des Artistes Français in 1903. Unfortunately, it was poorly received by the critics, who often compared it negatively with Rodin's sculpture. The writer Romain Rolland, for example, applauded the strength of the work and the feeling of passion and sadness emanating from it, but he deplored "a definite taste for ugliness and something weak and improvised in the tension, which is somewhat the caricature of Rodin's genius."[18] Henri Cochin noted that Rodin, absent from both Salons, could be recognized in many imitators, including Camille Claudel.[19] But Charles Morice appropriately objected: "They criticize her for resembling Rodin. These people are amazing who want that no one comes from no one. I would, on the contrary, blame artists who would have remained untouched by the lessons of the greatest statuary artist of this century!" According to him, "her bronze group *L'Age mûr*, marked with a quivering bitterness, is worthy of the good name earned by this valiant woman."[20]

A new edition of six bronzes of *L'Age mûr*, in reduced size, was undertaken in 1907 by Eugène Blot when he realized that the state would never come through with the promised commission. Blot had first come to

Camille's atelier in 1900, accompanied by the critic Gustave Geffroy. He bought two small statues from her that day, and his ensuing friendship with the artist became the source of much-needed consolation. Blot's casts of *L'Age mûr* were exhibited in his gallery in the fall of 1907 and again in December of the following year. Unfortunately, the reduced size of the edition diminished the impact of both movement and projected emotion. But such compromises had become part of Camille's artistic routine, considering that survival was taking precedence over other considerations. For her, the first decade of the new century would turn into a rapid disintegration of body, mind, and creativity, generated by an ever-growing load of financial difficulties and all kinds of disappointments.

Meanwhile, after the 1900 Universal Exhibition, Rodin's pavilion was transplanted to his garden at Meudon. The Villa des Brillants was becoming a pole of attraction for artists, writers, and admirers who wanted to interact with the great man; his ateliers turned into factories to handle the requests pouring in for his sculpture. At sixty, worshiped like a god, Rodin let himself be swept away by the whirlwind of fame that engulfed him. The last years of his life carried their own form of disintegration as he lost his ability to differentiate between friends and flatterers and fell prey to the "woman's snare" he had so carefully avoided earlier.

Rodin in the mirror, 1887,
photographed by Jessie Lipscomb

DURING THE LAST decade of the nineteenth century, the streets of Paris became the stage of an unexpected social revolution triggered by the immense popularity of the bicycle. This popularity had been immediate in masculine circles, and by the late 1890s, women were determined to join the fun. Suddenly it became obvious to every bicycling-minded woman that confining clothing had to go. Coming out of their chrysalids of corsets and petticoats, women increasingly took to the streets dressed in masculine garments, free at last to move and be physically active. Of course, it did not happen without resistance from the general population, and "the first women who went out dressed like this caused a scandal," a journalist remembered. "In some suburbs, the locals, outraged by this type of exhibitionism, threw stones at women cyclists. Coming home one morning, I had to protect one of these unfortunate women and give her asylum until the crowd, hissing and booing, went away."[1]

Politicians also hated to lose their control over women's wardrobes, and the Minister of Interior saw fit to proclaim, on 27 October 1892, that "the wear of masculine clothes by women is tolerated only for the purpose of velocipedic sport."[2] Even songwriters attempted to bring their rebellious female companions back to reason with an avalanche of odes to the petticoat. "Frou-frou," a popular song celebrating the sensual appeal of the petticoat, was soon on everyone's lips: "Frou-frou . . . a woman with her petticoat . . . frou-frou . . . seduces every man . . . but a woman looking like a boy . . . has never been attractive. . . ." Attractive or not, modern women were singing the song and keeping their new attire. Eventually, everyone got used to the new clothes, and in 1896 Maria Pognon, presiding over the Feminist Congress, could raise a toast to the "egalitarian and leveling bicycle."[3]

Camille Claudel may have followed with her eyes some of these

Quai Bourbon from across the Seine

modern women as they rode past her, but she did not imitate them. Although the wearing of masculine clothes would have been much more practical for sculpting, she showed no interest in this type of freedom, and she stuck to her long cumbersome skirts until the end. Engaged exclusively in her art, she lived like a recluse in her atelier on the boulevard d'Italie, shunning the clatter of social transformation. Unfortunately, the neighborhood was also changing, quickly losing the rural charm that it had once displayed, and Camille decided to move again. In January 1899, after a brief stay on rue de Turenne, where the rent and the storage of plasters were probably too high for her small budget, she moved into a two-room apartment at 19 quai Bourbon, on the Île St. Louis. Quai Bourbon would be her last atelier. There, in the heart of Paris, Camille found again the pastoral atmosphere she had once enjoyed on boulevard d'Italie.

The Île St. Louis was then, even more than now, a peaceful refuge in the middle of a hectic city. Its magnificent seventeenth-century mansions, abandoned to neglect and decay, were often partitioned as rentals for less affluent dwellers. One of these rentals became Camille's atelier. Nestled on the ground floor, to the left of a large gate facing the water, the atelier opened its windows to the soothing commotion coming from the river. Hurried pedestrians sometimes slowed down to watch the barges carrying

Camille Claudel, *Persée et la Gorgone* (detail). Marble, 1902. Collection A.G.F., Paris

their loads of merchandise, and Camille's rare visitors were often seduced by the serenity of the place. Henry Asselin, who befriended her in 1904, later remembered his first visit and the cheerfulness of the sculptor when she was working away from curious eyes. Like everyone else, and probably with more conviction than female cyclists, she was singing "Frou-frou."

> It was springtime, and through the opened windows entered the sweet scents of renewal, the rustle of the leaves in the tall poplars, and the songs of the birds. A woman, with hair disappearing under a scarf tied under her chin, was shaking a dust rag out a window, although it was 3 p.m. To the voices of nature, her slightly husky voice answered: she was gaily singing "Frou-frou," a popular song in those days. It was Camille Claudel.[4]

Another visitor, the journalist Gabrielle Réval, noticed the smell of the apples heaped on the barges floating down the river. Réval had come to Camille's atelier with the intention of writing an article about the woman she viewed as one of France's great sculptors. When Réval entered, she first glimpsed "a confused form, bent over a marble, and chestnut hair tied back

Camille Claudel working on *Persée et la Gorgone*

by a red ribbon." The form interrupted her task and faced the visitor: "You find me at work; excuse the dust on my blouse," Camille said as she put down her file. "I sculpt my marble myself; I hate to trust a work to the 'zeal' of a *praticien*." She smiled and turned her eyes toward Réval:

> Two magnificent eyes, of a pale green evoking the new growth of the forests. These eyes surprise by their limpidity, they have a Virgilian charm because they immediately recall the freshness of the woods. But at the very moment her eyes attract you, an instinctive gesture of the artist seems to stop your friendly impulse, and you remain with the bizarre impression of a deeply personal nature which attracts you by its grace and repels you by its animal shyness. The entire character of Mademoiselle Claudel lies in this half-wild withdrawal.[5]

Réval admired the splendid marble group set in front of her. It was the marble version of *Sakuntala*, renamed *Vertumne et Pomone*. "The group in white marble is wonderful because of both its grace and its power," Réval wrote. "The adolescent's torso lives and palpitates, and the young man supports the fainting woman with such passionate adoration. The work is of an incomparable purity of line." Ending with a tribute to the sculptor, Réval concluded: "Mademoiselle Claudel is a complete figure of feminine genius."[6]

The article, which appeared in the review *Femina* in 1903, was one of several major pieces devoted entirely to Camille Claudel at the turn of the century. All of the writers shared an unreserved admiration for a woman they viewed as a genius, a great enthusiasm for her sculpture, a certain curiosity for her person, and a concern for the difficulties they could guess behind her spartan way of life. While the novelist Henry de Braisne proclaimed the originality and the vigor of Camille's sculpture,[7] the well-known critic Camille Mauclair called her "the greatest woman artist of the present time."[8] But it was Mathias Morhardt's forty-six-page article published in 1898 that demonstrated the most unbridled enthusiasm for the sculptor. With a detailed account of Camille's life and work, Morhardt tried to stir the curiosity of the general public and to lure collectors to her door. Although Camille was unquestionably gaining recognition as an important sculptor, by 1899 her circle of buyers had not grown beyond the small group of the loyal supporters she had met when she worked with Rodin: Morhardt himself, the banker Joanny Peytel, the industrialist Maurice Fenaille, the painter Fritz Thaulow, and the civil servant Henri Fontaine. Comte and comtesse de Maigret joined the group when each commissioned a bust and, soon after, a Perseus.

Aside from *L'Age mûr* and *Vertumne et Pomone*, Camille's most recent works exhibited at the Salon were not as interesting as her earlier ones. *La Profonde Pensée* (Deep Thought) and *Le Rêve au coin du feu* (Dream by the Fire), two charming small pieces that depict a melancholic woman by a fireplace, lacked the stunning originality and the symbolism of her other small sculptures. Straight genre scenes, they could also be turned into lamps, and thus were more decorative pieces than sculptures. But, as Paul Claudel noted: "One must live!"[9]

Of the larger works, the bust of a nymph called *L'Hamadryade* or *Ophélie*, which was exhibited at the Salon in 1898, blends tradition with Art Nouveau. The nymph's head, weighted down by a strange adornment of twisted hair and foliage, leans forward, her mouth open in a grin. The complicated marble cutting of the nymph's hairdo allowed Camille to display her technical skill, but the piece remains rather conventional.

Seemingly conventional, *Persée et la Gorgone*, made for the Countess de Maigret, was first presented in plaster at the Champ de Mars Salon in 1899, then in marble in 1902. This large sculpture portrays the Greek hero Perseus, who killed the Medusa by using his shield to send her own reflection back at her and then cutting off her head. Camille represented the victorious Perseus standing over the dead Medusa and brandishing her head. The piece originally included a bronze shield held in Perseus's hand, but somehow the shield broke off. However, the interest of *Persée* lies beyond the piece itself. On the one hand, it recalls the *David and Goliath* of Camille's adolescence. Although that early terra-cotta work was already in poor shape when Morhardt saw it in Camille's atelier, his description of David points to strong similarities with the new Perseus: "Standing upon the toppled body of the giant [Goliath], who, with his left arm, still tries to protect his head cut off by the young hero [David], triumphs in a gesture of enthusiasm and victory."[10] The Medusa has replaced Goliath, and Perseus has replaced David, but the gestures remain the same. On the other hand, a disquieting touch added to the severed head of the Medusa transforms

Camille's latest work into a personal nightmare. The Medusa's hair, made of the twisting snakes of the legend, frames a face deformed with age, grief, and madness, and this face bears Camille's own features. Caravaggio, before her, had represented himself as the severed head of the mad Medusa, but Camille's decision to emulate the great painter at this point of her life betrays a poignant foreboding of the tragedy that was going to strike, as well as an awareness of her present physical decline. Indeed, a photograph taken when she was working on *Persée* reveals the damage that worries and deprivations had done to her once beautiful face. Henry Asselin noticed it right away when he first came to her atelier:

> She seemed nervous, flustered, and continuously moving, with singularly brusque gestures. She removed her scarf and freed her hair, still very black and thick, poorly held up with combs and pins. She was then forty. . . . But she looked fifty.
>
> Life had marked her, wilted her mercilessly. The extreme neglect of her garment, and her indifference to her own appearance, an olive complexion, faded, with early wrinkles, underlined a sort of physical decline which could be, at leisure, attributed to fatigue, sorrow, disappointment, disenchantment, total indifference to her surrounding world. And yet, there was not a trace of despondency in this active and charming woman, sturdily built and surprisingly spontaneous. Besides, her large dark blue eyes shaded with black had lost none of their beauty, and none of their troubling radiance, a radiance sometimes almost disconcerting. Because it was the expression of a complete and absolute honesty, which never bothered with manners and nuances.[11]

Because Camille's spontaneity and charm soon erased the first impression of premature aging, she remained in Asselin's mind as "the one who laughed while giving life to a man's face, the one who offered champagne to her guests without thinking of tomorrow, the one who reached the highest spheres of the mind, but could also express herself with grace and wit."[12] A valiant woman who kept her sense of humor and her cheerfulness in the midst of countless difficulties.

The same impression comes out of the many letters Camille sent to her trusted friend Eugène Blot in the early 1900s. Financial troubles had become a daily occurrence at that point, with little hope for relief in the immediate future. The expenses of simple survival, such as paying the rent or buying food, haunted her as much as paying the assistants or models she occasionally still hired. As her art dealer, Blot was one of the few possible sources of income for Camille, and she often turned to him in moments of need. Yet her letters display an amazing exuberance, an ability to laugh at herself and a total obliviousness to protocol. She never begs but turns every one of her requests into a laughing matter. "I would like to know if it is by accident that you forget to send me the last fifty francs left on our poor little account," she writes in one letter. "Oh là là! Don't forget that the mailman, the garbage man, and the street cleaner of quai Bourbon will expect me to give them something on New Year's Day."[13]

Later she convinced him to buy the delightful bronze of a flute player, which she had just finished. This piece—*La Joueuse de flûte*—also called *La Sirène* (The Mermaid), was Camille's favorite, according to Blot, perhaps because of the irresistible gaiety and freedom exuding from the young woman entranced by her music. The money received for *La Sirène* did not last long, so Camille wrote again: "You are deluding yourself if you think you will not hear from me any more; you don't think I will leave you alone just because you bought my Mermaid." This time she asked him to buy another figure by a fireplace—he already owned two. Another day she wondered whether Blot could get the state to commission her *Persée* in bronze, but, confusing the piece with *L'Age mûr*, she warned him that "Rodin is waging a vicious war against this statue."

Sometimes, the threatening figure of a bailiff named Adonis Pruneaux shows up in her letters. "Send me one hundred francs on our future deals," she urges Blot, "otherwise I will disappear in a cataclysm. Stanislas Margotin is asking for the payment of a bill that threatens to swallow me entirely; the shopkeeper screams that she delivered several eggs which have not been paid for; Adonis is again going to seize me (we won't be saying this time that Venus is after him)."[14] The threat was only too real, and Camille had to appear once more in court, an incident that she related with much wit to Blot, after noting that "bills of one thousand francs are extremely rare on the Paris square and they often pass by quai Bourbon without stopping."

We went in summary judgment with sinister looking fellows. . . .
Conclusion: considered as an exploiter of the poor, I was condemned
to pay 200 francs to the poor man I had awfully tortured. I had to bor-
row them from a friend who found the story rather fishy and advised
me to be more conciliatory in the future.

Ever since this moment, each time he sees me with my plasters,
he turns his back on me. It is in fact agreed that I am the plague, the
cholera of the benevolent and generous men who are interested in art
and that, when I show myself with my plasters, even the Emperor of
the Sahara would flee.[15]

Camille's ability to turn her sardonic wit against everyone, including
herself, had not diminished since the days of her travels in England.
Although her physical appearance had altered, her voice had remained the
same. The mature woman recounting her ludicrous tale of judges and half-
hearted friends displayed the same playful spirit as the young woman who
wrote self-descriptive answers in the album of her friend Florence Jean.
Because Camille liked and trusted Blot, she could joke with him and speak
to him without fear. Thus, in a more serious mood, she spoke honestly and
soberly of her condition as a woman artist:

In truth, I would prefer to have a more appealing job, which would
attract people rather than make them run.

If I could still change careers, I would prefer it. I would have
done better to buy beautiful dresses and beautiful hats that would
underline my natural qualities rather than devote myself to my passion for doubtful constructions and somewhat forbidding groups.

This unfortunate art is made for long beards and ugly faces
rather than for a relatively well-endowed woman.

Forgive these bitter and belated thoughts: they will not soften
the ugly monsters that sent me on this dangerous path.[16]

In spite of Blot's devotion, Camille's sculpture did not sell. Much
later, in 1935, Blot explained his frustrations to Morhardt: "I was proud to
edit her work and happy to help her, because she sold so little, and for such
low price, superb pieces . . . so I never got half of my investments back . . .

but I could count on her friendship. . . ."[17] Blot remained her friend to the end and was one of the few people who kept her trust.

Besides Blot, there were others still eager to help Camille financially around the turn of the century. One of those men was Rodin. In May 1899, he sent her two women who had approached him for art lessons. One, the Scottish sculptor Ottilie McLaren, became quite bewildered by what happened. At first, all seemed to go well: Camille was hesitant but welcoming, her art enchanted McLaren, and plans were made for the first lesson. "I think she will be stunning," McLaren wrote to her fiancé back in Scotland. "I was awfully pleased to find that, though she had worked so much with Rodin, she was not just an imitation of him." McLaren immediately understood the importance of the pieces she saw in Camille's atelier. "[Her work] is big and simple," she added, "and seems to have that womanly quality which I like so immensely."

A day before the lesson, Camille changed her mind. She preferred her solitude, she said. "It seems that for the last three years she has cut herself off from everyone, even Rodin," McLaren lamented, "and Rodin was anxious as much for her sake as for ours that this should come on." Rodin persisted and managed to convince Camille to reverse her decision; but a few days later, she changed her mind again and wrote from Villeneuve "that on no condition whatsoever would she give lessons."

Worried and embarrassed, Rodin apologized to the women: "He says he thinks poor Miss Claudel is overworked and that she is really ill, that this mania against seeing anyone is really an illness and that she can't be held altogether responsible for it," McLaren explained. Meanwhile, Rodin offered to give the women weekly lessons free of charge. This happy turn of events made McLaren quip: "What remains is to woo and win Rodin and pray that Mademoiselle Claudel stays off her head in the country!!!"[18]

After the affair of *L'Age mûr*, Camille became even more difficult to help because she would have nothing to do with Rodin, and he had to be very crafty in order to channel some badly needed funds in her direction. For a short time, Morhardt remained the intermediary. With Rodin's money, he bought back the plaster of *La Vague* from Henri Fontaine, along with the reproduction rights.[19] When Morhardt, in turn, was rejected by Camille, Joanny Peytel took his place. It was thanks to the Rodin-Peytel arrangement that Camille was able to hire the sculptor François Pompon to carve the two marble versions of *Persée*, when poor health prevented her from doing it herself.[20] It was also thanks to this arrangement that Camille received monthly payments in 1902; a letter from Peytel to Rodin describes the mysterious ways they used to appease Camille's sensitivity in this matter:

> I have just seen Mademoiselle Claudel. According to your desire, I told her that a friend who is interested in her charged me to buy the bust of her brother in bronze, and to give her every month for twelve months the sum of 500 francs. She insisted on knowing who was the friend; I refused to tell her, according to your instructions. She hesitated for a short time, then accepted. I gave her the first 500 francs and I told her that for eleven months, the first time on February 28, she would receive the same sum of 500 francs every month. I gave, in front of her, the useful instructions to the bank. Your benevolent intentions toward this interesting artist will therefore be fulfilled and I think that no generosity could be more opportune.[21]

After 1902 Rodin stopped helping Camille altogether. That year Camille had declined an invitation to exhibit in Prague alongside Rodin's works, because she feared another "machination." Obviously still seething about *L'Age mûr*, she wrote to the organizer of the exhibition:

> I will tell you frankly that I would have preferred to be successful here with a piece that cost me a huge amount of money and effort, and which was supposed to be, for me, the point of departure for other commissions, rather than sending to Bohemia some ordinary works.
>
> It is true that in Prague, if I agreed to exhibit side by side with Monsieur Rodin, he could claim as much as he wanted that I was under his protection and make believe that my works are due to his inspiration; there I would stand a chance to have a success that coming from him would return to him.
>
> But I am in no mood to be deceived any longer by the crafty devil and false character (*master to all of us*, he says), whose greatest pleasure is to take advantage of everyone.[22]

After this embarrassing letter, Rodin gave up on Camille. By that time, he was inundated with admirers—especially women admirers—and he preferred their loud praises to Camille's public insults. Yet within Rodin's circle, some still tried to find commissions and buyers for Camille. In 1904, when the town of Puget-Théniers was getting ready to raise a monument to Louis-Auguste Blanqui, a revolutionary and a local hero, Gustave Geffroy immediately approached Camille. As a long-time friend and admirer, the art critic thought she would be perfect for the task. Tempted but hesitant, Camille pointed out that her poor health might not withstand the physical exertion demanded by the creation of a large monument. However, after reading Geffroy's biography of Blanqui, she decided to accept the commission. Blanqui's life appealed to Camille; like her, he was a rebel. "I view Blanqui as an instinctive rebel," she wrote to Geffroy, "he does not know against what he is revolting, but he feels he is misled, in a world immersed in falsehood, and he fights ceaselessly without knowing where is the truth."[23]

As ideas for the monument were forming, Camille proposed a stone sculpture leaning against something—in the manner of the sculptor Jules Dalou—and a fee of 20,000 francs. Because she needed to travel to Puget-Théniers, in the south of France, in order to choose a site for the monument, she prudently insisted on a written official commission and an advance of 1,000 francs. The money would allow her to buy two or three dresses and hats to be presentable for the occasion. By April 1905, because the town of Puget-Théniers was showing no enthusiasm for Camille's proposal, Geffroy intervened and obtained the advance requested.[24] It was Eugène Blot who delivered the money to Camille. As could be expected, the sum was spent within a few days.

Other problems needed to be resolved because the town representatives proposed a cheaper monument in bronze, while Camille wished to work only with stone. To reduce expenses, the sculptor offered to make a bust rather than a large monument, but this idea was also rejected. Consequently, Camille decided not to go to Puget-Théniers. When Blot returned for a visit to her atelier, she informed him of her decision, adding that she did not intend to make a maquette because Rodin would steal her commission.[25] Discouraged, Geffroy transferred the commission to Aristide Maillol, who created a monument called *L'Action enchaînée* (Action in Bondage).

Another man tried to help Camille and continued to do so until his death in 1913. That man was her father. Louis-Prosper Claudel, then in his late seventies, was troubled by his wife's rejection of their oldest child, and he worried about Camille's health. On 2 August 1904, he expressed his distress in a letter he sent to Paul, then in China:

> My dear Paul,
>
> Gloomy, sinking into despondency, sadness, discouragement in face of the last events and for other reasons as well, I turn to my usual source of strength in my moments of moral weakness, your book L'Arbre. . . .
>
> We are supposed to go to Gerardmer next month, invited by Marie, who has let a chalet for us all. It is very kind of her, but it is with a heavy heart that I will leave Camille to her isolation.
>
> How unfortunate that these arguments, these conflicts within the family, cause me such great sorrow.
>
> If you could help me restore harmony among us, what service you would render me. . . .
>
> Adieu, I send you my love. Will I see you again and when? a big worry at my age.[26]

While Louis-Prosper Claudel was willing to share his sadness with Paul, he kept his financial concerns to himself. The truth is that by 1902, his personal fortune had shrunk considerably. Although in 1874, the Villeneuve cultivated land register listed him among the most heavily taxed landowners in the area, by 1902 the same register listed him only for two modest fields of wheat and alfalfa.[27] Most of the Claudels' land was gone and soon only their home and another house would remain. Yet Monsieur and Madame Claudel lived a humble, thrifty life and often decried other people's extravagances. The money, no doubt, had been spent on their children.

Of the three children, only Louise did not seek a career. Although she married young, her husband, Ferdinand de Massary, died eight years later, and she was left a widow with a child to support. Under these circumstances, her parents probably helped her financially. As for Paul, his studies and diplomatic career must have cost his parents a considerable amount of money before he became financially independent. But it was Camille who represented the greatest financial drain, considering that Blot and his few purchases could not possibly keep her afloat. In 1909 Louis-Prosper Claudel explained to Paul what must have been a routine for quite a few years: "We pay her rent, her taxes, and even her butcher bills, and small sums we send her from time to time which she asks in unstamped letters. She asks for 20 francs, we send 100 francs; or she asks for nothing and we send 100 francs anyway, often several times in a trimester."[28]

Almost entirely dependent upon her family to survive, with sculpting expenses by far exceeding the profit she made from her sales, Camille had reached an impasse. For her, the severance of all ties with Rodin and his friends had been catastrophic. No matter how devoted Eugène Blot might be, he did not have Rodin's power. To improve her financial situation, only teaching or working in someone else's atelier was still available; but her fragile health and her reclusive habits made either virtually impossible. Anyway, she was certainly not ready to let go of her dream. Although she claimed on occasion that she wanted to follow her brother to his consulates—assuming Paul agreed!—or join one of her cousins in Spain, these outbursts were not meant seriously. Doggedly, she kept on going, living only for the present.

It is interesting to note that at no point did Camille turn toward other women artists. Possibly because of her poor relationship with her mother and sister, she did not trust women. "As soon as a generous man tries to help me out," she had written to Rodin in 1897, "a woman is here to hold his arm and prevent him from acting."[29] Her female models were meek, without civic or political power, and totally dependent upon their fathers and husbands. Yet, things were changing, and as some women were throwing their old confining clothes out the window, other women were challenging the traditional roles assigned to them.

One of these women was Hélène Bertaux, a sculptor better known as Madame Léon Bertaux. In the 1890s, Madame Léon Bertaux launched an assault against one of the most visible bastions of male chauvinism—the École des Beaux-Arts. This remarkable woman had already done much for women artists, considering that she had opened a school of sculpture for women in 1873 and created her own art society, L'Union des Femmes Peintres et Sculpteurs, in 1881, to help women exhibit their work. But there could not be any true victory without equal opportunity for education and recognition. For this, women had to gain acceptance to the École des Beaux-Arts. Since no law prevented them from entering the famous École, Bertaux was left to confront a much more formidable obstacle: tradition.

For years, Bertaux faced hostile officials entrenched in their privileges. When, in 1889, she asked for the creation of a special class for women, she was told that new studios would be too expensive. On the other hand, the idea that women could share studios with men was declared unthinkable. Incensed by the mere thought of it, Charles Garnier, the creator of the Paris Opera House, had claimed that "putting young men and women under the same roof would be setting fire next to powder, and this would produce an explosion engulfing art entirely."[30] Unperturbed, Bertaux modified her request and kept trying, only to face the same ill will. Unlike Camille, she was a crafty diplomat, and she pretended to play the official game rather than to challenge it openly. Each time a request was turned down, she presented a slightly different one. Eventually officials realized she would outlast them, and they compromised.[31] In 1897, the École des Beaux-Arts opened its doors to women, but still excluded them from life studies. Three years later, this last obstacle was lifted and, in 1903 women could finally compete for the Prix de Rome. The first woman won it in 1911. She was sculptor Lucienne Heuvelmans.[32]

This huge victory came too late for Camille. In any case, like other prominent women artists, she did not identify with women's struggles, and she did not join their battles or their exhibitions. She would have been appalled by the compromises Bertaux was willing to make in order to move forward. These compromises were especially visible at the exhibitions of the Union des Femmes Peintres et Sculpteurs, where women rarely ventured outside of sanctioned subject matters—religious, literary, and genre—and where second-rate works were too readily accepted. Camille remained resolute in fighting in the same Salons as male sculptors, and with the same freedom of expression, although it was becoming obvious that she was losing the battle.

PAUL CLAUDEL RETURNED from China in April of 1905. Instead of going home directly, he rushed toward Belgium, driving an automobile through the night, in the mad pursuit of a lost dream. The dream was called Rosalie Vetch. She was married with four children, and she was pregnant with Paul's child.

Paul had met her in 1900 on the ship that took him to China. Beautiful, intelligent, and vibrant, she attracted everyone's attention. At first, Paul had disliked her spoiled mannerisms and kept his distance; but a friend, wishing to thaw the ice between them, had slipped Rosalie's shoe into his pocket. Soon, the thirty-two-year-old Paul was bewitched.

Years later, Paul confided to a friend that "he had known he was lost and had fallen on his knees with his arms raised to the sky when he learned that Rosalie and her husband were coming to Fuzhou."[1] Paul had been named French consul in Fuzhou, a seaport on the China Sea facing the island now called Taiwan. According to traditions of hospitality, he welcomed Rosalie and her husband and offered them shelter in the house provided to him by the consulate. They stayed four years. Although Francis Vetch, Rosalie's husband, proved to be a shady character, Paul protected him at the cost of his own reputation. Completely obsessed by the forbidden seductress living under his roof, entangled in the most unlikely trio, Paul prayed for a miracle. "Even the sight of Hell under my feet would not have separated me from this enemy!" he told his friend André Suarès. "God had to intervene violently; it is true that I prayed for this."[2]

The intervention took place in August 1904. On the first of August, Rosalie left alone for France. Both husband and lover were planning to join her a few months later. The long trip from Fuzhou to France took her first to Japan, then across the Pacific to Canada. From Shanghai, Nagasaki, and

Kobe, Rosalie mailed loving letters to Paul, poking fun at the other passengers and rejoicing that her charms still cast their spell upon everyone. She wrote regularly until she reached Canada. Then silence. Soon the letters Paul and Francis sent her were returned unopened. On 24 February 1905, they finally learned the painful truth: Rosalie had met someone else on the return trip and was living with him in Belgium.

Mad with sorrow and anger, husband and lover joined forces to find the faithless object of their love. They reached France in April and drove nonstop to Rosalie's apartment, only to find that the couple had just escaped. In a state of disarray, Paul turned to his usual source of consolation: a community of monks recently organized nearby in Chevetogne. The kindly monks must have convinced him to change his ways, because Paul returned to Paris, leaving Francis behind in Belgium. "Providence wanted to hit me through the flesh in order to overcome my malice," he declared later.[3] But verses he had written soon after the news of Rosalie's betrayal reveal the excruciating pain he was then enduring: "I am here, the other is elsewhere, and the silence is terrible."[4]

Almost exactly one year after these painful events, on 15 March 1906, Paul married Reine Sainte-Marie Perrin, the daughter of an architect and a fervent Catholic. He had just spent the winter writing the play *Partage de Midi*, where Rosalie was transcended into the unforgettable femme fatale Ysé. Years later Paul chose to view Rosalie's decision to leave him as a noble gesture intended to save his soul. "I could not have done it," he wrote in 1940. "It took me 20 years, these 20 years which passed until [I wrote] *Le Soulier de Satin* to break this tie, or rather transform it. . . . I am convinced that morally and even physically, each man is made for only one woman, and each woman for only one man. The giving up, for God, of this essential and reciprocal craving is something terrible, a salutary but incurable break." Then, suddenly switching mood, he added: "Too bad! God is the greatest and He is the one I have chosen forever. . . ."[5]

Paul's passionate feelings for Rosalie may have improved his understanding of his sister's relationship with Rodin, because he soon directed his attention toward Camille. His numerous attempts to help her in 1905 reflect his concern over the physical and mental changes he could not help but notice. "The poor girl is sick, and I doubt she will live much longer," he wrote to a friend in November. "If she were a Christian, there would be no reason to be distressed. With all her genius, life for her has been so full of trials and disappointments that we can't wish for it to be prolonged."[6]

At the Salon des Champs Élysées, in April, Paul had the opportunity to admire Camille's *Vertumne et Pomone*, the beautiful marble version of *Sakuntala* commissioned by the comtesse de Maigret. The new title referred to the mythological couple Vertumnus and Pomona, divinities of the garden and protectors of fruit trees. During the happy days Camille had shared with Rodin at La Folie Le Prestre, Pomona had been one of the four statues guarding the crumbling mansion and watching over the creation of *Sakuntala*. A wind of nostalgia, therefore, seems to breathe over the marble group with this belated title. "It is a consolation to find, away from all the noise, a moving work done with love," the critic Maurice Hamel wrote in *La Revue de Paris*. "How touching and beautiful is Pomona! . . . The sculpting of the marble is both sweeping and tight. One feels the hand of the artist and not just the scissors of the *praticien*. It is a real masterpiece."[7] Eugène Blot agreed with Hamel's praises; he financed two different bronze editions of *Sakuntala,* a large version and a reduced one. The former was presented at the Salon d'Automne in 1905, and the state bought one of the casts in December.[8] It was given the ambiguous title of *L'Abandon*, meaning both passionate abandon and desertion, which refers to the sensual posture of the woman as well as to the earlier betrayal by her king. In Camille's own life, where desertion had taken the place of love, past and present seem to merge with this ambiguous title.

Camille's modest success at the Salon des Champs Élysées gave Paul the impetus to write an article about his sister's sculpture, "Camille Claudel Statuary Artist." Published in *L'Occident* in August, the article names Camille as the "first worker" of a sculpture that moved away from public places and found a new surrounding in private interiors. Unable to restrain his dislike for Rodin, Paul throws a few rocks in the direction of "the one whose name I withhold."[9] His sculpture is heavy, Paul writes; it pushes back the light. It is the work of a man endowed with a devious mind and a poor imagination. According to Paul, Camille's sculpture is very different because it welcomes light and radiates the inner dream that inspired it.

Encouraged by the compliments he received from readers, Paul prepared a more virulent diatribe against Rodin. "One has to be feared," he wrote to the poet Francis Jammes in October, "and I will use the biting tooth that puzzled you for this purpose. I keep it for villains among whom Rodin will be first served. I wrote a second short article, which I will present here and there until I decide to publish it."[10]

Paul never published the article, which is just as well, considering that the bitter piece reduces Rodin to the level of a simpleton who appeared good only because the other sculptors around him were so bad. "I have nothing to say of this art," Paul added. "They say it is really serious. As for me, in this carnival of rumps, I find the work of a nearsighted man who sees only what is most obvious in nature. All of Rodin's figures hold their heads upside down as if they were pulling beets with their teeth, and turn their posteriors toward the magnificent stars."[11]

On the other hand, Paul truly admired Camille's sculpture. To a friend who asked for pictures of her works, he emphasized that she was a woman of genius. "I say it in spite of the limited liking I have for her person," Paul confided, "because I think she is much superior to Rodin, whose statue of Claude Lorrain in Nancy is so pitiful. I will try to introduce you to her when you come to Paris, but she is so difficult to approach."[12]

Obviously, the relationship between brother and sister had its share of problems. Yet Paul took Camille along when he and a couple of friends— the Francquis—traveled to the Pyrenees in August. Seeking a spiritual retreat as well as forgiveness for his unfortunate affair with Rosalie, Paul intended to participate in the national pilgrimage held at Lourdes while visiting the Pyrenees. As the travelers spent a few days in the spa town of Eaux-Chaudes, the name of the town (Hot Waters) stirred ironic feelings in Paul. "I made a good choice for my retreat this summer," he wrote. "Eaux-Chaudes, tears."[13] Yet the wild mountains with their abundant springs and their breathtaking views made this retreat particularly soothing to the weary siblings. As Paul prepared for the pilgrimage, Camille and the Francquis left for Gavarnie, spending two days in the village overlooking this "colosseum made by nature," as the poet Victor Hugo called it.

Back in Paris, Camille started to work on her brother's bust. Paul, then thirty-seven, had changed considerably since the days of his first diplomatic appointments. "Young, he looked like a stick, now he looks like a sledgehammer," the novelist André Gide, who saw him in December, joked in his journal. "Short but fairly large forehead; face without any nuances, as if cut with a knife, bull neck ending straight with the head, where one sees

Camille Claudel,
*Bust of Paul Claudel
at the Age of 42.*
Bronze, c. 1912.
Private collection
and Musée Rodin,
Paris

passion grow and congest the brain. Yes, I think it is the dominant impression: the head is part of the trunk."[14] Paul's bust did not look like a sledge-hammer. On the contrary, it granted much nobility to Paul's features. Four years later, this bust attracted the attention of the painter Henri Lerolle, a friend of the Claudels. Lerolle wished to have it cast in bronze but by then Camille had turned her back on sculpting and was opposed to the idea. She finally recanted, and the piece was cast in 1910.[15]

In December 1905, Eugène Blot organized an exhibition in his gallery located on the boulevard de la Madeleine. Thirteen works by Camille and twenty-two by sculptor Bernard Hoetger had been selected for this special exhibition. Although it was not a one-woman show for Camille, it was her first retrospective, and the thirteen works represented her creation of the last decade. Among them were *L'Imploration, Persée, L'Abandon, La Valse, Les Causeuses,* and *La Sirène.* In the preface to the catalogue, Louis Vauxelles showed a perceptive appreciation of Camille's sculpture, underlining "her science, her will, her high intellectuality," terms usually reserved for male sculptors. "This rustic and impulsive woman of Lorraine," he added, "who has not found the place she deserves, who has known distress, destitution, who fought alone, scornful of Salon cliques, is one of the most authentic sculptors of our time." [16]

After the exhibition, an article by Charles Morice expressed an admiration mixed with much discouragement:

> Camille Claudel is a great artist. A few of us have been saying it for a long time, and we would like to believe that no one does not know it; we would be wrong; we remain just a few. Nothing more unfair than the fate of this truly heroic woman. She never stopped working and her stubborn labor is visible in works that belong to the most beautiful of contemporary sculpture; she remains poor, and her production is compromised owing to her precarious conditions of living. And yet it must be known, and I would like to shout it in the hope of seeing this iniquity end. [17]

Disheartened by the public's lack of interest in the retrospective, Charles Morice wondered "why art collectors, at least the enlightened ones,

Camille Claudel, *Clotho*. Marble, 1897. Lost

don't rush to enrich their collections with these pieces, today easily afford-able and which, later, in the painful 'later' of glory and tomorrow, will most certainly reach vengeful prices!"[18]

For Camille, hopelessness set in, and after 1905 she stopped exhibit-ing at the Salon. Soon, she would stop creating altogether. As her creative powers crumbled under the weight of hardship and seclusion, her obses-sions about Rodin flared up again; she accused him of having stolen the mar-ble statue of *Clotho*. This representation of one of the three Sisters of Fate who wove man's destiny had been commissioned at the 1895 banquet in honor of Puvis de Chavannes, and Rodin had put up half of the money. While Morhardt and Rodin had intended to give the piece to the Luxem-bourg Museum, they also feared it might not be easily accepted. "Clotho is almost finished," Morhardt wrote to Paul Claudel in 1897. "We are going to send it to the Luxembourg Museum. But here too, won't we face difficul-ties?"[19] They did. Although *Clotho* had been exhibited at the Salon in 1899, by 1905 it had not yet been accepted by the museum. Instead, it remained in storage in Rodin's atelier.

On 27 June 1905, shortly before leaving for Spain, Rodin expressed his worries to Morhardt:

My dear Morhardt,

Would you please give your advice concerning the matter we discussed, Mademoiselle Claudel's marble statue.

It will be difficult for me to have it admitted to the Luxem-bourg museum now or ever. I am facing an opposition that will never end. It would be better for you to come and see me.

Please, extend my greetings to Madame Morhardt.

A. Rodin[20]

Soon the matter became urgent, and a second letter reached Morhardt: "I have just received the insulting letter of Mademoiselle Claudel, who tells me I stole her marble statue," Rodin lamented. "It is in my atelier and I have not yet been able to have it admitted into the Luxem-bourg."[21] Accustomed to Camille's sudden fits of anger, Morhardt did not get too ruffled. "Mademoiselle Claudel's accusation of having 'stolen' her statue is extravagant," he wrote back. "I think there is no cause to get excited. This statue, for which you gave your money . . . according to me must remain in your hands until the day we can have the state accept it. If you don't mind, we will take care of this at the end of summer with Mirbeau and Geffroy."[22]

By December, nothing had been resolved, and Rodin had to remind Morhardt of the problem. On the eleventh of December, encouraged by the news that one of Camille's bronzes—*L'Abandon*—had been acquired by the state, Morhardt wrote to Léonce Bénédite, then director of the Luxembourg museum and asked him to admit the sculpture to the museum. Unfortunately, Bénédite's answer hinted at bureaucratic problems and was far from encouraging: "I need to contact Monsieur Dujardin-Beaumetz since I don't know whether he will accept your offer without going through the Conseil des Musées or decide to submit it. In the latter case, I know what the result will be. . . . We can, in any case, bring the marble statue to the museum temporarily. There, it will be seen, if you wish."[23] The next day, on December 16, Morhardt asked Rodin to send *Clotho* to the Luxembourg museum and, on the nineteenth, Rodin wrote back: "I sent Mademoiselle Claudel's piece to the Luxembourg yesterday."[24]

Years later, in 1929, Judith Cladel contacted Morhardt for the book she was writing on Rodin. She was curious about Camille as a woman and as an artist. In his answer, Morhardt mused about *Clotho:* "What happened to *La Parque* [Clotho] done in marble for the Luxembourg museum—and which I paid with the subscription collected from Rodin, Puvis de Chavannes, Albert Besnard, and so many others? The Conseil du Musée had, of course, rejected its admission. But Léonce Bénédite assured me he had it placed on the stairway of his cabinet and that sooner or later. . . . Maybe you'll find it there, dear Mademoiselle, since you wish to bring her great and noble memory back to life."[25]

But five years later, Judith Cladel was still looking for *Clotho*. On 6 June 1934, she alerted the Ministry of Fine Arts about its disappearance. Cladel had hoped to include *Clotho* in a retrospective she was organizing of Camille's work, but "the piece is not in the collections of the Luxembourg, and the search done by Monsieur Louis Hautecœur brought no result. At the Rodin museum as well, no sign of *La Parque*."[26] Morhardt, also alerted, shared his concerns with Cladel, but neither of them was able to find *Clotho*. To this day, it has not been found.

WHEN CAMILLE READ in a newspaper that her bronze of *La Fortune* was used as publicity by a shopkeeper, she mockingly expressed her satisfaction that "*La Fortune*, which always eludes her, can be used as publicity by someone else."[1] This pun was hiding the truly critical circumstances of the sculptor, her physical and mental health having deteriorated to the point that she could no longer create new works. Although the Ministry of Fine Arts was finally extending to her a sincere helping hand, it never amounted to more than a few "charitable handouts." In 1904, after the critic Roger Marx had requested an "urgent aid for Mademoiselle Claudel,"[2] she received 150 francs; on two other occasions, she received respectively 100 francs and 150 francs. All the notes attached to these paltry awards emphasized the need to spare the artist's pride. "Don't write the word 'aid,'" they each under-lined.[3] But the small amount of the gifts had a humiliating ring.

A more substantial offer from the state occurred during Camille's ret-rospective at the Blot Gallery in December 1905. In the course of his visit to the gallery, Dujardin-Beaumetz promised Blot he would work out a com-mission for Blot's protégée. Three months later, Blot wrote to remind him of his promise to "the great and poor Claudel," stressing the urgency of the need and the certainty of supporting the creation of a beautiful work of art.[4] Dujardin-Beaumetz followed through and, on 26 April 1906, the state awarded a complete commission to Camille for the plaster and the bronze of a statuette. This first state commission would also be the last sculpture Camille had the strength to complete, and the correspondence taking place between her and the Ministry of Fine Arts during this period reveals that her delusions had finally turned into a psychotic paranoia centering on Rodin.

Notified by the Ministry that she was granted 1,500 francs for the plaster model of a statuette, Camille wrote back on May 18, in an attempt to receive more money:

Mr. Under-Secretary of State,

Your letter dated 30 April, informing me of a 1,500-franc commission for a statuette, arrives just in time. I have just finished a highly original study in clay, but I could not give it to you for the modest sum you suggest. I ask for an extra 500 francs, because I spent a considerable amount of money on this study, hiring an exceptionally beautiful French model, who charged very high prices (but it is an original creation).

If you decide in my favor, please let me know, and I will be at your disposal.

Sincerely,

Mlle Claudel

19 quai Bourbon

P.S. I was sick due to ill treatments I endured and to the lack of the care I required; I therefore could not answer any sooner.[5]

Camille stretched the truth in order to solicit an extra 500 francs. Far from being an original study, the sculpture was a duplicate of *Sakuntala*, but without the king. The woman, now alone, is on the verge of collapsing. She is held up by the branch of a tree, which has replaced the loving arms of the missing king.

The figure was renamed *Niobide blessée* (Wounded Niobid) after the daughter of Niobe, the mythical Greek princess who offended Apollo and Artemis. In retaliation for Niobe's insulting pride, the young Niobid and her siblings were shot by the gods' dreaded arrows and the disconsolate mother was turned to stone. The parallel between the Niobid's lingering death and Camille's own painful collapse is obvious, while this last creation ends the cycle of *Sakuntala*. From the tender sensuality of the first piece modeled during the happy days with Rodin, to the hopelessness of the last piece, *Sakuntala* underwent several transformations that closely followed Camille's own life. As *Vertumne et Pomone*, the white marble revived the nostalgic memories of the goddess Pomona standing in a niche of the wall of the crumbling Folie Le Prestre, where Camille lovingly sculpted with Rodin. With *L'Abandon*, the bronze became a symbol of both passionate abandon and desertion. Finally, with *Niobide blessée*, the female figure has turned into a woman tormented by the gods and left alone to die.

Camille Claudel, *Niobide blessée,* (detail). Bronze, 1907. Musée de Poitiers

Art Inspector Armand Dayot, who came to Camille's atelier to view the sculpture, later wrote: "The piece is beautiful and, looking at it, I could only rejoice that I found it already made in the atelier of the artist, and that I did not ask for a new sculpture, which, unquestionably, she would not have been able to complete."[6]

Camille's plea for an extra 500 francs was denied, but she accepted the commission anyway. A month later, in dire need of money, she asked for a partial payment, and Dayot was dispatched to her atelier to view the progress she had made. His recommendation on 30 June 1906 supported the sculptor's request and underlined its urgency. "It is a work full of *remarkable* qualities," he wrote. "I deem it appropriate to accept it and to urgently grant the artist, now in great need, an 800 francs advance on the total price. The work is, I repeat, almost done."[7] A few days later, Camille received a partial payment, and in October she informed the Ministry that her work was finished. "Please, tell me where I must send this statuette," she worried, "and please, pay me the balance, because I am going to change apartments and I will not have room to keep it any more."[8]

Niobide blessée was sent to the Dépôt des Marbres on October 16, and Camille was paid, although not fast enough, as far as she was concerned. In February 1907, she accepted the 3,000 franc commission offered by the state for the bronze of *Niobide blessée.* Unfortunately, when she attempted to retrieve her plaster from the Dépôt des Marbres, she ran into a bureaucratic snag, and her request was denied. Convinced that Rodin was behind the administration's refusal to return the plaster, and unable to find the order sent to her by the Ministry, she concluded that "it had been taken away by fraudulent means." Urging the Ministry to disregard any claim produced with the "stolen" order in hand, she embarked on a tale of persecution and deceit perpetrated, she claimed, by Rodin:

> After trying by all possible means to steal several of my ideas and some studies he coveted, and after finding a fierce resistance in me, he expects, by force, and by the poverty he imposes on me, to reduce me to deliver what he wants. These are his usual ways. This is the revolting exploitation undertaken by this great genius in order to get the ideas he lacks.
>
> I therefore wish to protest against this disgraceful mistreatment and request the immediate delivery of my plaster statuette, which, according to me, is not at the Dépôt des Marbres, but in the atelier of the great man, where he is taking a cast of it, as he did with my other works, one after another.[9]

The bureaucratic blunder leading to these wild allegations was quickly straightened out, and Camille recovered her plaster. In September she wrote to the Ministry that the bronze was finished, but at the end of her letter, she returned to her obsessions and tacked on a very strange accusation:

> I take this opportunity to tell you that I know the author of all the thefts and depredations committed in the Louvre. There is only one: he pays poor people to do his dirty work; afterward, the objects are sent back to him. He has tons of them, more than the architect Thomas. Dalou knew him: he is a knight of the underworld. When he dies, you will recover everything you have lost.[10]

Camille, of course, found herself in an embarrassing predicament when the police asked for details. Realizing that she was hallucinating, the police noted that "she received the information she related in her letter from a woman she met in the Luxembourg garden. But she did not know the woman and could not provide even a vague description. Under these conditions, no information was collected regarding the person reported by Mlle Claudel, and the latter's behavior allows us to consider his existence as problematic."[11]

The allegations were dropped, but Camille was plainly going through an acutely aggressive phase of her illness, and she persisted in her belligerence. Forgetting the time-consuming processes of the French bureaucracy, she demanded to be paid immediately for her bronze. When she was not, she turned her wrath against Art Inspector Eugène Morand. In the absence of Inspector Dayot, Morand had been charged with providing the administrative report on *Niobide blessée*, but a virulent exchange of letters with Camille forced him to decline this mission. In an attempt to explain his decision to the Ministry, Morand noted that he wrote two very courteous letters to the sculptor. "These two letters," he added, "were answered with such vulgar postcards, and with envelopes containing such foul-smelling filth, that I want to have nothing to do with Mlle. Claudel, who behaved in the same manner and at the same time with M. Rodin."[12] The "foul-smelling filth" of these letters was in the form of cat feces; Camille sent the letters anonymously, but their content left no doubt as to their origins. Outraged by her behavior, Morand threatened to file a complaint to the public prosecutor if it ever happened again.

Right away, the Ministry returned Armand Dayot to Camille's affairs. *Niobide blessée* was delivered to the state in December 1907, in spite of Camille's bickering about the slowness of the payments. In April 1910, the plaster was given to the Bougie Museum in Algeria, then a French colony, but the bronze waited another twenty-five years to be placed on the site of the naval prefecture in Toulon.[13]

Camille's heightened aggressivity in 1907 was also noticeable in a letter she sent to Marguerite Durand, founder of the feminist review *La Fronde*. In October of the preceding year, Durand had requested photographs for an article she intended to write on Camille, and the sculptor had been delighted. "I am happy to learn from you that something cheerful is being prepared for me," she had rejoiced.[14] A few months later, her tone had changed, and she did not try to hide the irritation she felt at answering Durand's bothersome questions. "The questions you ask seem to me pointless, useless for your article. Why does anyone need to know who owns my art? You have enough to say with what I told you during our last visit; it is much more interesting than enumerations and useless details."[15] After this cutting honesty, she saluted Durand with an abrupt "receive my salutations"—quite unlike her first letter, which had closed with "please, kindly receive my sincere friendship."

Camille Claudel, *Louis-Prosper Claudel at the Age of 79*. Charcoal on paper, 1905. Private collection

Camille's letter also alluded to her health. She had been sick and forced to stay in bed most of the time, she said. In fact, she was still sick, and she plainly needed care that she was not receiving. Both her mother and sister had stopped seeing her once they realized the extent of her departure from traditional values. In their eyes, her thirst for freedom had stained the family, and they no longer wanted to have anything to do with her.

In the early 1880s, the painter Marie Bashkirtseff had pointedly written in her *Journal:* "The woman who becomes so emancipated, the young and pretty woman, I mean, is almost ostracized; she becomes strange, noticed, blamed, crazy, and therefore, even less free than if she did not shock the idiotic customs."[16] Bashkirtseff, only twenty-two when she wrote these lines, is one of the few women artists who became involved in women's organizations, both as an artist and as a feminist. Yet when she penned art reviews for the feminist newspaper *La Citoyenne*, she signed them Pauline Orelle. Openly taking the step of emancipation would have been too risky for the young Bashkirtseff; she preferred to hide behind an assumed identity. Camille Claudel, on the other hand, openly challenged "the idiotic customs" in both her private and her professional life. She dared to become the mistress of a man who lived with someone else—an unforgivable sin, according to bourgeois values. Banished from her family circle, she could have found solace in her artistic pursuits, but here too she refused to bow to the dictates of propriety. Her sexually daring pieces shocked the academic art world and turned state officials against her. As a result, she solicited state commissions in vain, until she finally proposed an acceptable piece: a woman alone—vanquished and dying.

Marie Bashkirtseff's insightful observation takes on a prophetic poignancy when applied to Camille. The sculptor's defiance of the sexist values of her time had indeed made her "strange, noticed, blamed, crazy," and so on. Her freedom had evaporated along with her dreams, and she was surviving only because of her father's unwavering affection. Unlike the women of the family, Louis-Prosper Claudel wanted to help his daughter. Overwhelmed by his wife's animosity against Camille, he did not know what to do. He was therefore very grateful when Paul, who had briefly returned to France in 1909, requested money to buy a few things for his sister. "Until now," Monsieur Claudel wrote to Paul, "nobody wanted to bother with her. It has been ages since I wanted for your mother to see her, check her clothing, her furniture—because, for me, I have never been able to be heard by Camille without triggering revolting scenes. . . . I would like for Camille to come and see us once in a while. Your mother won't hear of it, but I wonder if it would not be the best way to calm down, if not to cure, this rabid madwoman."[17]

Louis-Prosper Claudel understood that Camille's seclusion contributed to her mental deterioration. He believed, perhaps rightly, that a return to Villeneuve and to normal human interaction might improve her mental state. If Camille still stood a chance of reversing her decline, emotional and physical support had to be extended to her right away. Unfortunately, Camille's vindictive mother refused to see her or to welcome her in her home, and the old man was not able to impose his will upon the rest of his household. Therefore, with almost no visits from relatives, and no friends aside from Eugène Blot and Henry Asselin, Camille was once more left in the most acute isolation.

Desperate for warmth and affection, she turned to the bums she met in the street and invited them to boisterous parties whenever unexpected money came her way. On these occasions, she welcomed her guests dressed in extravagant attire, with ribbons and feathers in her hair, and she generously served champagne to everyone. The next day, after these demonstrations of prodigality, she returned to her poverty and her obsessions.[18]

Although Camille was still making clay and plaster pieces during this period, none of these works remains. After *Niobide blessée*, she destroyed all her subsequent statues with a hammer. At the beginning of each summer or after a crisis, she pounded away at everything she had created in the preceding year, and then she called someone to carry the debris away and bury it. In a letter Camille wrote after the death of her cousin Henri Thierry, she describes how this ritual started; her words suggest that she performed the massacre both as a form of sacrifice and as an act of rebellion against the world:

> When I received your death announcement, I got so mad that I took all my wax studies and threw them in the fire. It made big flames, I warmed my feet at the fire, that's the way it is when something unpleasant happens to me, I take my hammer and I squash a figure. Henri's death cost me a lot. More than 10,000 francs.
>
> The great statue followed his little wax sisters because Henri's death was followed by more bad news: for no reason, all of a sudden, they stopped giving me money. I find myself suddenly penniless. It's Rodin's gang that worked my mother over to get this result. Many other executions occurred afterward, and a pile of rubble accumulates in the middle of my atelier, it is a real human sacrifice.[19]

As she pounded away at her own creation, Camille vehemently affirmed her right to live outside the values of her time. For a few brief moments, driven by her destructive mission, she may have believed that she controlled her destiny. When the massacre was over and the debris had been picked up, she sometimes disappeared for days or even weeks. She lived in filth, scavenged for food in garbage containers, and ranted against Rodin and his "gang," claiming they wanted to kill her and to steal her statues. To protect herself against them, she turned her atelier into a fortress: "security chains, machicolations, wolf traps behind every door," she told Henri's widow.[20]

One morning, Asselin came to her atelier for a posing session— Camille was making his bust. She would not open the door, and Asselin had to spend a long time talking to her from the other side. Finally, she unlocked the door. She was shaking with fear and holding a broom studded with nails. She told him: "Last night, two men tried to force my shutters. I recognized them: they are two of Rodin's Italian models. He told them to kill me. I am in his way: he wants to get rid of me."[21]

More than ever, in Camille's mind, Rodin loomed as the Enemy. Nothing remained of the beloved friend and mentor, nothing but a frightfully devilish figure out to get her. With the twisted sense of logic that paranoia patients can sometimes demonstrate, Camille looked back on her long years in Rodin's atelier and the many hours she had spent working for him. She saw herself stripped, starved, and dispossessed by the very person who now dominated the art world. In her view, he had stolen her work and her ideas, and he was even conspiring to destroy her life.

Camille had indeed produced work for Rodin in the past, and Rodin had most probably abused his power in the case of *L'Age mûr*; but the seed of truth, which sparked Camille's hatred and fueled her paranoia, generated the most extravagant accusations. Camille's delirium is especially visible in a letter she sent to Paul about 1910. Once more she voiced her fears regarding the fate of *L'Age mûr*, and then she carried on against everyone in general, Rodin in particular. Artists, dealers, models, cleaning women, all came to her atelier with only one purpose: to steal her work and become rich from it. "Last year," she wrote, "my neighbor, Sir Picard, Rodin's buddy and brother of a police inspector, entered my atelier with a passkey. There was a woman in yellow against the wall; since then he made several women in yellow exactly the same as mine and exhibited them. His profit: 100,000 francs." A young boy who brought her wood fell under the suspicion of spying on her on behalf of Rodin. A cleaning woman was accused of putting a narcotic in her coffee to steal one of the sculptures while Camille was asleep, and selling it off for another 100,000 francs. "With *L'Age mûr*," Camille concluded, "it will be the same, they are all going to do it one after another. Every time I create a new work, millions are rolling for casters, founders, artists and merchants; but for me . . . $0 + 0 = 0$."[22]

It is true that Camille's new creations were disappearing, considering that she destroyed them herself. But her confused mind often could not remember that she was the one who had orchestrated their disappearance. It is also true that she had imitators in the art world, although it is doubtful that they made "millions." In 1904, for example, Agnès de Frumerie exhibited five statuettes of gossiping women, in the exact same style as Camille's *Causeuses*.[23] But what should have been a mere source of irritation to the sculptor became a torrent of hallucinations triggered by her paranoia.

In the case of Rodin, her delirium took the same exaggerated dimensions. She called him a scoundrel, a thief, even a murderer. At the end of her letter to Paul, she concluded:

> The unsavory character draws heavily from me through various means and shares it with chic artists, his buddies who, in exchange, have him decorated, give him ovations and banquets, etc.
>
> Ovations for this famous man cost me an arm and a leg, and for me there is nothing at all!!! . . .
>
> And the nerve of using my groups for more than twenty years to make me end my career on my parents' charity. What nerve! You will tell them "you owe her something for all you took from her for so many years, otherwise her atelier will remain hermetically closed."[24]

"All you took from her" included much more than her artistic career, but Camille could not talk about it, and this may partly explain the intensity of her obsessions. She had given her youth to Rodin, and she had received unequivocal promises from him. Even though he had been supportive of her work until *L'Age mûr*, he had failed her in the most sensitive realm of her psyche. The breach of promise and especially the abortion were all the more damaging to her in that they had to be kept secret. But Camille knew how much Rodin had "taken from her," and she was never able to forgive him.

Another letter written by Camille during the same year is full of incoherent accusations. Ever since the Dreyfus affair, Camille viewed Jews, Protestants, and Freemasons as the enemies of France. By 1910 they had become her personal enemies, and she was sure they were all plotting to poison her, especially Rodin, whom she now labeled as Dreyfusard and Protestant, although he was neither. "As for me, I have had it," she wrote to her cousin Henri. "I am still sick from the poison I have in my blood, my body is burning; it is Rodin, the Protestant, who gives me the poison, because he hopes to inherit my atelier, with the help of his good friend, the lady de Massary."[25]

Camille accused her sister, Louise de Massary, of striking a deal against her with Rodin. In Camille's mind, Louise had already poisoned her own husband and was now trying to poison her. As for her cousin Henri, who had been in the hospital, Camille was sure he too was being poisoned, so she urged him to avoid the medicine brought by his doctors and to drink his own herb teas instead. When Henri Thierry died two years later, there was no doubt in her mind that he, indeed, had been poisoned.[26]

In September 1909, Paul Claudel, back from China, mustered the courage to visit his sister's atelier, and he recorded in his *Journal:* "In Paris, Camille mad. Wallpaper ripped in long strips, the only armchair broken and torn, horrible filth. Camille huge, with a dirty face, speaking ceaselessly in a monotonous and metallic voice."[27] Paul had permanently left China after spending three years in Tien-Tsin, eighty miles from Peking. His new position as a consul, first in Prague, then in Frankfurt, made it possible for him to see his relatives more often, although these occasions were rarely happy ones. "Camille ran away at 4 a.m.," he wrote in 1911. "No one knows where she is."[28] The sight of his elderly parents also added to his worries: "The two old people alone in the old cracked house, with the old servant and the cricket in the ashes of the kitchen. In Villeneuve I am always *overwhelmed by pathetic.*"[29]

There were many good reasons for Paul to be overwhelmed: his father, old, despondent, and unable to improve Camille's circumstances; his embittered mother and sister, Louise, unwilling to extend a comforting hand; the neighbors on quai Bourbon constantly gossiping about the madwoman downstairs. "What was this first-floor apartment with shutters always closed?" the neighbors complained. "What was this haggard and careful woman you saw only in the morning when she went to get her miserable food?"[30]

Something needed to be done. Although Louis-Prosper Claudel had long resisted the idea of committing Camille to a mental asylum, he was becoming too feeble to resist much longer. Talks about confinement reached Camille as early as the beginning of 1913, shortly after the death of Henri. "Right now," Camille confided to Henri's widow, "Sir Rodin convinced my parents to have me committed; they are all in Paris to arrange it. Thanks to this summary process, the scoundrel would gain possession of the work of my whole life."[31] Although Rodin had nothing to do with it, Paul had contacted the director of the Ville-Evrard asylum around that time and sought the spiritual support of a saintly Parisian priest named Daniel Fontaine. "Pray for my family, so barely Christian," he wrote from Frankfurt on January 24, "for my sister who is more than half-crazy, for my eighty-seven-year-old father, who refuses to fulfill his religious duties."[32] On February 26, he wrote again from Frankfurt to elaborate on what he viewed as the nature of his sister's illness:

> As for my poor sister, I will probably be forced to go to Paris to commit her to an asylum. In reality I am convinced that, like most cases of madness, hers is truly a case of possession. It is really curious, anyway, that the two best known forms of madness are pride and terror, self-aggrandizement disorder and persecution disorder (I am not speaking of frequent eroticism). She was a great artist, and her pride and contempt for others were limitless. It became worse with age and misfortune. When I returned four years ago, she was already mad, and what struck me most was that her voice had completely changed. Right now, she does not go out and lives in a dreadfully filthy apartment, with doors and windows locked. You see how painful this must be for my parents.
>
> I am exactly like my sister, although more of a weakling and a dreamer and, without God's grace, my story might have been hers or even worse.
>
> Pray for us.
>
> —Is it possible to exorcise from afar?[33]

A few days later, Fate called again on Paul: Louis-Prosper Claudel had been seriously ill for a week.

> I delay my departure for no reason, laziness or secret desire to arrive there too late. On the first of March, urgent telegram. I leave in the evening. On the river Marne, magnificent dawn. . . . Walk up to Villeneuve. Arrive at 8:30. My father died almost suddenly at 3 a.m. without confession, although he expressed a desire to do so several times. His yellow face, his contemplative, *self-communing* look, the mortal cold of this cadaver.[34]

Louis-Prosper Claudel died on 2 March 1913 and was buried two days later. Camille was not informed of her father's death, and so she did not attend the funeral.

ONE OF THE RESIDENTS at 19, quai Bourbon was Dr. Michaux, a well-liked doctor who had treated Camille on several occasions. Appalled by the awful mess in Camille's atelier, Dr. Michaux had strictly forbidden his ten-year-old son to go into the place. His interdiction, of course, produced the reverse effect, and the child managed to sneak into this magic cavern full of sculptures, cats, and spider webs.[1] One day, the eccentric mistress of the forbidden kingdom disappeared, but the child could not know his father had played a major part in her disappearance.

According to the 1838 French law governing confinements to mental institutions, any person armed with a medical certificate could have a family member committed. Immediately after Louis-Prosper Claudel's funeral, Paul Claudel contacted Dr. Michaux for this purpose. There was no time to lose, because Paul had to return to his diplomatic post in Germany. The required medical certificate, written and signed by Dr. Michaux on March 7, provides numerous arguments supporting Camille's commitment:

> I, Doctor of Medicine from the University of Paris, certify that Mademoiselle Camille Claudel is suffering from very serious mental disorders; that she wears wretched clothes; that she is extremely dirty since she never washes; that she sold all her furniture, except for an armchair and a bed; that, in spite of this, she receives from her family, besides the rent for her apartment paid directly to the landlord, a pension of 200 francs per month which would be enough for her to live comfortably; that she spends her life locked inside her apartment and without fresh air, since the blinds are tightly closed; that for the past several months she has not gone out during the day, but sometimes comes out in the middle of the night; that, according to letters she recently wrote to her brother and according to comments she

made to the concierge, she is always afraid of "Rodin's gang;" that, for the past seven or eight years, I have noticed several times that she thinks she is being persecuted; that her condition, dangerous to herself because of the lack of care and sometimes of nourishment, is also dangerous for her neighbors; and that it is necessary to commit her to a mental institution.[2]

Dr. Michaux's report focuses upon Camille's antisocial behavior: wretched clothes, dirty dwelling void of furniture, seclusion, and fear of going out during the day. Although his arguments point to a definite need for treatment, he fails to explain how a fearful woman who comes out only at night could be a danger to her neighbors. At no time in her life did Camille ever threaten to hurt anyone; it is hard to see how she could have been a danger to society.

The following day Madame Claudel signed the request for the committal of her daughter:

> I, Louise Cécile Athanaïse Cerveaux widow Claudel, living in Villeneuve-sur-Fère (Aisne), 73 years old, declare in my position as mother that my intention is to commit to the Ville-Evrard Asylum Camille Claudel, 48 years old, living in Paris at 19 quai Bourbon and, consequently, pray the director of this institution to accept her and have her treated for her Mental Alienation.[3]

Camille was to be taken to Ville-Evrard just before the weekend, but a minor correction requested by the director of the asylum delayed the proceeding. Without being aware of it, Camille was granted two more days of freedom. She would be committed on 10 March 1913, eight days after her father's death. On Monday morning, still unaware of what was coming, she posted a letter to her cousin Charles Thierry, brother of Henri who had died the preceding year. Between 1910 and 1913, Camille appears to have renewed old ties with the Thierrys, who welcomed her quirky correspondence with tolerant goodwill.

> My dear Charles,
> You inform me of Father's death; this is the first time I hear of

it, no one told me anything. When did it happen? Try to find out and give me some details. My poor Father never saw me the way I am; he was always led to believe that I was an odious creature, ungrateful and mean; it was necessary so that the other one could inherit everything. . . .

I would not dare to go to Villeneuve; in any case, I would have to be able to do it; I have no money, not even shoes. I have been placed on a reduced pension; sorrow is my fate. If you know anything, tell me; I will not try to write because I would be rebuffed, as usual.

I am surprised that Father died; he was supposed to live a hundred years. There is something suspicious about it. Love to you and Emma.

K-Mille[4]

Around eleven that morning, an ambulance stopped in front of the quai Bourbon atelier, and "hospital employees entered through the back of the room and seized the terrified occupant, who for a long time had been waiting for them among plasters and dried-up clay. The mess and dirt were indescribable. On the wall, hung with pins were the fourteen Stations of the Cross, cut with scissors from the front page of a newspaper."[5]

Confused and, numb, Paul witnessed his sister's abduction and accompanied her to Ville-Evrard, which was right outside of Paris. What he had feared for several years had finally taken place, and by his own intervention. In a state of shock, he stared at the pitiful patients he met when he reached the asylum: "The madwomen at Ville-Evrard. The old senile woman. The one who chattered continually in English with a soft voice, like a poor sick starling. The ones who wander around without saying anything. Sitting in the hallway, with her head in her hand. Horrible sadness of these souls in trouble and of these fallen spirits."[6]

"I have been miserable all week," Paul confessed to his *Journal*.[7] In an effort to find some solace, he wrote again to the priest Daniel Fontaine. "My sister was committed to Ville-Evrard without resistance and without scandal," he noted with some relief.[8] His attention was mostly focused upon the fourteen crucifixes pinned on the wall of the atelier and on other signs that Camille might be returning to religion. Saving her immortal soul was much more important to him than saving her miserable body, but Camille had different ideas. On March 14, she wrote again to her cousin Charles Thierry:

> My dear Charles,
>
> My letter the other day seemed to be a foreboding, because scarcely was it posted than an automobile came to take me away and drove me to a mental asylum. I am, at least I think I am, in the Ville-Evrard asylum. If you wish to come and see me, you can take your time, because it will be long before I get out of here; they have me and they are not going to let go.
>
> If you could bring me a portrait of my aunt, my godmother, to keep me company, you would make me happy. You would not recognize me, you who saw me so young and so radiant in the Chacrise sitting-room.[9]

Camille's godmother, Julienne du Jay and her sister Marguerite du Jay, had always been kind to Camille. They were related to the Thierrys by marriage and lived in their Chacrise estate until their death in the 1880s. Camille's humble request at this terrible time of her life is particularly moving and points to the few avenues she had left to find warmth and solace. Charles reacted quickly, and a week later Camille could thank him for sending the coveted portrait. "Poor women," she wrote, "they were so kind, so modest; I felt so good with them. Ah! if they were still alive, I would not be the way I am; they had such generous hearts. You are good to give me the portrait. You are like your mother; if you were still the landlord, I would immediately settle down with you in Chacrise. Forget all this. . . ."[10] Letting go of her nostalgia, Camille turned to her fears. She had no illusions about her committal, and she analyzed her situation with a prophetic lucidity:

> I am scared, I don't know what is going to happen to me; I think I am about to end badly, all of this is suspicious; if you were here, you would see. What was the point of working so hard and of being talented, to be rewarded like this? Never a penny, tormented all my life. Deprived of all that contributes to happiness and still finish like this.
>
> Do you remember the poor marquis du Sauvencourt, from

Château de Muret, your former neighbor? He just died after being locked up for thirty years! It is horrible, one cannot imagine it.[11]

Camille's fears were somewhat mellowed by Charles's imminent visit. On March 17, Charles had received the authorization from the head doctor of the asylum—Dr. Truelle—to come and visit her the next time he was in Paris. Unfortunately, this authorization was withdrawn a few days later, when the order was given to completely sequester Camille. She was to have no communication with the outside world, no correspondence, no visits, except with her mother, brother, and sister. The Claudels had requested Camille's sequestration because they objected to the Thierrys' way of life and feared the possibility of scandal. Charles, who had traveled all the way from Reims to see his cousin, was not even given news of her health.[12] Again, the law gave little protection to patients, and sequestration was usually granted by the head doctor upon the request of a family member. Many doctors then believed that isolation was a proper therapeutic measure to ensure the peace and well-being of the patient; therefore, they often complied with such requests. Only the official correspondence taking place between the concerned parties and the administrators was protected by law. All other correspondence could be destroyed "for the sake of the patient."[13]

It is true that Camille had reached the point where she could not function on her own any longer. Her obsessive letters, her constant ranting against everyone, her regular disappearances, and the filth in which she lived clearly proved that she needed care and treatment. The first observations recorded on the day of her arrival at Ville-Evrard supported Dr. Michaux's certificate and diagnosed her as suffering "from a systematized persecution delirium, mostly based upon distortions of facts and fabulations, with conceited ideas and self-gratification."[14] As she had done so often, Camille blamed Rodin for all her troubles, but her violent ranting against him presented a new, surreal dimension to her delirium: she had lost track of time; she saw no difference between a millennium and a decade. According to Camille, Rodin had already exploited her three thousand years earlier, even before the Deluge. He forced her to work in his atelier when she was eighteen; he beat and kicked her; he attempted to poison everyone in her family, but she had not noticed it until recently. He had her committed so he could steal what little remained in her atelier. As the head of a gang of thieves, he had power over everyone, even her relatives.[15]

All the medical reports written on the day of Camille's arrival present similar narratives. They also emphasize Camille's filthy appearance, her reclusive habits when she lived on quai Bourbon, where she barricaded her door and had food delivered through the window. Camille even had to be taken out of her atelier through the window to be placed in the ambulance.

In view of this situation, committal could hardly be avoided. However, there is a significant difference between regular committal and sequestration. It is important to recognize that Camille never represented a direct danger either to herself or to society. She never threatened to hurt anyone, nor did she ever attempt suicide, both of which could have explained sequestration measures. In 1905, when prompt help could have slowed down and possibly reversed her inexorable decline, her unforgiving mother had stubbornly refused to pull her out of her seclusion. This same mother, now blind to her own insensitivity and to the critical part she had played in Camille's illness, resolved to condemn her daughter to the most absolute form of seclusion: sequestration in a world of madness. "I don't find it inhuman to deprive my daughter of visits, which could only get her agitated," Madame Claudel wrote to Dr. Truelle. "When she was home, she received no one, even the local retailers, who put the food they brought in a box on her windowsill. . . . Why couldn't she do without visits now, especially these?"[16]

According to the law, however, Camille's fate was in Paul's hands. As the only male in the family, he had the supreme authority to act on her behalf. But Paul's options were limited: he could either take Camille along, as he moved from consulate to consulate, or leave her behind in a mental asylum. By then, Paul was the father of four children, and his wife showed no interest in nursing her "crazy sister-in-law" back to health. In any case, between diplomacy and writing, Paul's life had become an endless whirlwind. Social evenings, ceremonies, rehearsals, openings, all absorbed his time and kept him in the public eye. Under these circumstances, it would have been impossible for him to take Camille along. Yet, while committal to an asylum may have been the only alternative for the time being, nothing in Camille's behavior defends the decision to cut her off from the outside world. Her sequestration was decreed only to prevent the scandal that might happen.

Camille Claudel, *Niobide blessée*. Bronze, 1907. Musée de Poitiers

It happened anyway. It took a while for Charles Thierry to figure out what to do, but six months later he alerted the local newspaper *l'Avenir de l'Aisne* to Camille's plight, and he produced the last three letters she had sent him as proof of her sanity. On 19 September 1913, the paper's first article sought, most of all, to stir the readers' emotions when it reduced Camille's case to "a monstrous and hardly believable thing: as she was working under the full possession of her talent and intellect, men came to her home, brutally threw her in a car in spite of her indignant protests, and, ever since this day, this great artist has been locked up in a crazy house."[17]

The news reached Parisian newspapers a month later, when the journalist Paul Vibert received a letter condemning the frivolous committals occasionally fostered by the 1838 law. The letter was signed only with the initials "A.L.," but Vibert decided to publish it in the editorial of *Le Grand*

National on 8 December 1913. "There are two ways of eliminating a person from society," the writer forcefully wrote. "The first way is murder. The second way is legal committal, later converted, according to needs, to sequestration. Arbitrary committal is regularly initiated by people who wish to get rid of a troublesome relative for reasons of revenge or cupidity."[18] The author of the letter—later identified as A. Lelm—focused especially upon sequestration, justly pointing out that it deprived the patient of any means of contacting the people who could help him. At the end of his letter, Lelm revealed his personal interest in Camille's committal. With enough precision to expose the various protagonists to the public, he narrated Camille's abduction from her atelier, condemned her mother and her brother, and quoted parts of a letter Camille had sent to Charles Thierry.[19]

For a few days, a dialogue between the Parisian newspaper and its provincial counterpart *l'Avenir de l'Aisne* set the stage for an informal trial of the Claudel family. "We are resolute, my friends and I, to tear this unfortunate great statuary artist from the claws of the mental asylum where her family had her locked up," *le Grand National* proclaimed. Unfortunately, these seemingly good intentions were muddled by the newspaper's anticlerical agenda. With a lack of logic reminiscent of some of Camille's prose, the newspaper managed to blame the Church and the Army both for the 1838 law and for Camille's fate.

Apparently unaware of Paul Claudel's strong Catholic beliefs, a journalist for the same newspaper appealed to him. "Considering the circumstances," the journalist wrote, "it is up to him to stop the odious sequestration, which has lasted much too long and looks like a clerical revenge, to unmask the revolting scheme, and to punish the guilty, whoever they are."[20]

As could be expected, Paul did not answer. He endured the scandal as a form of expiation for his sins, and he referred to it in these terms in his *Journal:* "Atrocious calumnies against us regarding Camille's committal to Ville-Evrard, from Lelm and the Thierrys, in *l'Avenir de l'Aisne* and various blackmailing newspapers, denouncing a 'clerical crime.' It's all very well. I received so many undeserved praises that calumnies are good and refreshing; they are the normal lot of Christians."[21]

It is difficult to determine whether, at this point, Paul viewed Camille's confinement as temporary or definitive. He himself probably did not know, and he may not have wanted to think about it. Instead, he clung to the reassuring thought that Camille did not have long to live. As early as 1905, he had written to a friend: "The poor girl is sick, and I doubt that she could live much longer."[22] As time went on, Paul never ceased to refer to Camille's physical decline in his *Journal*, even though doctors' reports often contradicted him.

Paul's behavior toward his sister appears even more disconcerting because of his religious interpretation of her illness. In an earlier letter sent to Daniel Fontaine, he had shared his belief that she was possessed, and he seemed particularly struck by the noticeable change in her voice. "Is it possible to exorcise from afar?" he had asked Fontaine.[23] The same idea of possession was repeated many years later in the case of the great love of his life—Rosalie—who, as the mother of a daughter he barely knew, had resurfaced in his life. By the 1940s, Rosalie had become a frail, wasted, old woman, difficult to handle but demanding attention. "She is in the possession of a nasty devil," Paul declared.[24] As in Camille's case, he managed to convince himself that, for Rosalie, "the end was not very far."[25]

Perhaps even more revealing is the letter he wrote to his friend Marie Romain-Rolland in 1939 after she confessed to having had an abortion. To the strongly Catholic Paul, abortion was equal to murder, and he did not mince words in his answer: "Note that a person who is very close to me committed the same crime and that she has been paying for it in a house for the insane for *26 years*."[26] It is clear that Camille's confinement and sequestration had become, in his mind, a necessary expiation for the "crimes" she had committed in her emancipated life. In the eyes of many, mental asylums were the designated prisons for moral crimes, especially in the case of women, and the archives of these institutions sometimes provide examples of sane women who spent years of their lives within their walls. In England, for example, a scandal occurred in the 1970s, when it was discovered that two women had been confined in a mental asylum for fifty years, at the request of their families, because they had given birth to children out of wedlock.[27]

While Paul undeniably found it painful to have his sister committed, his violent intolerance clouded his judgment and distorted his feelings. Numerous testimonies point to this least flattering side of his character, which led him to fits of rage, bias, and complete lack of Christian charity.

Because of these tendencies, Jules Renard had severed his friendship with him at the time of the Dreyfus affair. The novelist André Gide also expressed more than once his repulsion at Paul's dogmatism. Four months before Camille's committal, Gide wrote in his *Journal*: "[Paul Claudel's] speech is a continuous flux, which no objection, or even questioning, can stop. Any opinion other than his own has no reason for being and no excuse in his eyes."[28] In 1905 Gide's recording of a meeting with Paul had been even more cutting: "He speaks endlessly; other people's thoughts cannot, for one moment, stop his own; a cannon would not divert it. To speak to him, to attempt to speak, you are forced to interrupt him. He politely waits for you to finish your sentence, then he returns exactly where he had left, to the very word, as if the other one had said nothing."[29]

In view of Paul's character and beliefs, Charles Thierry's attempt to help Camille was clumsy at best and pushed Paul to completely entrench himself in the status quo. Viewing both Lelm and Thierry as blackmailers, Paul waited for the storm to pass, and so the attempts to have Camille released failed. One year later, Paul sent a letter from Hamburg, confirming that Camille was still sequestered at Ville-Evrard: "We have been bothered for a year by two scoundrels who were disturbed in their blackmailing plans by my sister's committal," he informed his recipient. "After trying the press and the court in vain, they are now engaged in another direction, which will be no more successful. I am now accused only of sequestration."[30]

According to the law, in a case of crisis or conflict between the family and some other group, the court could name a special guardian—someone close to the patient, but not an heir—to protect the patient's rights and supervise the family. The patient herself or a family member had to make the request. But this proceeding rarely occurred, because a confined individual was seldom aware of her rights, especially if she was sequestered, and few people were willing to face the wrath of the family and assume the serious responsibilities of guardian. In any case, Camille was never provided with this type of guardian, and she remained totally cut off from the outside world.[31] By October, craving any visit, she appealed to her doctor:

Dear Dr. Truelle,

Long ago, I asked you to bring a person from my family. I have been buried here for more than nine months in the most awful despair. During this time, they took my atelier and all my belongings.

I absolutely need to see a friend. I hope you will not refuse to grant me this request.

Sincerely,

C. Claudel[32]

In December, she repeated her pleas, but to no avail. Unaware that the order of sequestration had been applied to her, she wondered why she never received any answers to her letters and why nobody ever came to see her. In August she chided Charles Thierry for his fickleness. "You promised to come and see me: you must have been joking," she reproached him. "Months went by and you did not come."[33] Not only had Charles been forbidden any visit to Camille, but his letters, like all the others sent to her, had also been intercepted by the administration of the asylum.

By the summer, Camille was feeling the full weight of her sequestration. She did nothing all day, remained alone in a corner, and rarely spoke to other patients. Her only distractions were the long walks she took in the park of the hospital and the errands she was sometimes allowed to run with the nurses. Distressed by the absence of visits, especially her mother's, Camille sometimes disclosed her grief to the nurses. "This patient," the night nurse reported, "says that she greatly misses her mother, that if she was not prevented from coming to see her, her mother would come, she is persecuted by people around her."[34]

The truth was, unfortunately, very different from what Camille believed, for her mother adamantly refused to go to Ville-Evrard. "What would I do at Ville-Evrard?" she wrote to Dr. Truelle. "I know Camille would not enjoy seeing me. She has done us a lot of harm, and she would go on if she could. Therefore, what would I say to her? I am very happy to know that she is where she is; at least she can't harm anyone."[35]

Until Camille's committal, Madame Claudel had been unable to gain any kind of control in the family. She was made to endure Camille's willfulness, her lies, and the dreadful scandals she had brought to them all. For the first time, Madame Claudel found herself in charge, and she was not about to rescind her power.

EARLY IN JUNE 1914, Mathias Morhardt requested an audience with Philippe Berthelot, head of staff at the Ministry of Foreign Affairs and a good friend of Paul Claudel. "If it is no problem to you," Berthelot answered, "come and see me at the Ministry, any morning at 11, and I will be happy to talk to you about Mademoiselle Camille Claudel."[1] After Camille's committal, Berthelot had become a member of the Family Board named by the court to administer Camille's modest fortune. While the law was often deficient regarding the protection of mental patients' personal rights, it did a better job in protecting their personal assets. In this regard, Camille received the services of a Family Board composed of six persons from both sides of the Claudel family. This board supervised Camille's financial circumstances, protected her possessions and inheritance, and planned for the payments of her living expenses in the mental asylum. Representing her father's side of the family were Paul Claudel; Louis Claudel, manufacturer; and Alexandre-Albert Bedon, landowner. Representing her mother's side were Félix-Pierre Leydet, lawyer; Henri Lerolle, artist; and Philippe Berthelot.[2]

As in the past, Morhardt was acting on behalf of Rodin, who had been alerted to Camille's plight by the newspapers. Rodin, then in his seventies, was nursing his poor health at the residence of his old friend Dr. Vivier, and he was quite shaken by the news of Camille's committal. On 28 May 1914, he wrote to Morhardt: "Could you see that Mademoiselle Claudel receive some comfort until she gets out of this hell? I can give money to the cafeteria so that they serve her treats or help her in one way or another. I thought of you because, like me, you are her admirer."[3]

Morhardt's loyalty had not faltered during all these years and, when he found out that Philippe Berthelot was on the Family Board, he contacted him immediately. Their meeting was friendly, but the news Morhardt received about Camille's mental health must have been very distressing. His answer to Rodin left very little room for hope:

Dear friend and Master,

I have just seen Monsieur Philippe Berthelot, and I shared with him—strictly confidentially—your desire regarding the poor and admirable artist. He is going to make delicate enquiries on the circumstances, and we will come and see you together as soon as we have an exact idea of things.

But I energetically demonstrated to Philippe Berthelot that we must join our efforts above all—any hope for a cure being an illusion—to pay the proper tribute to the memory of this great artist. What I wish is for you to agree to reserve a room of the Hôtel Biron for the works of Camille Claudel. We would gather everything she has left. It is without saying that I would gladly give everything I have kept of hers. I am certain that our friends Fenaille, Peytel, etc., will do the same. And it will be a beautiful museum worthy of being your neighbor. Don't you agree?

Yours faithfully,

M. Morhardt[4]

Since 1908 Rodin had rented the ground floor of Hôtel Biron, an eighteenth-century mansion located on rue de Varennes, surrounded by an extensive tangle of greenery that was home to a large population of colorful birds and wild rabbits. He had been led to this Eden by the sculptor Clara Westhoff and her husband, the German poet Rainer Maria Rilke. The gentle poet had once been Rodin's secretary, but like many other loyal servants of Rodin, he had been fired on a whim. Too generous to hold a grudge, Rilke immediately thought of the sculptor when he took over his estranged wife's studio in Biron, and he invited Rodin to come for a visit. Enthralled by a place that reminded him of the mansion he had shared with Camille, Rodin moved into the ground floor by the end of 1908, soon dreaming of turning the edifice into his own museum. The dream threatened to evaporate the following year, when the Hôtel Biron fell prey to developers. Fortunately, thanks to the powerful friends Rodin had in the government, the property was saved from the developers, and the state

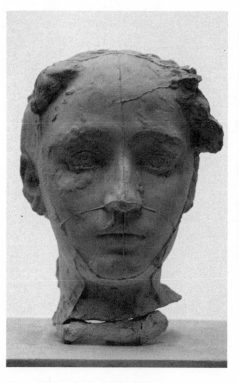

Auguste Rodin, *Camille Claudel*. Plaster.
Musée Rodin, Paris

Auguste Rodin, *Camille Claudel in the left hand of Pierre de Wissant* (figure from *The Burghers of Calais*). Plaster, c. 1900. Musée Rodin, Paris

acquired it for six million francs. Rodin remained temporarily in Biron, but he was making plans for something permanent through an astounding proposal to the state: if he was allowed to spend the rest of his life in Biron and turn it into a museum, he would bequeath all his works to the state, including the reproduction rights. It was an offer no one could refuse.

Sadly, while various ministers were slowly making plans to conclude the deal, Rodin himself came very close to ruining it. One day, a little American woman with frizzy red hair and outrageous makeup appeared at Hôtel Biron and made herself at home. She had married a French aristocrat, the duc de Choiseul, and the two of them managed to bewitch the sculptor. Declaring herself Rodin's muse, Madame de Choiseul reigned over the Hôtel Biron, while Rose was abandoned to new fears in Meudon. But the muse's plans were not merely sentimental for, with the help of her husband, she hoped to strip Rodin of many of his possessions. She might have succeeded had it not been for the vigilance of Rodin's friends, who managed to expose her treacherous intrigues. Humbled but relieved, Rodin broke with the duchess and returned to Rose at the end of 1912. He was then seventy-two years old. Unfortunately, this close call would not be the last one, because Rodin enjoyed being the center of attention for so many women. "My last years are crowned with roses," he declared. "Women, these givers, surround me and nothing can be sweeter."[5] Yet there were more takers than givers among these sirens, and their attempts at exploiting him in his old age resulted in an unbelievable series of intrigues, all narrated at length by his biographer Judith Cladel. Cladel, together with Marcelle Martin, Rodin's devoted last secretary, kept an eye on everything and managed to thwart the darkest of the schemes.

After the duchess's departure, Rodin returned to his museum project. Morhardt's idea of reserving a room at Biron for Camille delighted him, although he was not yet quite sure of its feasibility. After the problems with the duchess, Rodin also feared to discuss this issue openly by mail, and so he referred to Camille as "Mademoiselle Say" in his answer to Morhardt on 9 June 1914:

My dear friend,

I am happy that you took care of Mademoiselle Say, especially so discreetly, and that we join our efforts on her behalf with Monsieur Berthelot. As for Hôtel Biron, nothing is yet finished. The idea of taking a few sculptures of Mademoiselle Say makes me very happy.

This hôtel is very small and I don't know how we will do for the rooms.

We will have to add a few buildings for her as well as for me. But whatever the size, and if the thing gets done, she will have her place here.

I will make an appointment with you in a short time, and we will be able to talk. My regards to Madame Morhardt.

Yours cordially,

A. Rodin[6]

Two weeks later, Rodin sent a check for 500 francs to Morhardt, to be used on Camille's behalf. Another dance had to take place to bypass the Claudel family, since they were sure to oppose any gesture coming from the man they hated. Given anonymously to the Ministry of Fine Arts, Rodin's small gift served to pay for an annual subvention of 500 francs. This subvention by the ministry to Camille had been approved the preceding year, but had not been actually funded. Pleased with the results of the negotiations, Rodin intended to renew the gesture, but more serious events distracted him. In August 1914, war broke out.

Many Parisians, fearing a repeat of the ravages of the previous war, left in fear as the Germans relentlessly marched through Belgium and northern France. Rodin was among those who left. Soon after the beginning of the hostilities, he and Rose accompanied Judith Cladel and her mother to England, where they remained until November. At this point, tired of the cold and wet British weather, Rodin began to entertain the hope of making Pope Benedict's portrait, so he and Rose left for Rome. The pope's haughty and stubborn comportment forced Rodin to return to France without the finished portrait he had coveted, but the German advance had been halted, so Rodin was finally able to return home.

Back in Meudon, Rodin liked to reminisce about the old days. His secretary Marcelle Martin recalled that "he spoke of Mademoiselle Camille C., whom he had loved madly and his mind was filled with the past, good and bad alike." She remembered him falling into a deep reverie, overwhelmed by the weight of his own thoughts, then suddenly murmuring: "When women have bronze and marble and clay, the stuff of which creation is made, for rivals, they find a sculptor a mighty poor lover!"[7]

A few weeks before his death in 1917, Rodin was observed leading a visitor toward the terra-cotta bust he had made of Camille years earlier. "She is shut up at Ville-Evrard," the visitor remarked as he gazed at the sculpture. Stung, Rodin answered abruptly: "You could not recall a more unpleasant memory."[8]

Rodin's own mental health suffered to some extent after his first stroke in March 1916, and it took a turn for the worse after a second stroke in July. For days, Rodin would remain prostrated, oblivious of the people around him. Then, for no apparent reason, he would perk up and be himself again. Rose remained by his side, waiting for him to come out of his fog. Once, she confided to Judith Cladel that her old companion did not always recognize her. "He asks me: 'Where is my wife?' I answer: 'I am here; ain't I your wife?'—'Yes, but my wife who is in Paris, has she got any money?'"[9] Cladel refrained from enlightening Rose as to the identity of the "wife in Paris." Rodin was obviously worried about Camille. Although he had intended to renew his gift to her of 500 francs, he never got around to it; too many things had happened since the beginning of the war. The Hôtel Biron, especially, had been predominant in his mind, but the French government was slow to accept the incredible opportunity Rodin offered them; it took his first stroke to turn things around. Realizing there was no time to lose, officials finally hurried to approve his donation and the conditions attached to it. A draft of the deed was signed on 1 April 1916, three months before the sculptor's second stroke; the Hôtel Biron was finally becoming the Musée Rodin.

If no mention was made about setting aside a room for Camille's sculpture, it was not for lack of trying. Both Morhardt and Rodin yearned to see Camille's works vindicated in this manner, but they ran into the adamant opposition of the Claudel family. Several times in his correspondence with Judith Cladel during the early 1930s, Morhardt dejectedly referred to this heartbreaking experience. "I tried to reconcile Paul Claudel, at least, with Rodin," Morhardt informed Cladel in December 1929. "Rodin would have been elated to give a room from his museum to the great artist; we would have gathered everything we had of her—which is so little by its quantity, but prodigious by its quality. The Claudels answered with an absolute refusal."[10]

"Why didn't Paul Claudel accept the room Rodin offered in the Hôtel Biron for his sister?" Morhardt lamented four years later.[11] By then, the disappearance of Camille's *Clotho* had become evident, and Morhardt could not forgive Paul's hostility to Rodin's generous offer. "Paul Claudel is an idiot," he told Cladel bitterly. "When you have a sister who is a genius, you don't abandon her. But he always believed that he was the only one who had genius."[12]

Morhardt was not alone in his distress over Camille's ill fortune. Some of the generous men who had supported her in the past were still eager to do so, but their efforts came up against the impenetrable wall created by Camille's sequestration. Edmond Bigand Kaire, the friend who used to send Rodin barrels of wine from his vineyard, once wrote a letter to Marcelle Martin, appealing to her generosity on behalf of Camille. "I will only tell you today," he pleaded, "in the name of the sacred and immanent justice, that we must add to the amount the master granted to 'the great and beautiful artist,' as you so appropriately name her, or to the poor madwoman you know." Bigand Kaire had trouble continuing; the reading of old letters from Camille had left him in emotional distress. "I won't say anymore today," he decided, "I don't feel the courage because, during the reading I just made of the thirty letters I have kept of hers, the first ones dating back twenty-five years, I could not help but weep at the thought of such talent—verging on genius according to her master—sinking into madness for a lack of . . . of. . . ."[13] Too upset to finish his sentence, Bigan Kaire abruptly closed his letter. He must have been even more upset when he realized that Marcelle Martin was in no position to do anything for Camille. In any case, having given all that he owned to the state, Rodin was once more a poor man; he could not help anyone.

This poor man, a mere shadow of his former vigorous self, finally became Rose's husband. Thanks to Judith Cladel's efforts, the two were married on 29 January 1917. Because of war restrictions, the Meudon house was without heat, so the old couple spent their honeymoon in the only warm place they still had, their bed. Two weeks later, Rose died of pneumonia. Rodin followed her on 17 November 1917, also from complications due to the freezing cold of the house—the French government had failed to provide its greatest and most generous sculptor with heat.

Many years after these events, Eugène Blot attempted to contact Camille Claudel. In the moving letter he sent her, the art dealer recalled one of Camille's sculptures, the young woman on her knees stretching her arms toward the God who had flown away. Blot understood that it was a self-portrait, and he wanted to share something important with Camille. "One day that Rodin visited me," he told her, "I saw him stop suddenly in front of this portrait, contemplate it while softly caressing the metal, and cry. Yes, cry. Like a child. He has been dead for fifteen years. Truly, he will have loved only you, Camille, I can say it today. All the rest—these pitiful affairs, this ridiculous socialite life, he who really remained a man of the people—was the outlet of an excessive nature." Blot did not have any illusion of being heard by Camille, but he wished, perhaps, to soothe some of the old wounds. "Oh! I know too well, Camille, that he abandoned you," he added. "I am not trying to excuse him. You have suffered too much because of him. But I don't withdraw anything from what I said. Time will put everything back into place."[14]

AS THE FRENCH consul in Hamburg, Paul Claudel found himself in very unpleasant circumstances when war was declared against Germany. Accompanied by his wife, his young son, and four other people, he left the consulate "booed off by the crowd, which spit and threw rocks" at them.[1] They were finally shoved into a train bound for Copenhagen, with only a few cans of sardines, some bread, and two bottles of water. The painful journey would take them all the way to Denmark, Sweden, England, and finally Paris. On their way to Paris, signs of war became more ominous as they passed trains packed with British troops coming to reinforce the French defense. When he arrived in Paris, Paul found the city "deserted, silent, and purified."[2]

The patients of the Ville-Evrard Asylum were in the path of the German advance and had to be evacuated. First, they were temporarily transferred to Enghien, a few kilometers north of Paris, then far south to the Montdevergues Asylum, which was six kilometers away from Avignon. Camille Claudel was part of a group of women refugees admitted to the Montdevergues Asylum on 7 September 1914, two days after the beginning of the French counterattack remembered as the Battle of the Marne. Camille would spend the last thirty years of her life in Montdevergues. Thirty years anxiously waiting for her brother's rare visits. Thirty years yearning for the presence of a mother who never came. Thirty years defiantly surviving.

Montdevergues had first been the name of a small mountain. It was a deformation of "Mont des Vierges"—the Mountain of the Virgins—sometimes also called Montdevergues les Roses, probably because of the presence of rose fields in the area.[3] From the top of the mountain, the scenery was splendid. The writings of philosopher Jean-Jacques Rousseau had instilled in many French thinkers a belief in Nature's redeeming influence over the spirit. Daily contact with Nature through work and contemplation was thought to have a beneficial impact upon people's well-being. In the nine-teenth century, these ideas were being applied to the treatment of mental patients. Therefore, when Avignon's antiquated insane asylum had to be abandoned in the mid-1880s, Montdevergues seemed to be the perfect site for the construction of a welcoming, modern, and efficient mental asylum. "This most beautiful setting," an official wrote at the time of the land pur-chase, "will have the advantage of rejuvenating patients through its diverse scenery and viewpoints; and, through its vast expanse, it will offer all kinds of work and entertainment, which can bring about a cure."[4]

Perched on a hill, on an estate which encompassed a wooded moun-tain, a large stretch of arable land, and a vineyard, the asylum harmoniously molded its shape to the landscape. From the center, marked by a chapel sit-ting in a large garden, various buildings radiated uniformly toward the sur-rounding fields and hills. As Camille entered the asylum, she would have passed a large gate and stopped in the administrative buildings long enough to register. After crossing a courtyard, she would have reached service facil-ities, which included the pharmacy, kitchen, linen and laundry rooms, and lodgings for the nuns. In the same area, strictly segregated by sex, were two infirmaries, two workshops, two waiting rooms, and two bathrooms with ten bathtubs each. Behind these facilities, Camille would have discovered eight two-story pavilions arranged like spokes around the chapel, housing the male patients on one side and the female patients on the other. She would not have stopped there, however, because she had been assigned to a room in the Grand Pensionnat des Femmes (Boarding Facilities for Women) behind the church. For the moment, Camille belonged to the category of patients considered as "boarders." The pavilions and the Boarding Facilities sheltered five other categories of patients: the quiet ones, often in a conva-lescent stage; those receiving treatment; the senile or imbecile; the epileptic; and the patients living in special accommodations.[5]

Much care had been taken to provide the illusion of freedom: court-yards planted with trees and long walkways, with walls and ditches hidden behind lush vegetation. Treatment consisted mostly in expecting a beneficial impact from the environment, that is to say in encouraging the nonaggressive inmates to work in the fields and gardens owned by the asylum and to make use of the workshops. In these workshops, women could sew, wash, and iron clothes, while men could do wood and metal work, shoe repair, and tailoring.

Montdevergues Asylum in the early 1900s

Main entrance of Montdevergues Asylum

The more aggressive inmates, who could not work, were regularly calmed down with special bathing sessions called hydrotherapy.

The facilities had originally been planned for four hundred patients, with each pavilion housing one specific category of inmates. Unfortunately, as early as 1869, the asylum had grown to 750 patients. Although new constructions were added to the original facilities, the number of new arrivals to Montdevergues kept growing at an alarming rate, and the asylum never functioned as it had originally been planned. The introduction of electricity, a mechanized laundry, and steam cooking eased everyone's circumstances, but by 1929 as many as 1,650 inmates were crowded into facilities meant to accommodate half this number. As a result, category separation often had to be abandoned, and one could find epileptics mixed with psychotics or senile patients mixed with quiet ones.

Montdevergues had been planned to be self-sufficient. Most of the inmates in reasonably good health worked either in the fields and on the farms owned by the asylum, or in the workshops. Locksmiths made metal beds for the dormitories, carpenters crafted cupboards and coffins, tailors made clothing for male patients, and masons maintained the interiors of the facilities. Female inmates mostly made and mended clothing for everyone. They spun hemp and linen, wove them into cloth and turned them into outfits. As an incentive to participate in these activities, patients received a small stipend proportionate to the amount of work they provided.

Inmates rose at five in the summer and at six in the winter. Work lasted most of the day, with long pauses for meals and occasional board games. On Sundays, inmates could go to church, if they wished. On holidays, the daily routine was interrupted by the addition of a bit of fun. Everyone would go to the theater set up in the Women's Boarding Facilities to attend balls, concerts, or plays acted entirely by inmates. Long-awaited visits of friends and relatives also broke the routine, and those who were lucky enough could welcome their visitors in the parlor or in the sitting-rooms of the Boarding Facilities. These visits were strictly controlled, and no outsider was allowed to see a patient without a written authorization of a family member.[6]

From the time of her arrival in Montdevergues, Camille's energy had been focused on getting out. She wrote endlessly—to her friends, her relatives, anyone who might help her. Informed of her feverish writing activities, an alarmed Madame Claudel immediately contacted the supervisor of the women's facilities. "She tells me she writes quantities of letters all over the place," she worried. "I hope these remain in the asylum because I requested many times that none of these letters, which last year caused us so much trouble, be sent to anyone. Except for me and for her brother, Monsieur Paul

Claudel, she is not to write to anyone or to receive any communications or visits."[7] Consequently, most of Camille's calls of distress to the outside world never passed beyond the walls of her prison, and only a handful of the letters she wrote in the asylum survived. One, an assertive remonstrance to Paul, was written in 1915, one year after her arrival in Montdevergues. Although Camille chastised her brother for neglecting her, she loved him and hesitated to hold him responsible for her circumstances. Instead, she returned to her regular obsessions and shifted the blame to Rodin, believing he was manipulating her relatives as he had manipulated her in the past.

My dear Paul,

I wrote to Mother several times, to Paris, to Villeneuve, without receiving any answer.

And you, you came to see me at the end of May and you promised to take care of me and not to turn your back on me.

How is it possible that, ever since that time, you never wrote to me even once and you never came back to see me? Do you think that it is fun for me to spend months, even years without any news, without any hope!

Where does such cruelty come from? How have you been made to turn away from me? I would like to know this.

I wrote Mother to ask her to have me transferred to Sainte-Anne in Paris. This would give me the advantage of being closer to you and make it possible for me to explain the different points that still need clarifying. Furthermore, it would offer you the opportunity of saving money since one can be admitted to Sainte-Anne for only 90 francs per month. I don't say that it would be Paradise at this price, far from it, but ever since I left my atelier on quai Bourbon, I got used to anything. If I were sent to Siberia, it would not surprise me.

To tell the truth, I would prefer to return to civilian life and forget all these adventures.

You can tell Mother that, if she worries I might place a claim on our Villeneuve properties, she is mistaken; I would prefer to donate all I am supposed to inherit to [my nephew] Jacques and spend the rest of my life in peace.

I would even prefer to just be a maid than to go on living like this. Did you take care of my belongings you claimed to have moved to Villeneuve? Did you make sure they did not fall into the hands of the scoundrel who played this dirty trick on me so that he could steal them? He is really afraid of seeing me return before he can get hold of them. . . .

It's the reason why he delays my departure from the asylum; he is trying to gain time and, meanwhile, all sorts of unexpected things will happen. You will pay for your apathy; take care of yourself.

I expect a letter from you soon.

My regards to your wife and your children.

C. C.[8]

This letter clearly indicates that Camille's reasoning abilities remained intact as long as she did not speak about Rodin and other "persecutors." Although she was obviously distressed, her tone remained firm and dignified. Like many mental patients, she did not view herself as sick, so she was trying to make sense of her committal with other possible explanations. Since the most logical one was money, she assumed she had been sent to Montdevergues so her inheritance could be given to Jacques, her sister's son. Yet, even when Camille voiced these awful allegations, her tone remained composed. It is only when she accused Rodin that she revealed the extent of her paranoia.

Camille's mental health does not seem to have improved during the war years. Her certificate of admittance to Montdevergues, signed by Dr. Broquère on 22 September 1914, repeated the same laconic sentences of earlier medical reports: "suffers from a systematic persecution delirium mostly based upon false interpretations and imagination."[9] During the next five years, doctors recorded unchanged obsessions in their regular reports. "Recently, her persecution mania has turned against the personnel who cared for her at Ville-Evrard," one doctor wrote in January 1915. "She thinks those nurses are trying to poison her."[10]

Camille's fear of being poisoned had been going on for several years and would never disappear. Because of it, Camille was highly suspicious of the food served by the personnel, and she rejected everything except raw eggs and unpeeled potatoes. She prepared these unsavory meals herself, in the kitchen of the asylum, indignant and resentful whenever she was urged to eat the regular fare. The first mention of poisoning appeared in a letter Camille sent to her cousin Henri Thierry in 1910.[11] By this time, Camille's world had crumbled. Unable to control her life in any meaningful way, she believed it was being controlled from the outside—through poison from the hands of Rodin. In her head, poison and creation seemed to be linked. Rodin wanted to poison her, not necessarily to kill her but to control her and to steal her sculpture. He needed her ideas. Because he was all-powerful, he could hire anyone he wanted to do his dirty work, but the poison really came from him. Hence, she had to be very careful and to reject all food susceptible to contamination.

The link between poison and creation may also hold a more secretive significance. "I am still sick from the poison I have in my blood," she had written in her letter to Henri Thierry in 1910. "My body is burning; it is Rodin, the Protestant, who gives me the poison because he hopes to inherit my atelier. . . ."[12] Camille's affirmation strangely recalls the words used by Paul Claudel after his affair with Rosalie Vetch had so dramatically ended. A few months later, a still-tormented Paul had written to his friend André Suarès: "I, a horribly depraved man, my insides still burning from the blackest poison, speak to you of virginal weddings. . . ."[13] Like many before them, Camille and Paul were using the image of poison flowing in the blood, burning body and soul, to express sexual repulsion or desire. While Paul's use of imagery remained literary, Camille's seemed to have assumed a life of its own. In an existential analysis of *The Case of Ellen West*, Ludwig Binswanger drew an equation between the fear of eating and the fear of being fertilized or pregnant.[14] While the case of Ellen West was quite different from Camille's, the equation is well worth considering. Camille had become pregnant through Rodin. In those days, in view of her class values, it was a major catastrophe. As a woman, she had to bear the burden of this disaster, and one can only imagine the resentment she felt toward Rodin when she had to have an abortion. To make matters worse, it was many months before her body recovered from this ordeal—her letters indicate that she was c onstantly sick. Hence, she may have viewed fertilization by Rodin as a form of poison, an early attempt on his part to gain control of her life. Years later these feelings could have played a role in her recurring fear of being poisoned.

Camille's suspicions against the Ville-Evrard nurses were to have disastrous consequences on her future. Because the German advance had been stopped on the river Marne, Paris was no longer threatened, and patients were being sent back to Ville-Evrard. But Camille did not want to go. In January 1915, she beseeched her mother to let her stay in Montdevergues. In a genuine effort to make her happy, Madame Claudel petitioned the director of the asylum and dreamed about a possible improvement in her daughter's health: "Maybe her preference for the new environment in which she now lives, her participation in religious exercises, and the good Mediterranean climate will have a positive influence upon her mental health? Don't you think so, Monsieur le Directeur?"[15] The director agreed; therefore Camille remained in Montdevergues as a first-class patient, and she enjoyed her own private room.

The asylum had an elaborate class system, each class being assigned or denied certain privileges. As one moved downward from first to fourth class, the quality of the accommodations and especially the quality of the meals declined sharply. The food assigned to each class was painstakingly described in the regulations. For breakfast, first-class patients were served coffee or hot chocolate with as much white bread as they wanted, but third- and fourth-class patients had to get by with only a clear soup and inferior quality bread. For lunch, the first class enjoyed a soup, roasted meat with vegetables, cheese, and two desserts. The third class received a soup, a small amount of meat and some vegetables, while the fourth class was served alternatively meat one day and vegetables the next. For dinner, again roasted meat and vegetables with two desserts for the first class, while the fourth class had to content itself with a green salad, vegetables, and a choice of cheese or fruit. All classes were served wine, but the first and second classes received twice as much as the last two classes. For the privilege of placing a relative in the first class, families paid four times as much as for the lowest class, and these payments had to be made three months in advance.[16]

Although Camille was satisfied at first with the personnel and the facilities of Montdevergues, this did not last long. For all its qualities, the place was still a prison, and one very far from home. By September 1915, Camille had returned to her fear of being poisoned, and she yearned to be back in Paris. "Same mental state," her doctor wrote in his October report, "poisoning ideas, wastes food, especially eggs, thinks they are poisoned . . .

in spite of this, often does not eat, then
s not want to stay here anymore, wants

Paris, but not to Ville-Evrard, where
Instead, she begged her mother to take
director, Madame Claudel made it clear
This is not possible," she wrote, "I am
her request at any price. I would have
ave to endure whatever she wished."[18]
she could not go home, she took a clos-
in and around Paris. Sainte-Anne, a
of being cheaper than Montdevergues,
she pointed out to both her mother and brother. But for Madame Claudel, these financial considerations mattered much less than her own peace of mind. Her brutally honest answer to the director of the asylum left no room for compromise:

Monsieur le Directeur,

Yesterday, I received another letter from my daughter C. Claudel, telling me that she was very unhappy and wanted to be transferred to Sainte-Anne in Paris. I wonder, with much worry, how she can send me letters through other intermediaries than the doctor or yourself. I am extremely worried about it because she could just as well write to other people, who will use it to pursue the campaign they started two years ago against us.

I do not wish at all to take her out of your asylum, where she was happy a short time ago. I am not going to move her to a different institution every six months and, as far as taking her with me or putting her back in her apartment, as she used to be, never, never. I am seventy-five, I cannot assume the responsibility for a daughter with extravagant ideas and full of bad intentions toward us; a daughter who hates us and who is ready to do us as much harm as possible. If you wish to add an additional charge to give her more comfort, that is fine with me, but keep her, I beseech you.

She lived as if she was destitute, seeing no one for ten years, letting everyone who sold her food steal from her. Doors and windows were chained, locked, and people brought her food through a box placed upon a window. As for herself and her apartment, it was horrifying. She spent her time writing denunciations or letters to louts.

Finally, she has every possible vice. I don't want to see her again; she hurt us too much. I beseech you again, Monsieur le Directeur, to find out how she gets letters out, and to forbid her to write via any other way but the administration.

Sincerely,

L. Claudel[19]

This letter reveals the abyss between mother and daughter. Madame Claudel did not have the least understanding of her daughter's long struggle. Camille's life had been led in complete opposition to that of her mother; hence the disaster now striking Camille only reinforced Madame Claudel's own sense of righteousness. Even in the case of severe differences, one expects a certain amount of compassion from a mother for her own child. But in this letter, compassion is indeed scarce. Without realizing it, Madame Claudel transferred her own feelings to her daughter: hatred, desire for retaliation, revenge. She did not want to harm Camille, but she wanted to keep her as far away as possible and to leave her in a state of permanent helplessness. Yet she stuck to her own sense of motherly duty, requesting medical reports and sending coffee, chocolate, wine, and other such luxuries to Camille, as well as making sure she was in comfortable quarters.

Madame Claudel would have been astonished to discover feelings of tender concern for herself in a letter written by Camille during the same period to a friend and former Montdevergues patient who had just lost her mother. "To tell the truth," Camille confessed, "this death especially touched me because I am always afraid the same thing may happen to Mother. . . . What a tragedy if Mother died while I am locked up in here! What worry for me! because Mother won't admit it, but she is not happy!" Returning to the only dream she had left, the dream of leaving the asylum, Camille noted that no one had offered to let her go: "There is no talk of my getting out! I have been crying a lot since your departure. When you were here, it gave me courage! I took your place in the chapel, but I am far from having your confident bearing!"[20]

Camille remained in Montdevergues, but she did not give up hope. In 1917 she turned to her former doctor and neighbor, Dr. Michaux. Still unaware of the part Dr. Michaux had played in her confinement, Camille asked for his help because, as she touchingly wrote, she trusted him. She confided she had written to Monsieur Adam, a lawyer they both knew, and she hoped Dr. Michaux would join his efforts to Adam's to get her out of the asylum, given the disinterest of her own family in this matter. "They reproach me (oh dreadful crime) of living alone," she told him, "of spending my life with cats, of having a persecution mania! It is on the strength of these accusations that I have been incarcerated for five and a half years like a criminal, deprived of freedom, deprived of food, of heat, and of the most elementary commodities."

Camille maintained her eloquence through most of her letter. She was aware of the tremendous obstacles placed in the path of her freedom, so she accepted the possibility of remaining temporarily in an asylum. But she wanted it to be Sainte-Anne or another Parisian institution, not Montdevergues. "I must warn you against the nonsense being used to prolong my sequestration," she told Michaux. "They claim they will keep me confined until the end of the war; it's a joke and an attempt to fool me through false promises, because this war is not going to end, and when it does, my own end won't be far." As she returned to her pitiful condition, she added: "If by chance I was not able to write to you any more, please do not abandon me, and please act as fast as you can."[21] As could be expected, Camille never heard from Dr. Michaux.

Like other despondent Europeans, Camille came to believe the war would never end. In spite of her prolonged sequestration in Montdevergues, she caught enough snatches of news to identify with the pervasive hopelessness that affected everyone. In March 1915, she received a letter from Maria Paillette, a friend she had known as a young girl in Villeneuve. Maria was in mourning; her brother had been killed. With simple words, Maria told of the knock on the door of their family home: "It is the Villeneuve policeman, very upset and stammering. He did not need to say anything. Mother understood immediately. My little brother was killed. I can't believe it. How sad is this war! How long will it last?"[22] Camille feared receiving other letters like this one, and she worried about the fate of the few friends she still had in the world. "I hardly dare to ask of your news," she wrote one day to a cousin who never received her letter, "I tremble when I ask myself whether you are still alive, whether you have not disappeared in the horrible war that lays waste to our beautiful country."[23]

Villeneuve was only about a hundred miles from Verdun, where fighting in the trenches took so many lives. In May 1918, the Germans reached Villeneuve, pushing ahead of them hordes of refugees, including Madame Claudel and her daughter Louise de Massary—Paul was away in Brazil. This flight was a huge loss for the Claudels. Until then they had comfortably lived off the land, but with the new German offensive, their house was damaged, their land wasted, their animals killed, and their preserves and linens carried away by the enemy. Madame Claudel and Louise found refuge in a safer town, but the high cost of living drained the remainder of their savings. By October, one month before the end of the war, they were back in Paris, living together in Louise's apartment along the river. They did not know how they were going to pay for Camille's room and board in the second-class facilities, where she had been moved, and so Madame Claudel appealed to the Ministry of Fine Arts.

All through the war—sometimes with prodding—the ministry had paid the annual aid of 500 francs awarded to Camille in 1913. By the end of the war, Madame Claudel hoped to see the ministry pay all of Camille's expenses in Montdevergues, but the Claudels' circumstances were viewed as comfortable, so the request was refused. She tried again in March of the following year, pointing out that she had been ruined by the war. "I suffered all the miseries of the invasion," she complained. "I had to escape in a hurry, taking nothing with me, in light of the German arrival in May 1918. Upon my return to Paris in August, I found refuge in my daughter's apartment, since I did not have any home. I am eighty years old; it is terrible to be reduced to such an end after a long, comfortable life."[24] But the ministry turned her down again. By then, Camille had been moved down to the rank of third-class inmate and, as her mother pointed out in her letter, was on the verge of joining the most destitute inmates if her expenses were not paid. Yet at no point did Madame Claudel ever consider transferring Camille to Sainte-Anne or another reasonably priced Parisian institution.

IN SPITE OF the forceful letter she had written to her brother back in 1915, Camille did not hear from him for a long time. When Paul finally returned to France just after the armistice, his first concern was for his mother and sister in Paris and his second for the house in Villeneuve. He did not make it to Montdevergues until October 1920, seven years after his last visit. Between 1919 and 1920, Camille's mental state had significantly improved; her medical records emphasize her calm disposition and the decrease of her persecution obsessions. On 1 June 1920, Dr. Brunet made the suggestion to Madame Claudel that Camille be let out of the asylum on a trial basis. "Mademoiselle Claudel is calm," he wrote. "Her persecution ideas, though

Camille at
Montdevergues,
photographed
by William
Elborne, 1929

not completely gone, are much less pronounced. She would very much like to be with her family and to live in the country. I believe that, in these conditions, we could try to let her out."[1]

Madame Claudel immediately replied with a complete refusal. According to her, Camille's letters proved that she had not changed at all. "It is impossible to believe that she is healthy of mind and that she could behave reasonably," she claimed, "now no more than when she was committed to the asylum, where we put her because we could not endure her incoherence anymore."[2] Convinced that Camille would return to her old ways if she was released, Madame Claudel also pointed out her own difficult situation. "I am not living in my own home, but in my second daughter's; I am very old, often sick, I therefore cannot welcome the one who is in your asylum, nor can I authorize you to try and release her." Dr. Brunet nevertheless persisted. "If you can't take back Mademoiselle Claudel," he answered a few days later, "I believe it would be beneficial for the patient's mental health to bring her closer to her family, something she really wants. She has been very calm for quite some time, and the decrease of her delirious ideas could perhaps ultimately allow a trial release."[3]

Madame Claudel was as stubborn as any of the Claudels; she would not be swayed. "Each time I ask Mother to take me back to Villeneuve," Camille once quipped, "she answers that her house is melting."[4] Confronted with Madame Claudel's tenacious opposition to his suggestions, Dr. Brunet was forced to abandon the idea of a trial release. No doctor, in those days, would have discharged a patient without the authorization of her family. If the patient did not have the support of the relatives or friends with whom she was going to live, the director of the mental asylum would never dare to write in the register of the law that she could be discharged because she was cured.[5] Hence, instead of a trial release, Dr. Brunet proposed to move Camille to an institution closer to the Claudel family. "Mademoiselle Claudel continues to be calm, to behave correctly, and she rarely expresses her persecution ideas, which are much reduced," he insisted. "If you can't take her back, you could place her in a mental asylum closer to her relatives, who could come and see her sometimes. This absence of visits is indeed very painful for Mademoiselle Claudel."[6]

Dr. Brunet's last suggestion was better received by Madame Claudel. She was not against the idea of moving Camille closer to Paris, she said, but she needed some time to think about the problem and to find an institution comparable in price to Montdevergues. "I consider that she is not completely cured and that it would still be necessary to keep her under surveillance," she concluded.[7]

Madame Claudel also wanted to discuss the issue with her son, who had temporarily returned from Copenhagen. More open to his sister's pleas, Paul would have liked to move Camille to Prémontré, an asylum not far from Villeneuve, but his mother was quick to point out that Prémontré facilities had recently been reassigned to men only and therefore could not be considered. "In any case," she added, "all the doctors I have consulted, all without any exception, have declared that she was not cured and that she would most certainly become again as she was when she first entered Ville-Evrard." Thus having conveniently dismissed all the reports written by Dr. Brunet, Madame Claudel confessed: "I feel as sad as anyone to see her so unhappy (though she is probably exaggerating), but I cannot do anything else for her that I am not already doing, and if we let her out, the whole family would have to suffer, instead of just one."[8] Paul did not insist. A few days later, he traveled to Montdevergues to visit the sister he had not seen in seven years. He found her "skinny, gray, without teeth, and eating only the food she cooks herself."[9]

Dr. Brunet was replaced by Dr. Clément, then by Dr. Charpenel, and Camille's medical reports slowly reverted to the monotonous litanies of former days: "No notable change," we read on the first of April 1921. "Retains the same persecution ideas, believes she is the victim of an error, of a revenge, fears being poisoned and therefore often refuses the food that is brought to her, recriminates against her family."[10] One year later we read again: "Mademoiselle Claudel continues to present persecution ideas with fear of being poisoned. Calm and docile, although she sometimes recriminates against her committal and especially against being so far from Paris."[11] In September 1922, Dr. Charpenel sent a medical certificate to Jules Ferté, a lawyer and administrator of Camille's possessions. The document was strikingly similar to the early ones from Ville-Evrard, attesting that Camille was "suffering from a systematic persecution delirium based on delirious interpretations. A long-term confinement is still necessary."[12]

From all appearances, Camille had suffered a relapse triggered by anxiety and disappointment. With her hope for freedom shattered, and her longing for Paris and Villeneuve ignored, Camille had nothing left to hang on to; she returned to her obsessions. According to Elizabeth Packard, an American who was forcefully committed to a mental asylum in the 1860s, such reaction was common among women who were retained long after they should have been released. "I saw several such sink back into a state of hopeless imbecility from this cause alone," she said of her fellow inmates in Jacksonville, Mississippi. "Hope too long deferred made them so sick of life that they yielded themselves up to desperation as a natural, inevitable result."[13]

Although Camille never lost her survival instinct, there is no doubt that her feeling of desperation during this period intensified her paranoia. In spite of her recriminations against her mother and brother, she always stopped short of blaming them for the decisions they made on her behalf. She would not have survived if she had not trusted her only contacts with the outside world. Yet she could no longer hold Rodin responsible for her suffering; instead, she chose to blame his collaborators. The Protestant art dealer Hébrard, in particular, remained her bête noire for the rest of her life, and Philippe Berthelot, a member of the Family Board and Paul's friend, was added to the list of "her persecutors" after he dared use the plaster of *L'Age mûr* left in Camille's atelier to have a second cast made for himself.[14]

As late as 3 March 1930, in a letter she wrote to Paul, Camille reiterated her belief that her mother and brother had been manipulated by others. She had formed the habit of writing letters on March 3, the day she remembered as the anniversary of her committal. In reality, it was the anniversary of Camille's first day without her father, who had died on March 2; her committal did not occur until a week later. But Camille rightly believed that the death of the "Villeneuve oak tree,"[15] as she called her father, had resulted in her life sentence to the asylum. "Today, the third of March," she declared to Paul, "is the anniversary of my kidnapping to Ville-Evrard. Seventeen years ago, Rodin and the art dealers had me do penance in insane asylums. . . . [Berthelot] was only an agent whom they used to keep you at bay and get you to execute this audacious move, successful because of your credulity, as well as Mother's and Louise's."[16]

In Camille's mind, the "millionaire art dealers" who had mounted this plot preyed on her creativity, something they all sadly lacked. Not content with stealing her few possessions, they sent her to an asylum in order to retain control over her ideas. "It is the exploitation of women," she concluded, "the crushing of the artist whom they want to make sweat blood and tears."[17] Evidently convinced that anything she would create would be stolen from her, she always refused to sculpt in the asylum and, although clay would occasionally be brought to her, she never touched it. A few years before her death, she told Paul: "In reality, they want to force me to sculpt here, and seeing that they don't succeed, they give me all sorts of trouble. It will not convince me, on the contrary."[18]

Her refusal to sculpt was also an opportunity to reassert her personal freedom. Everything had been taken away from her, everything but her willpower. While her medical reports usually describe her as calm and gentle, they do not paint her as submissive. Except for a new acceptance of church activities, possibly indicating a return to faith or a simple need to break the monotony of daily life, nowhere do we read that she participated in any of the projects fostered by the asylum. She is usually described as being bored, as refusing to keep herself busy, her only occupations being the preparation of her own meals and the writing of letters. In all cases, she set herself aside from the rest of the inmates.

Eating her own food was as much an expression of Camille's free will as it was of the fear of being poisoned. And when she wrote letters, she regained the peace provided by solitude, away from the other unfortunate creatures of the asylum. Most of these letters would not have made it through the control of the administrators, but Camille sometimes managed to outwit her supervisors. Hiding, plotting, paying off a cleaning lady to mail the letters, were all demonstrations of a spirit that would not willingly submit to the tyranny imposed upon her. Even her delusions may have contributed to her survival, for they provided her with a tolerable explanation for what was happening.

Camille's new doctor, Dr. Charpenel, eventually proved to be as anxious about his patient's happiness as Dr. Brunet before him, and his medical reports took on a more personal tone. "Mademoiselle Claudel is calm, docile," he wrote in November 1923. "She is very bored. She says that she is far from her family and would like to be closer to Paris while, at the same time, living alone in the country. Although her persecution ideas have not disappeared, they are reduced and, since Mademoiselle Claudel does not seem likely to have violent or dangerous reactions, wouldn't it be possible to satisfy her to some extent?"[19] In October of the following year, he wrote again: "Mademoiselle Claudel receives very few visits these days. She emphatically asks for her discharge. She is disappointed not to have received any visit from her family, something that she expected at this time of year."[20]

The visit Camille expected finally took place in March 1925, five years after the preceding one. Paul's duties as ambassador to Japan had made it impossible for him to come any sooner. Returning to France via the Suez Canal, he disembarked in Marseille and soon reached Avignon and Montdevergues. "My poor sister Camille," he wrote in his *Journal* on March 24, "toothless, dilapidated, with the look of a very old woman under her gray hair. Sobbing, she throws herself upon my chest."[21] Again, Camille must have begged her brother to send her back to her dear Villeneuve. "This pretty Villeneuve," she once wrote, "there is nothing like it on earth."[22] But her pleas fell on deaf ears, for Paul knew his mother would never agree to it. He returned to Japan in January 1926, and Camille was left once more with her deferred dreams.

Neither Paul nor Camille knew that the family home would cease to be theirs before long. During the summer, Madame Claudel sold the Villeneuve house to Louise's son, Jacques de Massary. She informed Paul by letter of this transaction a few months later, while also referring to her coming death.

> I must speak to you about a business transaction I made this summer. I sold my Villeneuve house to Jacques for 60,000 francs. . . . I thought I had to do it to avoid the interference of the law in my succession, something that would be very expensive for you. It is a good price, not too high and not too low. . . . A good share for Camille still remains. I hope you won't reproach me.
>
> My clothes and my linens will be for Camille. What can we do for her? We can only ease her conditions, as we already do. Besides the pension payments, I send her clothes and comforting packages; anywhere she is, it will be the same, she will not be happy. I am tired of racking my brains to know what we could do without ever reaching another solution than the one we are already taking. We must wait; she can't be on her own, in her own house, with an atelier, she

would do what she has always done, tell lies about us and our friends, and everything else you know too well. Let us not speak about it anymore.[23]

But Paul wanted to speak about the sale of the house where he had spent most of his youth. Stunned that he had not been contacted before the transaction took place, Paul resentfully accused his mother of manipulating her children's inheritance in favor of Louise. His anger with his younger sister started a series of conflicts that would last for years. As is so often the case with quarrels between siblings, Paul's grudges against Louise brought him closer to Camille. Suddenly, he realized he had sadly neglected his older sister, and he resolved to do something about it. For a start, he decided to transfer her to the first-class inmate status and to take over her expenses. The switch, however, was not welcomed by Camille, who hated to change her accustomed routine. The letter she wrote to her mother on this occasion provides numerous details on the especially difficult living conditions she was experiencing at the moment, and it remains one of the most poignant she ever wrote.

My dear Mother,

I waited to write for some time because it has been so cold that I could not stand up any more. To write, I can't go to the room where everyone goes, where a meager little fire burns; there is a deafening racket. I am obliged to go to my room on the second floor, where it is so hellishly cold that my fingers are numb; they shake and can't hold the pen.

I did not warm up the whole winter; I am frozen to the bones, cut in half by the cold. I got sick. One of my friends who ended up here, a poor teacher from the Lycée Fénelon, was found dead in her bed from the cold. It is horrible. Nothing can give any idea of the iciness of Montdevergues. And it lasts seven months as a whole. You can never imagine what I suffer in these asylums. Therefore it is with surprise mixed with fear that I learned of Paul's decision to have me placed in first class. It is interesting to notice that, though you never set foot here, you know what I need better than me. You spend your money foolishly: who knows what you give? [24]

Camille explained to her mother why she did not want to be transferred to first-class status. According to her, first-class patients were the most unhappy; their dining room was cold and uncomfortable, and their food gave them dysentery. As for the furniture of a first-class bedroom, it consisted of an uncomfortable iron bed and a broken chamber pot. Camille demanded to be returned to the third-class category and to let Paul know about it. The thought of Paul triggered again within her the hope of being released from the asylum—the passionate and crazy hope, always deferred, yet always reborn. An avalanche of questions formed under her pen.

> Do you have any of his news? Do you know where he is right now? What are his intentions toward me? Does he intend to let me die in insane asylums? You are really cruel to refuse to give me a place in Villeneuve. I would not cause any scandal, as you believe. I would be so happy to start again an ordinary life that I would not do anything. I have suffered so much that I would not dare to move. You say I would need someone to serve me? What do you mean? I never had a maid in my whole life; you are the ones who always needed one.

Before Camille had the time to get her letter posted, she received a message from her mother, requesting a list of necessities for the next package. Camille asked for the usual fare of coffee, tea, butter, sugar, flour, oil, salt, bouillon, and soap, as well as a few treats such as mandarin oranges and a bowl of cherries in brandy. While these luxuries improved her diet of eggs and potatoes and probably made her feel better, they did not address her most fundamental needs—to be seen and heard and, most of all, to receive answers. "Insane asylums are created for the purpose of making one suffer," Camille observed sadly. "There is nothing to be done about it, especially when one never receives any visits." Her desperate mood persisted through the end of her letter as she added mournfully: "As for me, I am so dejected to live like this that I am no longer a human being. I can't bear the cries of all these creatures, it makes me sick. God! How I wish I were in Villeneuve!"[25]

One month later, on 3 March 1927, she was able to contact her brother. Without recrimination but with a clearly stated argument, she attempted to make the outsider Paul understand what the insider Camille had to endure.

Your intention is good and so is the director's, but in an insane asylum these things are hard to get; changes are hard to make. Even if they try, it is difficult to create a bearable atmosphere. There are established rules, there is an adapted way of life; it is extremely difficult to go against the rules! It is a matter of keeping at bay all kinds of atrocious, violent, shrill, and threatening creatures. For this, a very strict order is needed, occasionally even a harsh order; otherwise it would be impossible to control them. They all scream, sing, yell from morning to night and from night to morning. Even their parents can't stand these creatures because they are so unpleasant and so abusive. And how is it that I should be forced to put up with them? Without counting the trouble resulting from such proximity. They laugh, whine, tell endless stories. . . . What a bother it is to be in the middle of all this; you must let me out of this environment, where for fourteen years today I have been sequestered! I demand freedom. My dream would be to return to Villeneuve right away and never move from there. I would prefer a barn in Villeneuve to a first-class pension here.[26]

Camille still did not know that the Villeneuve house had been sold; she would learn it during her brother's following visit in August 1927. "Painful things of my sojourn in France," Paul wrote in his *Journal* on this occasion, "My old sister Camille in Montdevergues, with her sad-looking straw hat perched upon her skull and her yellow cotton dress."[27] Earlier he had returned to Villeneuve as a guest in the house of his childhood. "I saw the poor old Villeneuve house transformed by Jacques with a sitting room and a pergola," he wrote dejectedly. "It is completely over. Only one thing remains mine, this corner of the church where my father and my grandparents are buried. . . . There is a moment when the past ceases to be with us. The tie has been broken."[28]

Losing his childhood haven prompted Paul to find a permanent home for himself and his family. By then ambassador to the United States, he could afford something worthy of his prestigious position. In June 1927, he bought the château de Brangues, an old castle reshaped by relatively recent additions, and sitting within a large park shaded by ancient trees. In July, the family moved in. "For the first time," Paul happily declared, "I find myself surrounded with my wife and my five children under a roof belonging to me."[29] Camille must have been just as delighted, considering that the castle was located in the Alps, on the left bank of the Rhône, and its relative proximity to Montdevergues promised more frequent visits from her brother.

The Brangues purchase did not heal the wounds caused by the sale of the Villeneuve house, and the tension between the Claudels remained. By the next year, Madame Claudel chided her son for his resentful comportment toward them. "You reproach me for money matters," she complained, "and you don't hesitate to quarrel with us for these reasons. . . . Regarding Camille, you are not any better: my life is torture because of her, I think about it all the time and yet you wrote to me last year: 'I assume the responsibility for my sister's expenses, you will never hear again from your oldest daughter.'" As she was nearing her death, Madame Claudel would have liked to see her children interacting harmoniously. "I will be very happy if, before I die," she confessed, "I saw you all getting along well and full of affection for one another."[30]

Shortly after this remonstrance, Madame Claudel's health deteriorated because of an inoperable ovarian cyst. From the United States, Paul contacted Dr. Jacques de Massary, his nephew and the new owner of the Villeneuve house. Dr. de Massary did not hide his belief that Madame Claudel's end was not very far off. Switching to a different subject, he added: "I was very happy to learn from your letter that you did not hold against us any of the grudges or ill feelings that your behavior toward us, even your words, seemed to indicate. Their unfairness and lack of foundation pained us deeply."[31]

With ill feelings brushed aside, or so it seemed, Paul returned to France for his usual summer break, happy to spend a few more days with his mother. When he left her, he knew he would not see her again. "I kiss my old mother probably for the last time. Her poor arms are like those of a skeleton. She had Communion, and she received Extreme Unction."[32]

Louise-Athanaïse Cerveaux Claudel died on 20 June 1929. She was eighty-nine years old. According to her desire, her funeral was very simple, and she was buried next to her husband in the small Villeneuve cemetery. "God, have mercy upon the soul of Louise-Athanaïse Cerveaux," Paul wrote in his *Journal*. "She was poor, simple, deeply humble, pure of heart, devoted to her daily duties, working with her hands from morning to night. Her life was full of woe and knew very few joys."[33] Two days later, he wrote again:

"Said the office of the dead for mother's soul. . . . I was completely different from her in the essentials. But I looked like her through a multitude of small characteristics. Even physically, more and more as I am getting older."[34]

Louise de Massary was very shaken by her mother's death. "She knew the end was near," Louise wrote to Paul, who remained in Washington, D. C. "When she saw me close to her, sorrowful, she consoled me and told me not to grieve so much, that death had to arrive, that it was unavoidable, that it was her turn. . . ."[35] Louise also informed her sister of the sad events. Camille "seemed quite moved," Louise told Paul, "but she remains convinced that mother has been poisoned."[36]

Several years later, Camille commemorated the anniversary of her mother's death in her own words. "At this time of summer holidays, I always think of our dear mother," she wrote, "I never saw her again since the day you took the fatal resolution of sending me to mental asylums!" Camille also wondered what happened to an oil portrait she had done of her mother years ago:

> I think about the beautiful portrait I made of her in the shade of our beautiful garden. The large eyes expressing a secret sorrow, the spirit of forbearance that exuded from her person, her hands crossed over her knees in an expression of complete self-sacrifice: everything pointing to humility, to a sense of duty pushed to the extreme, so was our poor mother. I never saw this portrait again (nor did I see her either!). If ever you hear about it, tell me.[37]

The portrait was never found; it appears to have been destroyed by Madame Claudel.

IN MARCH 1929, Camille received an unexpected letter from England. After all these years, Jessie Lipscomb Elborne had managed to unearth her former partner's elusive address. The search, delayed many times, had required much perseverance, for all the Claudels had moved out of the dwellings they had occupied in the 1880s. As long as Rodin had been alive, Jessie had managed to sustain a tenuous link with her past Parisian life, keeping in touch with her former teacher through short messages sometimes accompanied by photographs. When, in June 1913, Rodin was called to London to select a site for the newly purchased cast of *The Burghers of Calais*, Jessie and her son Sydney joined Rodin for the dedication of the sculpture. Invited to stay at Wootton House, Rodin returned for a brief visit to the place that had sheltered his then-beloved Camille so many years before and signed the visitors' book at Saint Peter's Cathedral.[1] Jessie may have been informed of Camille's sequestration at that point, but the beginning of the Great War would have forced her to postpone any attempt to locate her old friend.

When the war was over, Jessie succeeded at last in tracking down Paul's address at the French Embassy in Copenhagen. Reluctant to talk about Camille, Paul scribbled a laconic answer to this ghost from the past: "My sister has been sick for many years and is right now in a hospital in the south. I thank you for your kindness. Yours ever."[2] Jessie, of course, had hoped for a more informative letter, but she did not get discouraged and she tried again. She must have tried several times before she finally received a postcard from Paul in 1926; an answer to a letter she had sent three years earlier. "It is with great confusion that I find your letter of 6 September 1923, among lost letters, and I don't think I ever answered it," he wrote apologetically. "Please excuse me. I thank you for not having lost, after so many years, the memory of the brother of a great and unfortunate artist."[3] The following year, Paul's answer to Jessie arrived more quickly: "My poor sister Camille is still in the same situation," he told her. "I hope you are happy in Peterborough, and I would find it agreeable to speak with you about the old days."[4]

Their exchange of polite missives could have continued much longer if Jessie had not taken the rather extraordinary decision to come and see Camille in Montdevergues on her way to visit Italy; her understanding husband had readily accepted the idea. Considering that both of them had traveled to Egypt three years earlier to visit the pyramids, this train journey was nothing to the vigorous couple, even at sixty-eight and seventy-one, respectively. Paul, having nothing to fear from them, easily gave his consent to the visit.

Deeply moved by Jessie's great news, Camille awaited her old friend's arrival with an eagerness mixed with melancholy. So many merciless changes had taken place during the long years of their separation; Camille wore them on her ravaged face. She feared Jessie might not recognize her, and she made a brave attempt to warn her.

> Dear Madame Elborne,
>
> I received your letter with great pleasure; you give me much solace: what will it be then, if it is true you are getting ready to come and see me.
>
> You have done well to think of me! . . . to come through here on your way to Italy! It will not be much longer and for me it will be a great joy. I can't believe that you will come all the way here, it seems impossible to me. If I had known it would have pleased you, I would have written to you immediately after my arrival here. Be sure to warn me in advance of your arrival so that I can help you reach me (it is not always easy!). . . .
>
> Have no illusions about me; you will not recognize the pretty bust you made of me long ago: it is gone. I have changed so much that I doubt you will recognize me! I don't want to distress you with the tale of my troubles.

It was easier for Camille to talk about the weather. "We have had a terrible winter," she added. "Recently a real cyclone hit us; a terrible wind

Jessie Lipscomb Elborne, *Sydney at 7.*
Bronze, 1897. Private collection

Jessie Lipscomb Elborne, *Sydney at 9.*
Plaster, 1899. Private collection

Jessie Lipscomb Elborne,
William Elborne. Bronze, 1907.
Private collection

230

uprooted all the trees in the garden; several centenarian pine trees were thrown to the ground like straw in the wind. The wind was so strong that it sounded like detonations; in Avignon, tiles fell upon pedestrians, and nobody dared to go out."

Camille also recounted the most significant events in the Claudel family: the death of her father, the approaching death of her estranged mother, the peaceful life of her sister now residing most of the time in Villeneuve with her son and his new wife. "She is happy," Camille said of Louise, "but for me it is not the same." A hint of envy toward her sister, perhaps, but expressed without the animosity that Louise often attributed to her. As for Paul, his purchase of the château de Brangues near Chambéry did not seem to make much difference in Camille's life. "His wife and his children spend the summer there, but they never come and see me," Camille confided to Jessie.[5]

Jessie and William arrived in Montdevergues as promised; according to regulations, Camille must have met them in the parlor of the asylum. Years later, Jessie reminisced about their encounter, but only to insist that Camille was not insane.[6] She did not speak about the initial shock of recognition, emotional embrace, apprehension turning into confidence; and none of this could be captured by William's poignant photographs. Yet, the mood of the reunion is palpable. An overwhelming feeling of melancholy emanates from the two women sitting by the cheerless stone walls of the asylum. With her arms folded around herself, Camille does not seem to see Jessie's hand softly reaching out to her. The long years of isolation have taken their toll; Camille looks empty and withdrawn.

Life had been kinder to the British sculptor, who had much to tell Camille. During the six years following her marriage in 1887, Jessie had given birth to four children. The first one was a girl, Helen, born in Manchester, where William was eking out a precarious living as a lecturer in pharmacy at Owen's College. Encouraged by Sydney Lipscomb to return to his studies, William moved his family to Cambridge. Three boys were born during this period—Sydney, William, and Jack—but none of them would get to know their generous grandfather, who died suddenly in 1890. Three years later, the family moved again, when William received a teaching position at the medical school of London University.

In London William and Jessie resided in crowded facilities and yearned for space and easier living, while Harriet Lipscomb, alone in the large Wootton House after her husband's death, yearned for company. A hard decision was finally made. In 1895 William abandoned academia for a position as a public analyst in Peterborough, and the family joined Harriet at Wootton House. Unfortunately, they quickly discovered that Harriet had grown rather despotic in her old age, and insisted on running the household along with Jessie until her death at seventy-two, in 1910.

With four children, Jessie's life had become endlessly busy, although she received the help of two young housemaids, something rather common in Victorian times. Jessie had inherited several properties from her father, but they were rented out to supplement William's modest salary. In fact, William and Jessie could not afford private school tuition for their four children, so they attended to their education themselves. Yet, between the scientific William and the artistic Jessie, the children received a solid general education, which included not only French and German but also drawing.

On the rare occasions when Jessie could escape, she went to the soothing haven she had created at the bottom of the garden: an artist's studio with wooden panels and top lights. There, slowly, patiently, she modeled family portraits: a small but expressive bust of her oldest son, Sydney, aged seven, in 1897; a bust of her husband, William, a year later; a touching portrait head of Sydney, now nine, the following year; and in 1907, a bust of William that would have made Rodin beam with pride. Sydney later remembered sitting on a chair that turned round and round while his mother lovingly modeled his features in the clay. He also remembered her doing the portraits of local people, but only one of these has survived to this day—the bust of Alderman Redhead, mayor of the city of Peterborough, and a rather dour-looking gentleman. Jessie's last sculpture, in 1925, was also a wedding present: a plaster head of Cavil, the new wife of her son Sydney.[7]

Although Jessie had spent her adolescence in Peterborough, she found herself isolated when she returned there after thirteen years of living in large cities. Her education, travels, and experience as a sculptor had turned her into an outsider in the eyes of the rustic locals. She missed Paris terribly, so she tried to provide her own home with Parisian touches in the decoration and furniture. Lit by candlelight and gaslight, Wootton House came to life for Christmas and birthday parties; Jessie would play ballads on the piano, singing along with her clear and mellow voice. At quieter times, she immersed herself in a Walter Scott novel or some other classic, reading voraciously, an activity also scorned by the local population. Jessie's only friends in the area remained her husband's sisters Polly and Lizzie, who lived in a small village not far from Grantham. The family sometimes traveled there by train, or by horse and cart, with the two oldest boys cycling part of the way.

It was a dull life for a woman who had seen the bustle and glitter of Paris and London. No doubt Jessie would have been better off living in a larger city, where her art and her sophistication might have been appreciated, yet she was devoted to both her children and her husband, and she clearly enjoyed nurturing them.

The children grew up, and the boys left home to study in Cambridge, as their father had done. One by one, the properties inherited from their grandfather were sold to pay for their education. As for Helen, she followed in her mother's footsteps and studied art in London, eventually becoming a teacher of drawing and sculpture, deeply involved in her work until her marriage in 1912.

With the children gone, Jessie picked up her quill pen every Sunday night and sat at her elegant early-nineteenth-century French desk to write letters. When the war came, she wrote nearly every week to Sydney, expressing her worries, describing town events, or chatting about less troublesome matters. These letters display an unwavering strength of character and show that she was clearly in charge of the household, managing the family's resources, making sure her properties were rented to responsible tenants, juggling the finances, and even taking care of the garden. The bulk of her writing, of course, focused on war events. With three boys in the war, Jessie remained alert to all the changes occurring during this tragic time. "We don't want you blown to bits," she wrote to Sydney in 1915, urging him to be transferred away from a dangerous arsenal.[8] But she was strong enough to know that Sydney, William, and Jack had to decide for themselves. "I do not want Jack to go," she said, referring to the front, "but I tell him he must do as he thinks best."[9] Even though the greater part of the fighting was taking place in France, war was visible everywhere. German zeppelins raided London, British soldiers poured into Peterborough—ten thousand of them—officers requested lodging at Wootton House. Jessie remained emotionally strong through it all. She was more fortunate than many in that her three sons came back unharmed.

Ten years later, overwhelmed with conflicting emotions, Jessie was sitting by Camille's side in the most unlikely place. Once they had lived the same life and shared the same dream; then came the abrupt change. It was not so much the silly quarrel that had driven a wedge between them, but the sharp contrast of their choices. Marriage had made Jessie respectable in the eyes of Victorian society. Although she had had her share of troubles like everyone else, she was enjoying the serenity bestowed by a stable and affectionate relationship. On the other hand, Camille had fought a valiant battle against the bigotry of the art world, and she had lost. Her determination to make it alone against all odds had contributed to her tragic fate. Camille's magnificent hands, now lying useless on her lap, had not touched clay for sixteen years, and her dreams had shrunk to the modest yearning for a quiet corner somewhere in Villeneuve, where her sister, Louise, freely returned every year. Jessie knew that Louise had not come even once to visit Camille in the asylum, and she decided to do something about it.

After her return to England, Jessie voiced her concerns to Louise in a letter containing the poignant photograph of Camille taken by William a few months earlier. Louise's seemingly caring answer left Paris on 9 December 1929.

Dear Madame,

I can't tell you how disturbed I was when I received my poor sister's photograph, and I could not hold back my tears. It is an absolute picture of grief and despair; never did I imagine that she was in such a state, never would I have recognized her.

Poor unhappy victim of her own imagination. If it was up to me, I would immediately go and get her, I would bring her back, I would take care of her to make her forget her ordeal.

But I am not free; doctors around me are formally opposed to this idea, insisting that she would soon become again as she was in the past, and she hurt us so much, my poor mother especially. It is also difficult to bring her back around Paris: she would become even more agitated if she saw herself closer to us.

She enjoys a relative freedom where she is; elsewhere, she would have to submit to the discipline of the establishment, and it is what she hates the most. After a short while, it would be the same thing as now.

Dear Madame, I am in Paris until the month of April; if you had the opportunity of coming here, I would be very pleased to see you again; we would speak together about the poor martyr. I thank you immensely for the photograph although it caused me so much sorrow.

Yours truly,
Louise de Massary[10]

In spite of her efforts to appear compassionate, Louise was not very convincing. She obviously wallowed in self-pity, caring for the "poor martyr" only as long as she did not have to see her, and shifting the burden of responsibility to anonymous doctors. Jessie could not have been fooled by her insincerity, but she also believed she might be more successful in her attempt to help Camille if she confronted Louise face to face. She therefore resolved to return to France in April of the following year. "I received a letter from Jessie Elborne," Camille wrote to Paul on the third of March. "She tells me she will come with her husband around the end of April! . . . Among all my relatives, not one is doing as much."[11] Unfortunately, Jessie's plan to see Louise in Paris did not work out because Louise was getting ready to leave.

Dear Madame,

I am leaving Paris on the 8th of this month, I therefore regret that I will not be able to see you.

I would, of course, be happy to see you and to speak about my sister, but I don't think anything whatsoever would result from our talk. We can neither change anything about her circumstances nor bring her closer to Paris, where boarding is extremely expensive. When she lived close to me, she never wanted to associate with me; for fifteen years, I never saw her even once; do you believe that she would be different now? Remember how jealous she was of me in the old days; it would be much worse if she saw me again. She is an unfortunate woman, a martyr, and I suffer a great deal because of it, but nothing can be done about it.

My brother and I are planning to go and see her this summer, an encounter I dread terribly because of my poor health; emotions shatter me.

Yours truly,
Louise de Massary[12]

Louise was evidently holding at least as many grudges against Camille as Camille may have held against her. It is hard to understand why Camille would have been jealous of her sister "in the old days," when she was both happy and productive. It is likely that it was Louise who had resented the attention her gifted sibling was receiving from everyone. The same insincerity permeates Louise's complaints about Camille's estrangement, considering that only Louis-Prosper Claudel was willing to welcome the sculptor in his home.

Jessie must have been disheartened by Louise's letter. It is difficult to ascertain whether she and her husband made the long trip to Montdevergues again, because no photographs remain and no letters refer to the visit. In the asylum, the visitors' register did not record any further visits by the couple.

Later that year, Camille informed Jessie that Louise had finally come to see her, bringing along her son and her daughter-in-law. "They are very nice," Camille wrote, "but I can't convince them to take me out of here which, for me, is the main thing." Paul had come twice that summer, once alone and the second time with two of his children. "He still holds the same feelings toward me," she lamented. "It is impossible to receive any hope for a departure." Jessie's heart must have sunk when she read the rest of the letter. "The Jewish gang is holding me here," Camille claimed, returning to her obsessions, "because, at the time of the Dreyfus affair, I refused to sign petitions in favor of this individual"[13]

The remainder of Camille's last letter to Jessie is missing, as are further traces of their renewed friendship, perhaps because of Camille's lack of interest in anything but the possibility of leaving the asylum. "I received several letters from you," she apologized to Jessie in her last letter, "and I must seem very ungrateful not to have answered. I waited for something happy to take place, so that I could tell you." The lack of surviving documents suggests that Jessie eventually chose to stay away. Although she and her husband traveled to Switzerland in 1932, it does not appear that they attempted to see Camille. Yet when Paul received an honorary degree from Cambridge in 1939, Jessie and William were present at the ceremony. "I recognized Paul Claudel at once," Jessie wrote to her son Sydney. "In spite of his white hair, his features had the old familiar kindly expression!" They watched their friend as he slowly made his way toward the chancellor, accompanied by seven other recipients, all dressed in scarlet robes and wearing the traditional black velvet cap. "After all was over, we went to Trinity Hall Lodge and Paul came out at once to us—very delighted to see us again. He now speaks a bit of English—learnt, as he laughingly said, when he was in America."[14]

Their ease at renewing old ties was all the more remarkable in that it was their first reunion in fifty-two years. Sadly, it was also the last. Paul's poor health prevented him from returning to England, and Jessie did not return to France.

PAUL CLAUDEL HAD spent the seven years from 1926 to 1933 in Washington, D.C., as French ambassador to the United States. By then he was celebrated everywhere as a major poet and playwright. Americans bestowed their own homage on him when, in 1928, both New York University and Princeton granted him honorary degrees. Money also became plentiful, with the château de Brangues the most visible display of Paul's new affluence. Diplomat, poet, father, grandfather, lord of a castle, Paul could have savored the bountiful harvest of his accomplishments if he had not remained the prisoner of his many grudges. He had not forgotten how Jacques de Massary, Louise's son, had purchased the Villeneuve house, and his rancor against the de Massarys had not subsided. As long as his mother was alive, he had maintained a somewhat civil relationship with his sister Louise. After their mother's death, the unavoidable clash occurred when the responsibility for Camille's living expenses had to be worked out between the siblings. For several years, Paul and Louise clawed at each other each time Camille's income proved to be too small to support her.

Camille's liquid assets consisted of the pension she received from the state—a pension that was boosted to 1,500 francs after the war—and the income generated by the investment of a modest capital, worth 50,000 francs. Like all capitals belonging to mentally ill patients, Camille's was protected by law and placed in the hands of an impartial administrator—in this case Jules Ferté. Only the accrued interests from investments could be used to pay the trimester bills of the asylum. In the past, Camille's liquid assets provided most of the money needed for this purpose, but after the war several sharp increases demanded by the asylum upset the balance. By 1924 Madame Claudel could no longer meet expenses, and Paul had begun to help her. "I have just received your letter and the 1,200 francs," Madame Claudel gratefully wrote to him. "Thanks a million. It arrived just in time because the increase of Camille's boarding costs has just hit. It is huge, an extra 1,200 francs! I will have to sell a few shares in order to pay it."[1]

After Madame Claudel's death in 1929, Louise took over some of the accounts. Considering her precarious financial situation and Paul's wealth, she expected her brother to continue the payments he had made in the past. Paul, on the other hand, had a different opinion. After a closer look at the accounts, he realized that Louise had pocketed Camille's state pension in order to defray the cost of the packages she mailed to her sister. Immediately, he contacted Jules Ferté, directing him to take charge of the payments made to the asylum with both the state pension and the interests accrued from investments. Not knowing what to do, Ferté informed Louise of Paul's request. Several bitter exchanges took place as a result. Louise forwarded Ferté's letter to Paul, begging her brother not to deprive her of Camille's state pension. "In view of your financial standing," she wrote in November 1931, "it seems to me that you can easily pay 7,000 francs each year without any problem."[2] Not swayed by her arguments, Paul turned his anger against the honest Ferté, reproaching him for writing to Louise. He sharply reminded Ferté that he alone had supported Camille in the recent past and, therefore, he alone ought to be contacted on these matters. Caught between the feuding siblings, the seventy-eight-year-old man replied that he had handled this thankless administrative task free of charge for many years and that he would gladly ask the court to find a replacement. Two months later, a new administrator was appointed.

After further inquiries, Paul concluded that Louise was legally responsible for half of Camille's expenses. It was early January, a time traditionally devoted to joyful holiday wishes, but Paul did not spare his sister on this account.

> My dear Louise,
>
> Before answering your last letter, I took the time to reflect and also to consult a French lawyer in New York. His opinion is perfectly clear. You received an inheritance from our father and our mother, you are therefore liable for its expenses jointly and equally with me. As long as Mother was alive, I wanted to spare her. Now that she is dead, there is no reason for me not to ask you to share the expenses of

the inheritance. I am therefore doing so with this letter and, if necessary, I will ask for a meeting of the Family Board regarding this subject. I have made up my mind.

I wish you and your family a happy new year.

P. Claudel[3]

Camille's modest income met her expenses by half. Because Paul refused to pay the other half and Louise claimed to be financially strapped, the siblings took a second look at Camille's capital and, as expected, disagreed on how to dispose of it. Paul, believing Camille would not live much longer, wanted to withdraw regular amounts from the principal; on the other hand, Louise wanted to turn it into a life annuity for Camille. Since the law protected Camille's capital, Louise's proposal appeared to be the only legal possibility, yet Paul would not budge. His stubbornness left no alternative but to call the Family Board to a meeting.

It had been years since the Family Board had been convened; in 1933, many of the original members were either not available or not interested. A new board had to be created by Monsieur Moulin, the new administrator for Camille's affairs, and someone had to represent Paul, who was still in the United States. The deliberations were to take place in front of a judge, who then would make the final decision. More bickering occurred when, in a letter he sent to Monsieur Moulin, Paul bitterly objected to the presence of Louise and Jacques de Massary on the Family Board:

I do not understand the right claimed by the persons in question to discuss my sister's situation and the manner in which I propose to settle it. Madame de Massary declares that her circumstances do not allow her to pay the boarding costs. Her son, Monsieur Jacques de Massary, has always declared, at the first opportunity, that he refused to contribute to the costs, and he is protected by law from this eventuality.

On the other hand, I have been the only one for the last ten years to contribute to my sister's boarding costs, and I assume that my behavior is the best guarantee for what I, as well as my heirs, will do in the future.

I therefore don't see how Madame and Monsieur de Massary

have the right to get involved in a matter in which they have no interest, and which is no concern of theirs. Since I am the only one to assume the expenses, it is logical that my opinion on the manner of using my sister's capital be the most weighty.

My sister Camille is sixty-eight; because I visit her every year—something the de Massarys have never done, having seen her only once in twenty years—I am in a better position to judge the state of her health, and it seems highly unlikely that she could still have ten to twelve years left ahead of her; meaning that she would reach the exceptional age of eighty.[4]

Paul was wrong on all accounts. Camille missed the exceptional age of eighty by only a few months; the judge, foreseeing this possibility, decided in favor of turning her capital into a life annuity. Paul was also wrong on the matter of the visits. Although he had come to see Camille more often than anyone else, he had, more than once, let several years go by between visits. It was only after the purchase of Brangues that he went more often to Montdevergues.

Losing his case could not have improved Paul's feelings toward Louise, yet, an unexpected event helped heal the breach between the siblings, when Louise had a heart attack a year later. Paul came to visit her in September 1934; as soon as he saw her, he knew the end was near. Louise had changed terribly; she looked old and weak, but her religious faith gave her the strength to face the unavoidable. She died seven months later, on 2 May 1935. "Providence kept her alive to allow her to have communion at Easter," Paul exulted in his *Journal*. "What a joy! What a benediction!"[5]

The funeral in Villeneuve involved the whole village. "The coffin carried by the women of the village. All filing past me," Paul recalled. "What bodies, what ruined figures, deformed by work! And the souls probably the same. The body in its narrow craft above the tomb, lowered for the last navigation. Embarked for the depth. Against the wall of the church."[6] Three years later, Jacques de Massary, Louise's only son, suddenly suffered a stroke. Paul rushed to Villeneuve, only to find his nephew immobile and silent on his bed. He died the next day. "I can still see him as a child, as I made him dance on the tip of my foot," the seventy-year-old Paul remembered, shaken by Jacques' early death.[7]

Paul became the only individual in charge of Camille's destiny at a time when his own health was failing him. Like Rodin, he suffered from anemia, a condition requiring a great deal of rest. He was therefore grateful for the strong support his children gave him. One of them, his daughter Marie—also called Chouchette—had taken an interest in her neglected aunt. During the 1930s, she sometimes surprised Camille with unannounced visits, bringing along her brother, Pierre, or her husband, Roger. Camille welcomed these rare gestures of affection with a childlike joy, expressed in the letter she sent to Paul after one of these visits in 1932:

My dear Paul:

Yesterday Saturday, I had a pleasant surprise. I was called to the parlor where Chouchette, Roger, and Pierre were waiting for me. Chouchette was very pretty, very well-dressed. Pierre has grown considerably; he looks very much like you. Roger was very nice with me. He immediately went to get food; he went to Montfavet and brought back oranges, bananas, butter, croissants, apples, and then he gave me a small amount of money. He did the shopping so quickly, I thought he was very resourceful. I hobbled along to welcome them, with a rheumatism in my knee, an old worn coat, an old hat from the Samaritaine, which fell down to my nose. Well, it was me. Pierre remembered his old insane aunt. This is the way I will appear in their memories in the next century.

He told me you will come soon.

I am waiting for you.

I am now going through an unpleasant time. They started to install central heating. There are workers everywhere and scaffolds all over the courtyard. God! it's so bothersome, I would like to be by the fireplace in Villeneuve, but alas! The way things are going, I think I will never get out of Montdevergues. It does not look good![8]

There are no recriminations against anyone in this letter, no grudges, only the irritation of being disturbed by messy construction work. Although Camille was distressed by the thought of never leaving Montdevergues, at the same time she seemed almost resigned to it. By the early 1930s, she appeared to have reached an inner peace, which protected her from her environment. Former nurses of the asylum later recalled her quiet figure sitting on a straw chair lost in an endless meditation. "She was very polite and she never became angry," one remembered.

Camille had been moved to Pavilion 10, a place that housed about sixty patients. She was the only one to have her own room in this building, although it was tiny and had no sink. "She should not have been placed in this section, where the most mentally deficient had been gathered," the same nurse complained. "They screamed, grimaced, and immensely disturbed her writing." This nurse had often supervised Camille doing her own cooking in the refectory. "We brought her vegetables and a little meat, and she liked to cook the potatoes in their skins on the stove of the refectory. She washed her clothes on the pile of stones she kept in her room, and that may be why she was not always very clean, because we did not have much soap."[9] Marie-Thérèse Benier, another retired nurse, explained that Camille never spoke of her private life, but she sometimes talked about sculpting. "She especially spoke of her last piece representing a peasant with a scythe on his shoulder," Benier added. "She said the muscles were the most difficult to duplicate."[10]

According to the nurses, Camille spent most of her time with her cats—six of them during this period—and wrote endlessly when she was not daydreaming or waiting for her brother's yearly visit. Whenever he did come, she was called to the office of the director of the asylum, because Paul found it repugnant to go to the parlor of the pavilion. Sometimes overcome with remorse, Paul confided his anguish to his journal: "Saw Camille in Montdevergues," he wrote in 1933, "terribly old and pitiful, with her mouth furnished with a few horrible stumps. Ashamed of myself when I see her so poor and I living in affluence, but what can I do? She is the one who wants to live in section 10. She tells me that 'it will be her last winter' and talks about her funeral."[11]

It was not Camille's last winter. Instead, the next spring proved to be especially warm to Camille, as the outside world remembered her with a special retrospective show organized by the Société des Femmes Artistes et Modernes in May 1934. On this occasion, Camille's unwavering supporter, Louis Vauxelles, praised the sculptor in *Le Monde illustré*.

With Berthe Morisot, Camille Claudel is the most beautiful name of feminine art at the end of the nineteenth century. Eugène Blot, the art dealer and defender of Camille Claudel, wrote justly that she was to Rodin what Morisot was to Manet. Each one, working next to a crushing master, keeps her own personality. Claudel also owes something to the master of Meudon; he marked her with his touch, formed her as he modeled clay. But this rustic woman from Lorraine, hard, willful, untamable, remained herself. Look at her busts of her brother, Paul Claudel, and of Monsieur de Massary; if they don't have the feverish passion of rodinian portraits, maybe they express more nobility, elevation, majesty; and the groups created by Camille Claudel are enduring masterpieces. . . .

Camille Claudel, who was unhappy and disappeared like a meteor from the world of ateliers, deserved the honor given to her by the Société des Femmes Artistes et Modernes. They are rightfully proud of this woman, whose authentic genius remains acknowledged only by a few.[12]

Soon after the exhibition, Paul sent Vauxelles's article to Camille. That the outside world still remembered her after all these years was a great source of comfort to her. Deeply moved, remembering the friendly face of Eugène Blot, his affection, his endless efforts to sell her sculptures, she picked up her pen and wrote him "a very touching and melancholic letter— mysterious too, because she did not give her address."[13] It had seemed to Blot that Camille had disappeared without a trace. Then the war, the death of Rodin, and his own health problems, which kept him away from Paris until 1926, complicated matters even further. "I had lost track of you," Blot had written two years earlier as he tried to reach Camille. "In the scheming world of sculpture, Rodin, you, and three or four others perhaps had introduced authenticity; this cannot be forgotten." With great emotion, he remembered Camille's works, especially *L'Implorante,* considered by some a manifesto of modern sculpture:

You were, at last, "yourself," totally freed from the influence of Rodin, as great in your inspiration as in your skill. The first cast enriched with your signature is one of the magnum opus of my gallery. I never look at it without an ineffable emotion. I think I see you again. The half-open lips, the trembling nostrils, the light in the eyes, all of this screams life in its greatest mystery. With you, we were going to leave the world of false appearances for the one of thought. What a genius! The word is not too strong. How could you deprive us of so much beauty?

Generous as always, Blot had ended his letter with a touching gesture: "What can I do for you, dear Camille Claudel? Write to me, take the hand I extend to you. I never ceased to be your friend."[14] Blot's letter probably ended in the pile of withheld documents, thus Camille remained unaware of the friendly hand stretching out to her. It took the retrospective at the Société des Femmes Artistes et Modernes to prompt her to write to him; but the sequestration orders given against her were still in force, and Blot's answers were probably never delivered.

During the same period, Judith Cladel was finishing her biography of Rodin. As one of the organizers of Camille's retrospective, Judith Cladel had tried to locate the marble statue of *Clotho*, which had been commissioned at the banquet for Puvis de Chavannes, with the intention of being given to the Luxembourg Museum. In her search for information on Camille and *Clotho*, she contacted both Mathias Morhardt and Eugène Blot. It is at this point that the disappearance of *Clotho* from the Luxembourg Museum became evident. Horrified by this disappearance, Judith Cladel proposed steps to have another work of Camille placed in the museum.

> While consulting the dossier of Camille Claudel at the administration, I noticed that the state had bought several of her works. If we don't find *Clotho*, after this summer we will need to organize, you and I, a small petition of artists and amateurs so that one of these works is placed in the Luxembourg, for example the beautiful bronze of *L'Abandon*. But will we know where it is? It's incredible; isn't there a nomenclature and a repertory of the acquisitions of the state and of the gifts it receives? And why doesn't Paul Claudel look after his sister's fame, considering she has been so touched by the expressed remembrance of her talent and by an event such as the "Exposition des Femmes artistes?"[15]

Cladel never managed to locate *Clotho*. In a last desperate attempt,

Morhardt published an article on this important piece, but it did not lead to the hoped-for result, and *Clotho* remains missing to this day.[16]

Cladel's book on Rodin was published in 1936. A small part of the book was devoted to Camille, who was presented to the public as Rodin's "great passion." "The pages I have in mind for her are very delicate to write," Cladel had written to Morhardt, "and yet I cannot remain silent on an aspect of Rodin's life that caused so many outrageous critiques."[17] Cladel solved the problem by omitting Camille's name, and it is safe to assume that Paul appreciated her discretion when he read the book. "Book of Judith Cladel on Rodin," he wrote in his *Journal* in July 1936. "This slow degradation. This sinister end. Influence of Camille."[18]

In August Paul arrived in Montdevergues with Roger, his son-in-law. Late summer and early fall were his chosen time to visit Camille; she in turn waited impatiently for these few hours of happiness. Yet even this would be taken away from her when Paul became ill with repeated bouts of anemia. Confined to his Parisian home for months at a time, Paul would not return to Montdevergues for seven long years.

Paul's anemia did not, however, seem to diminish his ability to flare up at the least provocation. "My state of health does not make me gentle and peaceful," he confessed to his friend Françoise de Marcilly in 1937. Being in a mood for confidence and probably seeking a form of indirect forgiveness from his Catholic friend, he pushed the confession further when he admitted having violently thrown his good friend Jacques Madaule out the door. The kindhearted Madaule had solicited Paul's signature for a petition against the bombing of Guernica perpetrated by the Spanish dictator Franco, and later so dramatically brought to life in Picasso's famous painting. Instead of being horrified by the bombing, Paul viewed the petition as a provocation and an offense to the memory of the priests who had been massacred by Basque sympathizers. He hated and despised the Basques, whom he viewed as "despicable Judases." Paul was both astounded and slightly embarrassed by his violent outburst, but he remained unrepentant. "It is sad to be seventy and to still be subject to these fits of hysterical rage, which were too familiar in the past and which positively make me lose my head," he admitted. "Because my fits of anger don't last just one day. They leave grudges behind, which can last for months and sometimes more. . . . Madaule does not know how close he came to receiving a large crystal inkwell across his face! Maybe it would have done him some good!"[19]

Such excesses call to mind Camille's paranoid vision of Rodin and the art world. The letter itself bears some resemblance to the letters Camille used to send to the Thierrys when she still lived on quai Bourbon."I am exactly like my sister," Paul had written to Daniel Fontaine in 1913, "although more of a weakling and a dreamer, and without God's grace, my story might have been hers or even worse."[20] The undercurrent of anger expressed by each of the siblings at various times of their lives had very different outcomes, mostly because they faced very different social pressures. Paul could channel his aggressivity toward a fanatic interpretation of religion, and he could transcend it in his writing. As a diplomat, he could also turn it into a diplomatic weapon. None of these avenues was available to Camille. Her art had long been the outlet for her aggressiveness, but when she made the switch from creating works of art to destroying them, her vulnerability became exposed. While Paul's eccentricities were forgiven, Camille's were condemned.

The Spanish Civil War foreshadowed other terrible events, even more dreadful in their magnitude, as Nazism swept across Germany. Camille, alone and unaware of the possibility of war, increasingly withdrew into her inner world. "Through the years, her state of health worsened," a nurse remembered. "She did not go out any more; she shut herself away from the rest of the world and lived only with her memories, letters, and photographs. She did not wash any more, nor did she change her clothes."[21] The conditions in the asylum did not lend themselves to cleanliness, as there was only one bathtub for the whole pavilion, and no hot water. Nurses and aides went to get water at the men's pavilion, and the female patients were taken to the "big bath" once a week, fifteen and even twenty of them at a time. "Her persecution mania got hold of her again at the end," another nurse noted. "She said people came at night, so she padlocked her door."[22]

These signs are visible in the last letter remaining from Camille, a letter that Paul slipped into the pages of his *Journal*. The letter started well, with Camille thanking Paul for some pocket money he had sent her. "I am waiting for the visit you promised for next summer," she added, "but I don't dare hope for it. Paris is far and God only knows what will happen until then?" This absence of visits triggered memories of her mother. "At this time of holidays, I always think of our dear mother. I never saw her again since the day you took the fatal resolution of sending me to mental asylums! I think about the beautiful portrait I made of her in the shade of our beautiful garden," she recalled nostalgically. This portrait had unfortunately disappeared, and the remembrance of this disappearance triggered an all-too-familiar outburst from Camille. "I don't think the odious character I often speak about could have been bold enough to claim it, like my other works. It would be too much, the portrait of my mother!"[23] Camille signed her letter "Your sister in exile" as she had earlier signed a postcard to Jessie Elborne "souvenir from exile."

WAR SWEPT ACROSS France like fire. In 1940, temporarily vanquished, France was split in half; with the free zone in the south and the zone occupied by the Nazis in the north. Paul left Paris for Brangues, which was located in the free zone, but he still did not go to Montdevergues. Yet he must have realized that the patients were suffering the dire consequences of war. Before the war, Montdevergues had enough revenue from its farms, vineyards, and fields to feed and support its growing number of inmates. But during the war, the German army placed such enormous demands upon the asylum, requisitioning such huge amounts of food that malnutrition progressed rapidly among patients. They died like flies, four or five each day.

In the summer of 1942, Paul received a disturbing medical bulletin from the asylum.

> Monsieur,
>
> Your sister's mental condition has slightly worsened after the start of a progressive intellectual decline, now predominant, while the old delirious ideas have much lessened and become secondary although essentially the same in their themes. Physically, her general condition has shown a marked weakening ever since rationing badly hit the psychopaths. Your sister has lost weight and has suffered from enteritis since the beginning of the year. Last July she had to remain in bed because of a condition related to food shortage. She received the clothes. I urged her to write to you, but she is very indifferent.
>
> Yours truly,
> Dr. L. Izac[1]

In December Paul was informed that Camille's health had declined further. "A letter from Montdevergues warns me that my poor sister Camille is going from bad to worse and makes me foresee her death, which will be a deliverance," Paul wrote in his journal. "Thirty years in jail in an insane asylum. . . . I remember this splendid young woman, full of genius, but such a violent and untamable character!"[2] Still, Paul did not go to Montdevergues.

Another disquieting medical report reached Paul in May 1943.

Monsieur,

The condition of your patient is very mediocre. She is progressively weakening. Her intellectual faculties are also weakening: loss of memory, senility. Her condition is serious and, considering her advanced age, the prognosis is guarded, heart complications being possible.

Yours truly,
Dr. L. Izac[3]

Again, whether it was caused by another bout with anemia or just lethargy, Paul did not go to Montdevergues. Luckily for Camille, another member of the large Claudel family reacted to the news with more compassion. It was Nelly Méquillet, the mother-in-law of Paul's daughter, Chouchette. In August, Nelly Méquillet left Nancy, her hometown, and traveled twenty-four hours to Montfavet, the village closest to Montdevergues. Reaching the village at 3 A.M., she had to wait in the train station for three hours before the doors of the asylum opened. "For you, it would not be so long," she wrote to Paul from Montfavet, urging him to come and visit Camille. "If you could, after the summer heat, give the joy of your presence to your sister, her last days would be solaced." Méquillet found Camille in a pitiful physical condition, probably close to death. "Nevertheless," Méquillet added, "she remains pleasant, and courteous, and her female doctor as well as her nurses are attached to her. She no longer shows any mental anguish or persecution mania. She seems at peace—when I told her I came on your behalf, she took both my hands, thanking me profusely and touchingly, you are the only person from her past whom she remembers." Explaining that Camille suffered from edema caused by poor nutrition,

Méquillet urged Paul to send regular packages of eggs, butter, sugar, jam, or cake to his sister—difficult in wartime, but easier in rural Brangues than in Nancy or Paris. "I go and see your sister every day," she told Paul. "She devours what I bring her—a little milk from my breakfast, grapes, but no butter here! Eggs also would be good."

The kind woman stayed a week in Montfavet, and Camille's happiness made it all worthwhile to her. "I was so happy to see her beaming face, so grateful for a little visit. I kissed her for you, my dear friend," she told Paul, "and I immediately gave her all my affection."[4]

Finally shaken from his lethargy, Paul arranged to go and see Camille in September 1943. A friend drove the car that took them to Avignon on the twentieth, in the evening, and they spent the night in a priory across the river. The next day, Paul reached Montdevergues around 10 A.M.

> The director tells me that his patients are literally dying of hunger: 800 out of 2,000! The female doctor, wise and frail. Camille in her bed! an eighty-year-old woman who looks much older! Her extreme decrepitude; and I knew her as a child and young girl in the glow of beauty and genius! She recognizes me, deeply touched to see me, and repeats constantly: My little Paul, my little Paul!! The nurse tells me she has lapsed into second childhood. Upon this large face where the forehead remains magnificent, brilliant, one notices an expression of innocence and happiness. She is very affectionate. Everybody loves her, I am told. Bitter, bitter regret of having abandoned her so long![5]

The regret of having abandoned his sister remained intense, haunting Paul's writings for some time. At the end of September, his *Journal* turned to Camille's sculpture, identifying it as "a confession marked by feeling, passion, intimate drama." As he called to mind Camille's most moving pieces, the same words returned under his pen: love, passion, genius, fate, madness. "During my last trip, I was struck by this large face, this enormous forehead brought out and sculpted by age. Did we do all we could, my parents and I? How unfortunate that I was constantly away from Paris!"[6]

Paul's remorse found its most convincing expression in the poignant confession he wrote in *Le Cantique des Cantiques* shortly after his visit to Camille:

Here my pen remains suspended, and my thoughts cannot break away from the ultimate visit I had with my poor sister Camille in the city of sorrow where, for thirty years, she has wasted away her ill-fated life. Now she is almost eighty and, in a last flash of reason, she remembered me; she is going to die, she calls me! I kiss this face, both terrible and—how can I say?—illuminated! This powerful forehead, whose majesty was brought out by age and where neither misfortune nor sickness could erase the noble mark of genius. She is happy to see me, and yet I disturb her; she can't wait to return to the important things demanding her attention. Returning home across the mountains, with all the vines and walnut trees loaded with fruits along the road stretching like a retracting gold ribbon, I painfully ruminate upon the past. I see again, coming out of childhood, this young triumphant face, these beautiful dark blue eyes, the most beautiful I have ever seen, mockingly falling upon this clumsy brother. I contemplate one by one all these works, each one a station of the horrible Calvary, a clay kneaded with blood and soul: the Abandonment to Destiny, the Waltz, the Wave, the three-figure group of the Age of Maturity, the Fireplace and, the last piece, most tragic of all, the one immediately preceding the catastrophe: Perseus. Perseus is standing, his left hand holding a mirror, and, faltering with surprise and horror, he raises with the right hand behind him the head of Gorgona, where he cannot but notice his own features. Because Destiny does not walk ahead of us, it follows us step by step, like the monster behind Dürer's horseman, and it presses upon us.[7]

For Camille, Destiny had completed its course. On 19 October 1943, two telegrams left Montdevergues; the first one reaching Paul at 11:30 A.M.: "Sister very tired. End is near. Head Doctor." The second one, announcing Camille's death, arrived at 5 P.M.: "Your sister deceased.burial Thursday 21 October."[8]

Paul did not go to the funeral. Only a few nuns silently followed the procession led by the chaplain of Montdevergues and an Alsatian priest. They walked half a mile toward the cemetery, the chaplain wearing a cope, the other priest a surplice. When they reached the cemetery, they turned toward the area set aside for the asylum and stopped in front of a freshly dug

Paul Claudel with the bust of Camille Claudel made by Rodin,
photographed in 1951

grave. Camille's frail remains were lowered into it; a last prayer was said; it
was over. On the tomb, a simple cross with the year of her death and her
tomb number: 1943–392.[9] "Mademoiselle Claudel was well treated," the
chaplain wrote to Paul after the funeral. "Good disposition, polite, she was
very much loved in the community, and the nurses took good care of her.
The chaplain writing to you visited her often and was always kindly welcomed. Her agony did not last long: she died peacefully after receiving the
last sacraments."[10]

Friends and relatives presented their condolences, but the most moving letter came from the generous Nelly Méquillet, whose kindness had
brightened Camille's last days. "I am going back to Montdevergues tomorrow," she wrote to Paul on October 27, "and I will pray for this great soul
who has suffered so much, on her tomb and in the chapel around which all
the pavilions are gathered as around their center of attraction."[11] Paul preferred not to go. Instead, he sent 500 francs to the chaplain for the celebration of a dozen masses on Camille's behalf.

Five years later, Paul thought of having Camille's remains exhumed
in order to give her a proper resting place. The priest of Montfavet

answered his letter with a clear explanation of the steps to be taken and the resulting cost: Paul should go directly to the government administration of Avignon to buy a burial plot. To this expense he needed to add the cost of a new coffin and a tombstone. Although Paul's response to the priest's letter is missing, he made a note at the end of the letter on 1 August 1948: "I send him 10,000 francs for masses for my sister Camille."[12] Paul did not say another word about a proper grave for Camille, and he never returned to this matter. It was his son, Pierre, who, in 1962, seven years after Paul's death, inquired about the possible transfer of Camille's remains to her native village, so that she could be buried in the family vault. The pathetic answer, ignominious in its consequences, reached the well-meaning Pierre on September 6: "In reply to your letter, in which you expressed the desire of transferring the mortal remains of Madame Camille Claudel, buried on 21 October 1943, in the Montfavet cemetery, in the area reserved for the hospital of Montdevergues, I regret to have to inform you that the above-mentioned ground has been reclaimed for the needs of the Cemetery Department."[13] Ten years after her death, Camille's bones had been transferred to a communal grave, where they were mixed with the bones of the most destitute. Joined forever to the ground she tried to escape for so long, Camille never, ever, returned to her beloved Villeneuve.

Paul's neglect regarding his sister's grave is hard to forgive. At first, when he gave a large sum for masses in Camille's name, it appeared that he reacted like a true Christian, turning his back on Camille's earthly remains and focusing instead on saving her soul. Yet, while Paul decided not to be burdened with his sister's grave, he took great pains, on the contrary, in choosing his own final resting place, naming the exact location—in Brangues, under a tree, next to his grandchild—and citing the precise words to be written on the stone.[14] Today his admirers pay homage to his memory at his noble grave; but of Camille there is not a trace. In Villeneuve, a simple plaque reminds the curious visitor that Camille Claudel once lived there, but her remains are still in exile, somewhere, just a few steps away from the place where she was sequestered for thirty years.

EPILOGUE

CAMILLE CLAUDEL'S OLD friends Jessie and William Elborne had survived the war. Their traveling adventures had ended, but they were able to enjoy a peaceful life in the comfortable Wootton House, with their children and grandchildren often at their sides. Jessie died at the advanced age of ninety on 12 January 1952. William followed her a week later. They are buried together in Seaton Church, England.

Paul Claudel survived the Elbornes by another three years. He died at eighty-six, on 23 February 1955. Long before his death, he had made his peace with Rodin, admitting in 1928: "Alas! I am forced to recognize that Rodin was an artistic genius."[1] A year after this declaration, he agreed to give a speech in praise of Rodin at the inauguration of the Rodin Museum in Philadelphia, and a few years after Camille's death, he led the way toward the organization of a new retrospective of her sculpture at the Musée Rodin in Paris. The exhibition, which presented forty pieces to the public, finally took place in 1951. Again, as in 1905, the public mostly stayed away.

In spite of this disappointing outcome, Paul took an important step the following year by donating several sculptures to the Musée Rodin, including the plaster of *Clotho*, the first version of the plaster of *L'Age mûr*, the bronze of the second version of *L'Age mûr*, and the marble of *Vertumne et Pomone*. The room Rodin had wanted to create in his museum for Camille Claudel's works had finally become a reality. With the purchase of other pieces in 1963—the bronze of *La Valse*, the small marble of *Persée*, the onyx version of *Les Causeuses*—and again in 1968—the small bronze of *L'Implorante* and the marble of *La Petite de l'Islette*—a substantial collection of Camille Claudel's sculpture had been gathered. The stunning onyx-and-bronze version of *La Vague* purchased in 1995 added a crowning piece to the museum's collection.[2]

It took the major retrospective of 1984, which opened in the Musée Rodin and traveled immediately afterward to Poitiers, to "reveal" the art of Camille Claudel to the French public. At that point, her popularity grew instantaneously and quickly spread to other European countries, as well as to Asia, especially Japan. In 1988 a very successful exhibition was organized by the National Museum of Women in the Arts in Washington, D.C., where sixty-seven of her works were shown to the American public for the first time. Because it is very risky to move these fragile pieces, it has not been possible to mount another major exhibition, although international shows of her sculpture continue to be mounted, comprising mostly works in private collections and posthumous casts.

Posthumous casting is a very sensitive matter in the world of sculpture. As the demand for popular pieces increases, posthumous casts can proliferate unless the sculptor had given specific directives for the reproduction of the works. Auguste Rodin, for example, encouraged the reproduction of his works in unlimited numbers, but Isamu Noguchi, Henry Moore, and Barbara Hepworth either forbade such casts or limited them. In all cases, their heirs had to abide by the sculptor's will.[3] Ethical questions arise when the sculptor has not left instructions in regard to posthumous casts. If, for one reason or another, the sculptor had not been able to cast his works during his lifetime, posthumous casting would presumably save them. Edgar Degas for one did not cast his clay and wax figures of dancers and horses, and these would eventually have disintegrated were it not for posthumous casts.[4]

In spite of her financial troubles, Camille Claudel, unlike Degas, routinely cast her pieces in bronze. Except for *Clotho*, all her important works were cast during her lifetime, so that posthumous casting was not necessary for their preservation. There is little doubt, however, that her financial difficulties often prevented her from casting as many bronzes as she would have liked, but this does not mean that she would have applauded a dramatic increase in the editions of her works. Since the early 1980s, when her fame skyrocketed, some 250 casts have been produced, and more are expected in the future. In light of the fact that she created only 260 to 280 pieces in clay, plaster, marble, or bronze during her lifetime, the large number of posthumous casts will soon surpass her lifetime production and thus considerably distort her œuvre. Considering her fear of being robbed and her hatred for Philippe Berthelot, which emerged after he had acquired a new cast of *L'Age mûr* while she was sequestered in the asylum, one cannot help but believe that Camille Claudel would have passionately opposed this type of activity.

On the bright side, her pieces are protected by a French law that limits new editions of a sculpture to twelve (eight for the market and four artist's proofs). Beyond this number, a piece is considered a reproduction, not an original. This law, passed in 1952, has been amended several times to require that the name of the foundry and the number and date of the cast be inscribed on the piece. To be recognized as original, these casts must be made from the clay or plaster created by the artist, not from another bronze. They must also retain the same dimensions as the original.[5] However, such laws are always difficult to enforce, and by the time violations become obvious, the sculptor's legacy may have been permanently altered.

As the sculptures increase in value, they too often attract the undesirable and sometimes fraudulent attention of unscrupulous people. In 1993 *L'Abandon* and *La Valse* were stolen from the museum in Poitiers; they were recovered two years later in Hungary and returned to their rightful place. The thief, a well-known theater director, had hired a professional to help him in his endeavor. They both went to prison.

Another well-known story surrounding Claudel's works began in 1988, when a female baker facing a financial emergency decided to sell one of her precious possessions: the bronze of a young woman on her knees, her hands stretched toward a missing god. The deceitful antique dealer she visited told her it was only a copy of *L'Implorante* by Camille Claudel and he gave her $8,000. Two weeks later, the same piece sold for $290,000 at an auction in Rambouillet. Informed by a friend that she had been duped, the naive baker fought back, took her case to court, and won. "We can no longer tolerate that professionals, especially from Parisian artistic circles, cheat a poor woman who knows nothing of the subject," her attorney Bensoussan said of the case.[6] This victory of a female David against art-dealing Goliaths would most certainly have delighted a sculptor who spent years of her life defying officials of the art world.

Defiance was probably the most visible characteristic of Camille Claudel. She defied the prejudiced society in which she lived in almost every step she took: her choice of a career in sculpture; her entrance into a previ-

ously all-male atelier and a liaison with the master of this atelier; her determination to sculpt the nude with as much freedom as her male counterparts;
her persistence in soliciting state commissions for works that were sure to
offend the warped notion of propriety favored by male officials. Each of
these choices challenged the prejudices of Claudel's time. The critics who
condemned her for not being able to create a new style, as Maillol and Bran-
cusi did, failed to understand that her battle was focused in a different direction. As a woman of the nineteenth century, she came up against the social
and artistic limitations imposed upon her. She struggled endlessly to be
accepted as a sculptor in her own right, without any gender qualifications
and restrictions. This is probably why she returned to large works even
though she had created small-scale masterpieces with *Les Causeuses* and *La
Vague*. Knowing that only large works were viewed as worthy of a great
sculptor and that miniature sculpture was often branded as decorative or
"feminine," she abandoned a genre in which she showed real innovation. As
it is, Claudel left behind sculptures that were frequently as daring as any of
Rodin's yet endowed with their own distinctive spirituality. "A work by
Camille Claudel in the middle of an apartment," her brother wrote, "is, by its
sole shape, like the curious rocks collected by the Chinese, a sort of monument to inner thought, the seed of a theme offered to all dreams."[7]

NOTES

PREFACE

1. Jacques Cassar, *Dossier Camille Claudel* (Paris: Séguier, 1987). This book was published posthumously as a dossier and includes numerous documents that are difficult to find. In spite of unavoidable shortcomings caused by the author's untimely death, it is a monumental achievement.

2. Anne Delbèe, *Une Femme* (Paris: Presses de la Renaissance, 1982; New York: Mercury House, 2000).

PROLOGUE

1. Letter to Eugène Blot, date uncertain (probably 24 May 1934), Judith Cladel papers, Lilly Library, University of Indiana, Bloomington. This letter, quoted in Reine-Marie Paris, *Camille Claudel* (Paris: Gallimard, 1984), pp. 63–64 (hereafter Paris, *Camille Claudel*), seems to be no longer in the library collection. Judith Cladel referred to this letter, when she wrote to Mathias Morhardt on 20 June 1934: "Louis Vauxelles has written in *Le Monde illustré* an article that made the poor and beautiful artist very happy; after this, her editor, Mr. Eugène Blot, received from her a very touching and melancholic letter—mysterious too because she did not give her address." It was the first and last letter Blot received from Camille after she was committed.

CHAPTER 1

1. Anatole Jakovsky, *Les Années folles de Montparnasse* (Paris: …ditions Rencontre Société Coopérative, 1957), pp. 23–24.

2. Paul Claudel, "Ma Soeur Camille," *Œuvres en prose* (Paris: Gallimard, 1965), p. 277.

3. Claude Debussy, *Lettres à deux amis* (Paris: Corti, 1942), p. 42.

4. Paul Claudel, "Ma Soeur Camille", pp. 277–80.

5. Gérald Antoine, *Paul Claudel ou l'enfer du génie* (Paris: Éditions Robert Laffont, 1988), p. 34.

6. Paul Claudel, *Mémoires improvisés* (Paris: Gallimard, 1969), p. 19.

7. Letter to Paul Claudel, 1938, *Journal*, vol. II, pp. 1005–6.

8. Cassar, *Dossier Camille Claudel*, p. 45.

9. Paul Claudel, *Journal*, vol. I (1904–1932) (Paris: Gallimard, 1968), p. 863.

10. Cassar, *Dossier Camille Claudel*, pp. 42–43.

11. Paul Claudel, "Mon pays," *Œuvres en prose*, p. 1006.

12. 29 June 1895. Jules Renard, *Journal (1887–1910)* (Paris: Gallimard, 1965), p. 280.

13. Paul Claudel, December 1937, *Journal*, vol. II, p. 214.

14. Paul Claudel, *Mémoires improvisés*, p. 19.

15. Cassar, *Dossier Camille Claudel*, p. 51.

16. Mathias Morhardt, *"Mademoiselle Camille Claudel"*, *Mercure de France* (March 1898), p. 710. Morhardt, a friend and admirer of both Camille Claudel and Auguste Rodin, was editor of the newspaper *Le Temps*. He also wrote the first biography of Camille Claudel.

17. Fère-en-Tardenois tourist office.

18. Paul Claudel, *Journal*, vol. I (July 1924), p. 636.

19. Morhardt, "Mademoiselle Camille Claudel," p. 712.

20. Ibid., p. 712.

21. Paul Claudel, *Mémoires improvisés*, pp. 19–20.

22. Ibid., p. 28.

23. Charlotte Yeldham, *Women Artists in Nineteenth Century France and England*, vol. I (New York and London: Garland Publishing, Inc.), p. 44.

24. Clarence Cook, *Art and Artists of Our Time*, vol. I (New York: Selmar Hess, 1888; reprint New York: Garland, 1978), p. 266.

25. Paul Claudel, *Mémoires improvisés*, p. 20.

CHAPTER 2

1. Pierre Miquel, *La Troisième République* (Paris: Fayard, 1989), pp. 111–73.

2. "La Capitale de l'Art", *Le Figaro* (1886), quoted in John Milner, *The Studios of Paris* (New Haven and London: Yale University Press, 1988), p. 27.

3. May Alcott-Nieriker, *Studying Art Abroad and How to Do It Cheaply* (Boston: Robert Brothers, 1879), p. 43.

4. Cecilia Beaux, *Background with Figures* (Boston and New York: Houghton Mifflin, 1930), p. 174.

5. Alcott-Nieriker, *Studying Art Abroad*, p. 55.

6. Louise Jopling-Rowe, *Twenty Years of My Life 1867–1887* (London: John Lane, 1925), p. 133.

7. Ibid., p. 48.

8. Clive Holland, "Student Life in the Quartier Latin," *The Studio* 27, no. 115 (1902).

9. Marie Adelaïde Belloc, "Lady Artists in Paris," *Murray's Magazine* 8, (Sept. 1890), pp. 374–76.

10. Beaux, *Background with Figures*, p. 173.

11. Marie Bashkirtseff, *Journal* (Paris: Mazarine, 1980), p. 316.

12. Ibid., p. 396.

13. Ibid., p. 393.

14. Frederic V. Grunfeld, *Rodin: A Biography* (New York: Henry Holt & Co., 1987), p. 173.

15. Holland, "Student Life in the Quartier Latin," p. 38.

16. Belloc, "Lady Artists in Paris," p. 378.

17. Ibid., p. 377.

18. "The Art Student in Paris" (Boston: Museum School, 1887), p. 33. This booklet was published by former students of the school, where there was still a slight difference between the fees for men and women in the Left Bank studio: men paid 16 francs a month and women 20 francs.

19. Clive Holland, "Lady Art Students' Life in Paris," *International Studio* 30 (1904), p. 228.

20. Colarossi family archives.

21. Ibid.

22. Antoine, *Paul Claudel ou l'Enfer du génie*, p. 34.

23. John Milner, *The Studios of Paris*, (New Haven and London: Yale University Press, 1988) pp. 211–16.

24. Barclay, "L'Atelier Bonnat," *Magazine of Art* 5 (1882), p. 138.

25. Alcott-Nieriker, *Studying Art Abroad*, p. 50.

26. Morhardt, "Mademoiselle Camille Claudel," p. 712.

27. Ibid., p. 713.

28. Ruth Butler, *Rodin: The Shape of Genius* (New Haven and London: Yale University Press, 1993), p. 529, n. 3. Both 1882 and 1883 had been given for Boucher's departure date, but Butler found a letter sent to Rodin from Boucher in Florence dated September 1882.

CHAPTER 3

1. Paul Claudel, "Ma Sœur Camille,"p. 280.

2. Edmond and Jules de Goncourt, 17 April 1886, *Journal*, vol. II (Paris: Robert Laffont, 1989), p. 1242.

3. Horace Lecoq de Boisbaudran, *The Training of the Memory in Art and the Education of the Artist*, L. D. Luard, trans. (London: Macmillan & Co., 1911), p. vii.

4. Ibid., p. 180.

5. Frederick Lawton, *The Life and Work of Auguste Rodin* (London: T. Fisher Unwin, 1906), p. 14.

6. Arthur Symons, *From Toulouse-Lautrec to Rodin* (London: John Lane, 1929), p. 226.

7. Gustave Coquiot, *Rodin à l'Hôtel de Biron et à Meudon* (Paris: Librairie Ollendorf, 1917), pp. 25–26.

8. Henri Dujardin-Beaumetz, *Entretiens avec Rodin* (Paris: Éditions du Musée Rodin, 1913), pp. 81–82.

9. Frederic V. Grunfeld, *Rodin: A Biography* (New York: Henry Holt & Co., 1987), p. 127. The letter was signed by Carrier-Belleuse, Chaplin, Chapu, Delaplanche, Dubois, Falguière, Moreau, and Thomas.

10. Ibid., pp. 127–30.

11. Jacques Lethève, *La Vie quotidienne des artistes français au dix-neuvième siècle* (Paris: Hachette, 1968), p. 168.

12. Ibid., p. 89.

13. Lethève tells us that about the year 1885, women models cost around 10 francs and male models 6 francs (p. 79). On the other hand, Lady Kathleen Kennet Scott spent about 1 franc a day for her meals in 1901 (Kennet Scott, *Self-Portrait of an Artist* [London: John Murray, 1949] p. 30).

14. Phebe D. Natt, "Paris Art Schools," *Lippincott's Magazine* 27 (1881), p. 273.

15. Lethève, *La Vie quotidienne*, pp. 79–82.

16. Grunfeld, *Rodin*, p. 188.

17. E. Somerville, "An Atelier des Dames," *The Magazine of Art* 9 (1886), p. 156.

18. Ibid., p. 273.

19. Grunfeld, *Rodin*, p. 193.

20. Letter to Florence Jeans, 25 December 1887, Musée Rodin Archives. The model was also used for *Giganti*.

21. Judith Cladel, *Rodin: Sa Vie glorieuse et inconnue* (Paris: Bernard Grasset, 1936), p. 86.

22. Ibid., p. 228.

23. Ibid., p. 265.

CHAPTER 4

1. Morhardt, "Mademoiselle Camille Claudel," p. 713.

2. Ibid., p. 714.

3. Anne Rivière, Bruno Gaudichon, and Danièle Ghanassia, *Camille Claudel: Catalogue raisonné*, 2nd ed. (Paris: Adam Biro, 2000), p. 63 (hereafter *Catalogue raisonné*, 2nd ed.).

4. Morhardt, "Mademoiselle Camille Claudel," p. 716.

5. Butler, *Rodin*, p. 181.

6. Originally, the Salon was a simple event connected with the creation of the Académie Royale by Louis XIV in 1648. Members of the Académie, appointed by the king, organized their own internal exhibitions. This process continued until the French Revolution eliminated the Académie Royale along with everything else "royal." Instead, the revolutionary government

opened exhibitions to all artists through a jury selection. After the Revolution, the Académie was eventually restored under the name of Académie des Beaux-Arts, and an annual Salon was organized by its forty members. Members of the Académie were automatically members of the Salon jury. Since academicians also appointed professors to the École des Beaux-Arts, the Académie, the Salon, and the École des Beaux-Arts formed a closely knit group that dictated their conservative views to the art world. Several reforms occurred during the Second Empire, but it was not until the Republican landslide of 1879 that a thorough reform of public instruction, including the arts, ended government control over the Salon. In 1881, the newly created Société des Artistes Français became the organizer of the Salon, which, at last, boasted a jury elected by artists.

7. Tamar Garb, *Sisters of the Brush* (New Haven and London: Yale University Press, 1994), p. 26.

8. Clive Holland, "Lady Art Student's Life in Paris," p. 225.

9. Kennet Scott, *Self-Portrait of an Artist*, p. 42.

10. Abi Pirani, "Jessie: Study of an Artist," M.A. thesis, University of York, 1987, p. 15. Abi Pirani interviewed Sidney Elborne, Jessie's oldest son, just before his death in 1986. Much of the information regarding Sydney and Harriet Lipscomb was provided by this interview.

11. Census returns, Local Studies, Peterborough Library.

12. The will was executed in 12 December 1890 in Peterborough.

13. Peter Waszak, "The Development of Leisure and Cultural Facilities in Peterborough. 1850–1900." B.A. thesis, The Polytechnic, Huddersfield, 1975.

14. Charles Dickens, "Artistic Professions for Women," *All the Year Round* 63, no. 1035 (29 September 1888), p. 297.

15. H. F. Tebbs, *Peterborough: A History* (Cambridge: The Oleander Press, 1979), p.150.

16. Yeldham, *Women Artists*, vol I, p. 25.

17. Christopher Frayling, *The Royal College of Art* (London: Barrie & Jenkins, 1987), pp. 54–55.

18. Ibid., pp. 54–55.

19. Ibid., p. 55.

20. Phebe D. Natt, "London Art-Schools," *Lippincott's Magazine* 25 (1880), p. 631.

21. Alice Green, "The Girl Student in Paris," *The Magazine of Art* 16 (1883), p. 287.

22. Louise Claudel, letter to Jessie Lipscomb, 27 January 1884, Elborne Archives.

CHAPTER 5

1. Musée Rodin Archives.

2. Elborne Archives.

3. Camille Mauclair, *Auguste Rodin* (Paris: La Renaissance du Livre, 1918), p. 96.

4. Paul Claudel, *Œuvres en prose*, p. 1278.

5. J.E.S. Jeanès, *D'après nature: Souvenirs et portraits* (Geneva: Perret-Gentil, 1946), p. 116.

6. Cladel, *Rodin*, p. 226.

7. Kennet Scott, *Self-Portrait of an Artist*, p. 42.

8. François Dujardin-Beaumetz, *Entretiens avec Rodin* (Paris: Éditions du Musée Rodin, 1992), p. 11.

9. Lawton, *The Life and Work of Auguste Rodin*, p. 164.

10. Ibid., p. 242.

11. Ibid.

12. Morhardt, "Mademoiselle Camille Claudel," p. 709.

13. Ibid., pp. 716–17.

14. Ibid., p. 717.

15. Goncourt, *Journal*, vol. II, p. 1242.

16. Edouard Rod, *Gazette des Beaux-Arts*, quoted in Hélène Pinet, *Rodin: les mains du génie* (Paris: Gallimard, 1988), p. 120.

17. Morhardt, "Mademoiselle Camille Claudel," p. 721.

18. Ibid., p. 719.

19. Ibid., p. 718.

20. Bertrand Tillier, *Ernest Nivet, Sculpteur: Des fenêtres ouvertes sur la vie* (Chateauroux: B. Tillier, 1987), pp. 50–51. It is important to note that the legal work day during this period was eleven hours.

21. René Gimpel, *Diary of an Art Dealer*, John Rosenberg, trans. (New York: Farrar, Straus and Giroux, 1966), p. 422.

22. Catherine Lampert, *Rodin: Sculpture and Drawings*, exh. cat., Arts Council of Great Britain (London. Yale University Press, 1986), p.92.

23. *Catalogue raisonné*, 2nd ed., p. 60.

CHAPTER 6

1. Cladel, *Rodin*.

2. Several dictionaries and encyclopedias place the date of her death in 1920. Among them, *Le Grand Larousse Encyclopédique* (Paris, 1960); *Le Dictionnaire des peintres, sculpteurs, dessinateurs et graveurs* (Paris, 1955); E. Bénézit, *Dictionnaire critique et documentaire des peintres, sculpteurs, dessinateurs et graveurs* (Paris: Gründ, 1976).

3. Grunfeld, *Rodin,* note on p. 214.

4. Five were found in 1988 in the home of Cécile Gold-scheider, former curator of the Musée Rodin, after her death.

5. It must be noted that the word "Salon" has previously been read "Dalou" by Reine-Marie Paris (*L'Œuvre de Camille Claudel,* p. 20). Later, Ruth Butler translated the phrase as "my Dalou, the sculpture, that is" (p. 184) rather than "my Salon and sculpture" (my translation). The difference is important because Rodin was working on Dalou's bust in 1883, so a reference to Dalou would date Rodin's liaison with Camille as early as 1883, that is to say, from the very beginning of their acquaintance. However, the word written by Rodin is more likely to be "Salon." Rodin's handwriting is difficult to read and does not differentiate between "n" and "u." It is also inconsistent, for Rodin can write the same letter in many different ways. A close comparison between Rodin's capital letters D and S in other documents produced several similar Ss, but different Ds, thus supporting the theory that the word used by Rodin ought to be read "Salon," not "Dalou." Like other artists of the period, Rodin may have occasionally referred to the works he prepared for the Salon as "mon Salon."

Possibly more important than the deciphering of Rodin's handwriting, other events suggest a later date for this document. Rodin was making the bust of his idol Victor Hugo at the same time that he worked on Dalou's, and considering the importance he attached to Hugo's bust, it would be strange for him to single out Dalou's bust and not Hugo's. In any case, the dramatic tone of the letter demands more than the mere abandonment of one single bust. Like any distraught man in love, Rodin is ready to abandon everything for the object of his love (Salon and sculpture). Finally, dating the beginning of the sculptors' liaison about 1885 is consistent with other events such as Camille's entry into Rodin's atelier in 1885 and Rodin's letters to Jessie, also starting in 1885.

6. Renard, 8 March 1891, *Journal,* p. 84.

7. Elborne Archives. Most of these have no dates and bear many corrections, making them difficult to read and to place in time. All the letters to Jessie included in this chapter belong to these archives.

8. Elborne Archives.

9. Ibid.

10. Ibid.

11. Musée Rodin Archives. This letter, like the ones Rodin showered upon Jessie, would reach its recipient within one or two days, less than what was required at the end of the twentieth century, when letters could take up to five days to cross the Channel. But the development of a strong railway system and of fast-moving ferries allowed this splendid achievement at a time when the volume of international mail was not as heavy as it is today.

12. Elborne Archives

13. Ibid.

14. Ibid.

15. No date, Musée Rodin Archives.

16. Louise Claudel, letter to Camille Claudel (in the Montdevergues asylum), no date, quoted in *Catalogue raisonné,* 2nd ed., p. 270.

17. No date (probably June 1886), Musée Rodin Archives.

18. Duncan S. James, *A Century of Statues* (Frome: Morris Singer Foundry, Ltd., 1984), pp. 5–11.

19. Elborne Archives.

20. Paul Claudel, "In the Isle of Wight," *Œuvres en prose,* p. 1015.

21. These letters were recently discovered by Stephen Back, grandson of Florence Jeans, and were given to the Musée Rodin in 1992. They were first published in *Catalogue raisonné,* 2nd ed., pp. 187–97.

22. Musée Rodin Archives.

23. Elborne Archives.

24. Ibid.

25. Ibid.

26. Ibid.

27. Musèe Rodin Archives

28. Elborne Archives.

29. 22 September 1886, Musée Rodin Archives.

30. Ibid., 3 October 1886.

31. Ibid. This document is one of the five recently recovered and returned to the Musée Rodin.

CHAPTER 7

1. No date, Elborne Archives.

2. No date (probably June 1886), Elborne Archives.

3. Pirani, "Jessie: Study of an Artist," p. 48.

4. 15 September 1887, Musée Rodin Archives.

5. No date, Elborne Archives.

6. Elborne Archives. This photograph was found by Abi Pirani. It was in poor shape because it had been rolled upon itself for years and had cracked in its folds. It has now been restored.

7. No date (probably end of May 1886), Elborne Archives.

8. 12 February 1887, Musée Rodin Archives.

9. No date, Elborne Archives. This letter, signed by Camille Claudel, is not in Camille's hand and appears to be a copy of the original.

10. 15 March 1887, Musée Rodin Archives.

11. No date, Elborne Archives.

12. 16 April 1887, Musée Rodin Archives.

13. Ibid., 6 July 1887.

14. Ibid., 12 September 1887.

15. Ibid., 12 February 1887.

16. Ibid., 15 September 1887.

17. 19 October 1887, Elborne Archives.

18. 20 November 1887, Elborne Archives.

CHAPTER 8

1. Goncourt, *Journal*, vol. III, p. 291.

2. Ibid., p. 291.

3. Morhardt, "Mademoiselle Camille Claudel," p. 719.

4. Paris, *Camille Claudel*, p. 41.

5. "Salon de 1886," *L'Art* 41 (1886), p. 67.

6. "Salon de 1887," *L'Art* 43 (1887), p. 231.

7. 8 November 1886, Musée Rodin Archives.

8. 25 December 1887, Musée Rodin Archives.

9. This drama was written by the poet Kalidasa.

10. André Michel, "Salon de 1888, la sculpture," *La Gazette des Beaux-Arts* (August 1888), p. 151.

11. "Salon de 1888," *L'Art* 44 (1888), p. 212.

12. Paul Claudel, "Camille Claudel," *Œuvres en prose*, p. 279.

13. No date, Musée Rodin Archives.

14. 17 October 1887, Musée Rodin Archives.

15. Butler, *Rodin*, p. 228. Boulevard d'Italie is now called boulevard Auguste-Blanqui.

16. Paul Claudel, Théatre, vol. I (Paris: Gallimard, 1967), pp. 21–27.

17. Paul Claudel, "Ma Conversion," *Œuvres en prose*, p. 1010.

18. Louis Chaigne, *Vie de Paul Claudel et génèse de son œuvre* (Paris: Maison Mame, 1961), p. 37.

19. 19 March 1888, Musée Rodin Archives.

20. Jacques Hillairet, *Dictionnaire historique des rues de Paris* (Paris: Les Editions de Minuit, 1970), vol. I, pp. 117–18.

21. Maurice Hamel, "Les Salons de 1889, la sculpture," *La Gazette des Beaux Arts* (August 1889), p. 26.

22. Goncourt, *Journal*, 23 June 1889, p. 285.

23. Ibid., 14 June 1888, p. 135.

24. 9 August 1889, Musée Rodin Archives.

25. 8 August 1889, Musée Rodin Archives.

CHAPTER 9

1. Goncourt, *Journal*, vol. III, p. 267.

2. L. Augé de Lassus, "Exposition de 1889," *L'Art* (1889), pp. 165–67.

3. 8 August 1889, Musée Rodin Archives.

4. Antoine, *Rodin*, p. 25.

5. Morhardt, "Mademoiselle Camille Claudel," p. 729.

6. Oslo University Library, in Grunfeld, p. 221.

7. *Correspondance de Rodin* (1860–99), Alain Beausire and Hélène Pinet, eds. (Paris: Éditions du Musée Rodin, 1985), vol. I, p. 130.

8. Paul Leroi, "Salon de 1892," *L'Art* 53 (1892), p. 18.

9. Morhardt, "Mademoiselle Camille Claudel," p. 730.

10. Henri de Braisne, "Salon de 1892," *La Revue idéaliste* (1892).

11. Octave Mirbeau, "Salon de 1892," *Revue encyclopédique* (1892).

12. Paul Leroi, "Salon 1894," *L'Art* 48 (1894), p. 74.

13. Mordhardt, "Mademoiselle Camille Claudel," p. 729.

14. 19 May 1892, cited in Cassar, *Dossier Camille Claudel*, pp. 91–92.

15. Antoine, *Paul Claudel ou l'enfer du génie,"* p. 81.

16. 27 October 1889, Archives Nationales, F21 4299.

17. Ibid., 8 February 1892.

18. Ibid., 20 March 1892.

19. 21 March 1892, *Correspondance de Rodin*, vol. I, p. 129.

20. Archives Nationales, F21 4299.

21. Ibid., 9 January 1893.

22. Ibid., no date.

23. Marcel Schwob, *Chroniques* (Geneva: Droz, 1981), p. 79.

24. Louis Vauxelles, Preface to the catalogue *Œuvres de Camille Claudel et de Bernard Hoetger* (4–16 December 1905).

25. For a detailed study of sexuality in Camille's sculpture, see Claudine Mitchell, "Intellectuality and Sexuality: Camille Claudel, the Fin de Siècle Sculptress," *Art History* 12, no. 4 (December 1989), pp. 419–47.

26. Lucien Bourdeau, "Description d'œuvres exposées aux Salons de 1893," *Revue encyclopédique Larousse* (1893), p. 823.

27. Renard, 19 March 1895, *Journal*, p. 272.

28. Bourdeau, "Description d'œuvres exposées," p. 823.

29. Claude Debussy, *Lettres à deux amis: 78 lettres inédites à Robert Godet et Georges Jean Aubry* (Paris: Corti, 1942), p. 94. The letter was written on 13 February 1891. Some speculated that the woman evoked in this letter was Camille. Others misread a 19 March 1895 entry in Jules Renard's *Journal* (see Cassar, *Dossier Camille Claudel*, p. 87) referring to "the musician who lived two years with Claudel, and who did not know that Claudel was a writer!" The Claudel in question was evidently Paul, the writer, not Camille. The musician was an obscure violinist named Christian de Larapidie, who lived with Paul Claudel in Boston, Massachusetts.

30. Debussy, *Lettres à deux amis*, p. 42.

31. Ibid., p. 44.

32. Ibid.

33. Morhardt, "Mademoiselle Camille Claudel," p. 734.

34. Octave Mirbeau, "Ceux du Champ de Mars et ceux du Palais de l'Industrie," *Supplément illustré du Journal* (May 1893).

35. Henri Bouchot, "Les Salons de 1893: la sculpture," *La Gazette des Beaux Arts* (1893), p. 118.

36. Charles Saunier, "La Sculpture aux Salons de 1893," *La Plume* (15 June 1893), p. 278.

37. Mirbeau, "Ceux du Champ de Mars," May 1893.

38. Ibid.

39. Debussy, *Lettres à deux amis*, p. 42.

40. Goncourt, 8 December 1893, *Journal*, vol. III, p. 891.

41. Goncourt, 8 March 1894, *Journal*, vol. III, p. 929.

CHAPTER 10

1. Bernard Champigneulle, *Rodin* (Paris: Somogy Éditions d'Art, 1994), p. 154.

2. Marie Laparcerie, "Les Modèles," *La Presse* (15 December 1902), quoted in *Rodin et ses modèles*, exh. cat. (Paris: Éditions du Musée Rodin, 1990), p. 31.

3. Goncourt, *Journal*, vol. III, (3 July 1889) p. 291.

4. Marcelle Tirel. *The Last Years of Rodin* (New York: Haskell House Publishers, Ltd., 1974), pp. 60–61.

5. Ibid., p. 94.

6. Cladel, *Rodin*, pp. 227–331.

7. *Correspondance de Rodin*, pp. 97–126.

8. Mathias Morhardt, letter to Judith Cladel, 18 August 1934, University of Indiana, Bloomington, Indiana.

9. Cassar, *Dossier Camille Claudel*, p. 89.

10. Goncourt, May 1894, *Journal*, vol. III, p. 957.

11. No date, Musée Rodin Archives.

12. Ibid.

13. 25 June 1893, Musée Rodin Archives.

14. The pregnancy could have occurred in 1890, 1891,

or 1892. Camille did not exhibit any work in 1890 and 1891, and lingering problems about her health are mentioned in 1892 and 1893.

15. Lucien Descaves, *Souvenirs d'un ours* (Paris: Les …ditions de Paris, 1946), p. 150.

16. Robert Descharnes et Jean-François Chabrun, *Auguste Rodin* (Lausanne: Edita, 1967), p. 122.

17. Cladel, *Rodin*, p. 228.

18. Antoine, *Rodin*, pp. 166–67. Gérald Antoine became a friend of Marie Romain-Rolland, and she gave him access to some of her correspondence.

19. Cladel, *Rodin*, pp. 42–43.

20. Ibid., p. 43.

21. Mordhardt, "Mademoiselle Camille Claudel," p. 736.

22. Gustave Geffroy, "Le Salon de 1894 et le Salon de 1895," *La Vie artistique* (1895), p. 148.

23. Roger Marx, "Beaux-Arts: la libre esthétique," *La Revue encyclopédique* (1 November 1894), p. 309.

24. Archives Nationales, 26 April 1894, F21 4299.

25. *Catalogue raisonné*, 2nd ed., p. 123.

26. Morhardt, "Mademoiselle Camille Claudel," p. 737.

27. Ibid., pp. 738–39.

CHAPTER 11

1. Paul Claudel, "L'Œil écoute," *Œuvres en prose*, p. 280.

2. No date (probably 1894), Paul Claudel Papers, Bibliothèque Nationale de France.

3. Camille Claudel, letter to Florence Jeans, 24 August 1893.

4. Morhardt, "Mademoiselle Camille Claudel," p. 730.

5. Paul Claudel Papers, Bibliothèque Nationale de France.

6. Morhardt, "Mademoiselle Camille Claudel," p. 740.

7. May 1894, Musée Rodin Archives.

8. Paul Claudel Papers, Bibliothèque Nationale de Paris.

9. Ministry of Public Instruction and Fine Arts, letter to Auguste Rodin, 5 January 1895, Archives Nationales, # 4299.

10. Mathias Morhardt, "Le Banquet Puvis de Chavannes," *Mercure de France* 261 (1 August 1935).

11. Mathias Morhardt, letter to Auguste Rodin, 20 March 1895, Musée Rodin Archives.

12. Morhardt, "Mademoiselle Camille Claudel," p. 746.

13. Roger Marx, "Salon de 1895," *Gazette des Beaux-Arts* (1895), p. 119.

14. Morhardt, "Mademoiselle Camille Claudel," p. 746.

15. Octave Mirbeau, "Ça et là," in *Des Artistes* (Paris: Flammarion, 1922), p. 209. First published in *Le Journal* (12 May 1895).

16. Ibid., pp. 210–11.

17. Morhardt, "Mademoiselle Camille Claudel," p. 746.

18. Letter to Octave Mirbeau, no date, cited in Paul Claudel, *Journal*, vol.II, pp. 626–27. Bookseller Matarasso gave the letter to Paul Claudel, who then copied it in his journal.

19. Shortly before 13 May 1895, the date of Mourey's answer to Rodin; *Correspondance de Rodin*, vol. I, p. 153.

20. No date, Musée Rodin Archives. This letter belongs to the group of documents that had disappeared from the museum, and were later recovered. Georges Leygues and Léon Bourgeois are former Ministers of Public Instruction and Fine Arts.

21. 5 July 1895, Archives Nationales.

22. No date, Archives Nationales.

CHAPTER 12

1. Renard, *Journal*, 19 March 1895, p. 272.

2. Ibid., 7 March 1895, p. 269.

3. Ibid., 19 March 1895, p. 272.

4. Ibid.

5. Tillier, *Ernest Nivet, sculpteur*, p. 53.

6. Cassar, *Dossier Camille Claudel*, p. 124.

7. Ibid., pp. 124–30.

8. *Le Journal*, 15 December 1895, quoted in Cassar, *Dossier Camille Claudel*, p. 130. Jacques Cassar found this plaster in 1975 in a shed of the museum. It was covered with dust and spider webs and humidity had damaged it considerably. The male figure had lost his left arm and his feet, and the female figure had lost her arms. Cassar brought this fact to the attention of the Ministry of Culture, and measures were taken to protect what was left of the work.

9. *Correspondance de Rodin*, p. 158.

10. 3 October 1896, Musée Rodin Archives.

11. 7 November 1896, Musée Rodin Archives.

12. No date (probably 1896), Musée Rodin Archives. One of the documents returned to the Musée Rodin after Goldscheider's death. Several parts are impossible to decipher and were deleted here. Camille was working on a marble version of *La Confidence* for the Danish painter Fritz Thaulow. The same year, she produced a second marble version, without screen, for the architect Pontremoli.

13. Camille Claudel, telegram to Auguste Rodin, 30 March 1896, Musée Rodin Archives.

14. Telegram, April 25, 1896, Musée Rodin Archives.

15. No date (probably early 1898), Musée Rodin Archives.

16. G. Jeanniot, "Le Salon du Champ de Mars," *Revue encyclopédique Larousse* 194 (22 May 1897), p. 413.

17. Morhardt, letter to Rodin, 13 June 1897, Musée Rodin Archives.

18. "Les femmes et les féministes," *Revue encyclopédique Larousse*, 28 November 1896.

19. "Camille Claudel," *La Revue idéaliste* 19 (19 October 1897), quoted in Cassar, *Dossier Camille Claudel*, pp. 407–10.

20. Mathias Morhardt, "La Bataille du Balzac," *Mercure de France* 256 (November–December 1934), p. 467.

21. No date, Musée Rodin Archives. Probably November 1897 since Rodin's answer is dated 2 December 1897.

22. Morhardt, Letter to Paul Claudel, 24 May 1897, Paul Claudel Papers, Bibliothèque Nationale de Paris.

23. Quoted in Cassar, *Dossier Camille Claudel*, pp. 408–9.

24. 2 December 1892, Musée Rodin Archives. One of the five letters returned to the Musée Rodin.

25. Paul Morand, *Mon plaisir en littérature* (Paris: Gallimard, 1980), p. 283.

CHAPTER 13

1. Champigneule, *Rodin*, p. 190.

2. Caran d'Ache, 13 February 1998, reproduced in Pierre Birnbaum, *L'Affaire Dreyfus* (Paris: Gallimard, 1994), p. 121.

3. Descaves, *Souvenirs d'un ours*, p. 213.

4. Renard, 13 February 1900, *Journal*, p. 570.

5. Camille Claudel, letter to Rodin, end of 1897. Musée Rodin Archives.

6. Edmond Bigand Kaire, letter to Rodin, 31 May 1898. Musée Rodin Archives.

7. Cladel, *Rodin*, pp. 228–29.

8. 7 December 1929, Cladel Papers, University of Indiana, Bloomington, Indiana.

9. Armand Silvestre, 1 November 1898, Archives Nationales.

10. Paul Claudel, "Ma Sœur Camille," p. 253.

11. Archives Nationales.

12. 26 December 1898, Archives Nationales.

13. No date. Archives Nationales. Camille received her answer from the Ministry on 18 April 1905.

14. Camille Claudel, letter to Maurice Fenaille, no date, in *L'Œuvre de Camille Claudel*, p. 260. "I would

like you to let me know with a note whether the marble bust with foliage has been returned to you. I had to withdraw it from the Exhibition, my two most important works, the bust of comtesse de Maigret and *l'Age mûr* acquired by the state having been rejected, I withdrew the others at the same time."

15. No date (probably 1903), Paul Claudel Papers, Bibliothèque Nationale de France.

16. Eugène Blot, letter to Dujardin-Beaumetz, 11 November 1905, Archives Nationales.

17. Quoted in Cassar, *Dossier Camille Claudel*, p. 161. This bronze is now in the Musée d'Orsay, Paris.

18. Romain Rolland, "Les Salons de 1903," *La Revue de Paris* (1 June 1903), p. 667.

19. Henri Cochin, "Quelques réflexions sur les Salons," *Gazette des Beaux-Arts* (July 1903), p. 39.

20. Charles Morice, "Le Salon des Artistes Français," *Le Mercure de France*, June 1903, p. 691.

CHAPTER 14

1. Henri Duvernois, "La Pudeur et la Vertu," *Le Monde Illustré* (12 May 1934), p. 5.

2. Eugen Weber, *France Fin de Siècle* (Cambridge, Mass.: Harvard University Press, 1986), p. 37.

3. Ibid., p. 203.

4. Henry Asselin, "La Vie douloureuse de Camille Claudel," Radio Broadcasts, 1956. Typed text in Paul Claudel's Papers, Bibliothèque Nationale Archives, quoted in Cassar, *Dossier Camille Claudel*, pp. 441–42.

5. Gabrielle Réval, "Les Artistes Femmes au Salon de 1903," *Femina* 55 (1 May 1903), p. 520.

6. Ibid.

7. Henri de Braisne, *La Revue Idéaliste* (1 October 1897), quoted in Cassar, *Dossier Camille Claudel*, pp. 407–10.

8. Camille Mauclair, "L'Art des femmes peintres et sculpteurs," *La Revue des Revues*, 3e trimestre (1901).

9. Preface to the catalogue of the 1951 exhibition (Paris: Musée Rodin, 1951) p. 12.

10. Morhardt, "Mademoiselle Camille Claudel," p. 712.

11. Radio broadcasts, quoted in Cassar, *Dossier Camille Claudel*, p. 442.

12. Ibid., p. 451.

13. No date, Musée Rodin Archives.

14. Ibid.

15. Ibid.

16. Ibid.

17. Eugène Blot, letter to Mathias Morhardt, 21 September 1935, Musée Rodin Archives.

18. Ottilie McLaren Papers, National Library of Scotland, Edinborough, May 1899.

19. Mathias Morhardt, letter to Judith Cladel, 19 August 1934, University of Indiana, Bloomington, Indiana.

20. *L'Œuvre de Camille Claudel*, p. 195.

21. 22 January 1902, Musée Rodin Archives.

22. *L'Œuvre de Camille Claudel*, p. 264.

23. Camille Claudel, letter to Gustave Geffroy, March 1905. Camille's newly found letters to Geffroy were published in Rivière et al., *Catalogue raisonné*, pp. 237–40.

24. Ibid., p. 239.

25. Judith Cladel Papers, Bloomington, Indiana.

26. *Cahiers Paul Claudel*, vol. I (Paris: Gallimard, 1959), pp. 115–17.

27. 1902, Archives Communales, registre des cultures, Villeneuve-sur-Fère, in Cassar, *Dossier Camille Claudel*, p. 210.

28. *Cahiers Paul Claudel*, vol. I, p. 118.

29. No date (probably November 1897), Musée Rodin Archives.

30. Virginie Demont-Breton, *Les Maisons que j'ai connues*, vol. II (Paris: Plon-Nourrit et Co., 1926), p. 198.

31. Édouard Lepage, *Une Page de l'histoire de l'art au dix-neuvième siècle* (Paris: 1911).

32. See Yeldham, *Women Artists*, vol. I, pp. 53–58; and Marina Sauer, *L'Entrée des femmes à l'Ecole des Beaux-Arts* (Paris: énsb-a, 1990).

CHAPTER 15

1. Antoine, *Paul Claudel*, pp. 128–29.

2. André Suarès and Paul Claudel, *Correspondance (1904–1938)* (Paris: Gallimard, 1951), pp. 48–49.

3. Antoine, *Paul Claudel*, p. 129.

4. "Ténèbres," *Corona benignitatis anni Dei*, quoted in Antoine, *Paul Claudel*, p. 133.

5. Letter to Marie Romain-Rolland, 14 June 1940, quoted in Antoine, *Paul Claudel*, p. 128.

6. Letter to Gabriel Frizeau, 15 November 1905. Paul Claudel, Francis Jammes, Gabriel Frizeau, *Correspondance (1897-1938)* (Paris: Gallimard, 1952), p. 69.

7. Maurice Hamel, "Les Salons de 1905," *La Revue de Paris* (June 1905), p. 650.

8. Mathias Morhardt, letter to Rodin, 11 December 1905, Paul Claudel Papers, Bibliothèque Nationale de France.

9. Paul Claudel, *Œuvres en prose*, p. 274.

10. Paul Claudel, letter to Francis Jammes, 14 October

1905, Claudel, Jammes, Frizeau, *Correspondance*, p. 64.

11. Paul Claudel, *Œuvres en prose*, p. 288.

12. Paul Claudel, letter to Gabriel Frizeau, 29 September 1905; Claudel, Jammes, Frizeau, *Correspondance*, p. 62.

13. Paul Claudel, letter to Gabriel Frizeau, 13 August 1905; Claudel, Jammes, Frizeau, *Correspondance*, p. 53.

14. André Gide, 1 December 1905, *Journal* (Paris: Gallimard, 1951), p. 186.

15. Paul Claudel, letter to Henri Lerolle, no date (probably 1909 since the bust was cast in 1910), Paul Claudel Papers, Bibliothèque Nationale de France.

16. Vauxelles, preface to *Œuvres de Camille Claudel et de Bernard Hoetger* (December 1905).

17. "Art moderne. Expositions," *Mercure de France* (15 December 1905), pp. 609–10.

18. Ibid., p. 610.

19. 24 May 1897, Paul Claudel Papers, Bibliothèque Nationale de France.

20. Ibid., 27 June 1905.

21. Ibid., no date.

22. Ibid., 5 July 1905.

23. 15 December 1905, Musée Rodin Archives.

24. 19 December 1905, Paul Claudel Papers, Bibliothèque Nationale de France.

25. 7 December 1929, Judith Cladel Papers, University of Indiana, Bloomington, Indiana.

26. Letter to the Head of Art Works, 6 June 1934, Archives Nationales.

CHAPTER 16

1. Henri Godet, "Salon d'Automne," *L'Action* (1 November 1906).

2. 15 October 1904, Archives Nationales, note from the Beaux-Arts.

3. All these notes are kept in the Archives Nationales.

4. Archives Nationales, 8 March 1906.

5. Ibid., 18 May 1906.

6. Ibid., 15 December 1907.

7. Ibid., 30 June 1906.

8. Ibid., 6 October 1906.

9. Ibid., 4 April 1907.

10. Camille Claudel, letter to the Ministry of Fine Arts, 20 September 1907, Archives Nationales.

11. Prefect of Police, letter to the Under Secretary of State, 24 October 1907, Archives Nationales.

12. Eugène Morand, letter to the Under-Secretary of State, 15 October 1907, Archives Nationales.

13. *Catalogue raisonné*, 2nd ed., p. 99. Anne Rivière discovered the piece in 1983, abandoned in the middle of a water basin and covered with calcium deposits. Although it was later restored, it did not regain its original appearance.

14. 21 October 1906, Camille Claudel Papers, Bibliothèque Marguerite Durand.

15. 2 June 1907, Camille Claudel Papers, Bibliothèque Marguerite Durand.

16. Bashkirtseff, *Journal*, p. 594.

17. August 1909, quoted in Cassar, *Dossier Camille Claudel*, pp. 208–9.

18. Henry Asselin, two radio broadcasts, reproduced in Cassar, *Dossier Camille Claudel*, p. 445.

19. Camille Claudel, letter to Henriette Thierry, December 1912, private collection, in *L'Œuvre de Camille Claudel*, p. 271.

20. Letter to Henriette Thierry, December 1912.

21. Henry Asselin, quoted in Cassar, *Dossier Camille Claudel*, p. 445.

22. No date, Paul Claudel Papers, Bibliothèque Nationale de France.

23. Marcelle Tinayre, "Salon de 1904," *Revue de Paris* (1904), p. 406.

24. No date, Paul Claudel Papers, Bibliothèque Nationale de France.

25. Camille Claudel, letter to Henri Thierry, no date (probably 1910), private collection, cited in *L'Œuvre de Camille Claudel*, p. 268.

26. Marguerite Thierry Fauvarque, letter to Jacques Cassar, 18 June 1974, quoted in Cassar, *Dossier Camille Claudel*, p. 235.

27. Paul Claudel, September 1909, *Journal*, vol. I, pp. 103–4.

28. Paul Claudel, 27 November 1911, *Journal*, vol. I, note on p. 1178.

29. Paul Claudel, June 1912, *Journal*, vol. I, p. 228. Italics indicate words written in English in the original text.

30. Paul Claudel, "Ma Sœur Camille," p. 277.

31. Camille Claudel, letter to Henriette Thierry, private collection, no date, in *L'Œuvre de Camille Claudel*, p. 271.

32. Paul Claudel, letter to Daniel Fontaine, 24 January 1913, Paul Claudel and François Mauriac, *Chroniques du Journal de Clichy; Claudel-Fontaine Correspondance*, "Annales littéraires de l'Université de Besançon" (Paris: Les Belles Lettres, 1978), p. 106.

33. Ibid., 26 February 1913, pp. 114–15.

34. Paul Claudel, 1 March 1913, *Journal*, vol. I, p. 247. Italics indicate words written in English in the original text.

1. Dr. Michaux's son, letter to Professor Mondor, 8 December 1951, Paul Claudel Papers, Bibliothèque Nationale de France.

2. Camille Claudel Papers, Préfecture de la Seine Archives, quoted in *Catalogue raisonné*, p. 246. Although Camille's medical records will not be available to the general public until 150 years after her birth, that is to say in 2014, parts of these records were published in 1984 by Reine-Marie Paris, grand-niece of Camille Claudel, with the approval of the other members of the Claudel family. More recently, the complete Ville-Evrard Archives as well as the Montdevergues Archives were published in the second edition of Claudel's *Catalogue raisonné* by Rivière, Gaudichon, and Ghanassia.

3. Ibid. It was called "voluntary committal" because the patient was committed upon the request of a family member as opposed to an "involuntary committal" imposed on the patient and his family by the government for reasons of security.

4. Camille Claudel, letter to Charles Thierry, 10 March 1913, quoted. in Paris, *Camille Claudel,* pp. 92–93. The signature is a playful spelling of her name. Three letters from Camille to her cousin Charles, written in pencil and at the time of her committal, were communicated to Reine-Marie Paris by Suzanne Mulsant.

5. Paul Claudel, "Ma sœur Camille," p. 277.

6. Paul Claudel, *Journal,* vol. I, p. 247.

7. Ibid.

8. Paul Claudel, letter to Daniel Fontaine, 13 March 1913, *Chroniques du Journal de Clichy,* p. 116.

9. Camille Claudel, letter to Charles Thierry, 14 March 1913, quoted in Paris, *Camille Claudel,* p. 93. One of the three letters written to Charles.

10. Camille Claudel, letter to Charles Thierry, 21 March 1913, quoted in Paris, *Camille Claudel,* pp. 93–94.

11. Ibid.

12. Dr. Truelle, letter to Charles Thierry, 3 April 1913, Ville-Evrard Archives, quoted in *Catalogue raisonné,* 2nd ed., p. 251.

13. Françoise Guilbert, *Liberté individuelle et hospitalisation des malades mentaux* (Paris: Librairies Techniques, 1974), pp. 218–25.

14. Dr. Truelle, Medical Certificate, 10 March 1913, Ville-Evrard Archives, quoted in *Catalogue raisonné,* 2nd ed., p. 306.

15. Dr. Truelle, Report, 10 March 1913, quoted in *Catalogue raisonné,* 2nd ed., p. 305.

16. 5 April 1913, Ville-Evrard Archives, quoted in *Catalogue raisonné,* 2nd ed., p. 251.

17. Article quoted in Cassar, *Dossier Camille Claudel,* pp. 243–44.

18. Ibid., pp. 244–46.

19. Ibid.

20. Ibid., pp. 248–50.

21. Paul Claudel, December 1913, *Journal,* vol. I, p. 268.

22. Paul Claudel, letter to Gabriel Frizeau, 15 November 1905, Claudel, Jammes, Frizeau, *Correspondance,* p. 69.

23. Paul Claudel, letter to Daniel Fontaine, 26 February 1913, *Chroniques du Journal de Clichy,* p. 114.

24. Paul Claudel, letter to Marie Romain-Rolland, 1949, quoted in Antoine, *Paul Claudel,* p. 379.

25. Paul Claudel, letter to Marie Romain-Rolland, November 1943, quoted in Antoine, *Paul Claudel,* p. 381.

26. Paul Claudel, letter to Marie Romain-Rolland, quoted in Antoine, *Camille Claudel,* pp. 166–67.

27. Phyllis Chesler, *Les Femmes et la folie* (Paris: Payot, 1975), p. 156. One woman was committed in 1921, the other in 1928.

28. Gide, November 1912, *Journal,* p. 384.

29. Gide, 5 December 1905, *Journal,* p. 191.

30. Paul Claudel, letter to Massignon, 20 May 1914, quoted in *L'Œuvre de Camille Claudel,* p. 277.

31. Guilbert, *Liberté individuelle,* pp. 255–60.

32. Camille Claudel, letter to Dr. Truelle, 14 October 1913, Ville-Evrard Archives, quoted in *Catalogue raisonné,* 2nd ed., p. 255.

33. Camille Claudel, letter to Charles Thierry, 27 August 1913, Ville-Evrard Archives, quoted in *Catalogue raisonné,* 2nd ed., p. 254.

34. No date, Ville-Evrard Archives, quoted in *Catalogue raisonné,* p. 308.

35. Camille Claudel, letter to Dr. Truelle, 21 July 1913, Ville-Evrard Archives, quoted in *Catalogue raisonné,* p. 253.

CHAPTER 18

1. *Bulletin de la Société Paul Claudel,* no. 28, 1967, p. 26.

2. Minutes from the fourth arrondissement, Paris, quoted in Cassar, *Dossier Camille Claudel,* p. 240.

3. Rodin, letter to Morhardt, 28 May 1914, Paul Claudel Papers, Bibliothèque Nationale de France.

4. Mathias Morhardt, letter to Rodin, 5 June 1914, Musée Rodin Archives.

5. Cladel, *Rodin,* p. 297.

6. Paul Claudel Papers, Bibliothèque Nationale de France.

7. Tirel, *The Last Days of Rodin*, p. 95.

8. Ibid., p. 25.

9. Cladel, *Rodin*, pp. 353–54.

10. 7 December 1929, Judith Cladel Papers, University of Indiana, Bloomington, Indiana.

11. Ibid., 21 June 1934.

12. Ibid., 18 August 1934.

13. Letter to Marcelle Martin (Tirel), 29 November 1916, Musée Rodin Archives.

14. 3 September 1932, Montdevergues Archives, quoted in *Catalogue raisonné*, p. 284.

CHAPTER 19

1. Paul Claudel, August 1914, *Journal*, vol. I, p. 295.

2. Ibid, p. 297.

3. André Castelli, *Montdevergues les Roses terre d'asile* (Avignon: Editions Comité des œuvres sociales du personnel du Centre Hospitalier spécialisé de Monfavet, 1990), pp. 1–3.

4. Jean-Louis Soubeiran, "Histoire de l'Hôpital Psychiatrique de Montdevergues," M. D. thesis, University of Montpellier, June 1968, p. 15. It must be noted that, aside from hydrotherapy—soaking patients in bathtubs for several hours—no treatment of any kind was given to mental patients prior to the nineteenth century. This approach was, therefore, very modern at the time.

5. Ibid., pp. 17–25.

6. Ibid., pp. 41–52.

7. 16 January 1915, Montdevergues Archives, quoted in *Catalogue raisonné*, 2nd ed., pp. 262–63.

8. No date (probably October 1915), Paul Claudel Papers, Bibliothèque Nationale de France.

9. Montdevergues Archives, quoted in *Catalogue raisonné*, 2nd ed., p. 311.

10. Ibid., 28 January 1915, quoted in *Catalogue raisonné*, 2nd ed., p. 312.

11. Letter to Henri Thierry (1910), private collection, quoted in *L'Œuvre de Camille Claudel*, p. 268.

12. Ibid.

13. Suarès and Claudel, *Correspondance*, p. 48.

14. Rollo May, *Existence* (New York: Basic Books, 1958), pp. 317–20.

15. 26 January 1915, Montdevergues Archives, quoted in *Catalogue raisonné*, p. 263.

16. Soubeiran, "Histoire de l'Hôpital Psychiatrique de Montdevergues," pp. 45–47.

17. 12 October 1915, Montdevergues Archives, quoted in *Catalogue raisonné*, p. 312.

18. Ibid., 11 September 1915, quoted in *Catalogue raisonné*, p. 266.

19. Ibid., 20 October 1915, p. 266.

20. Ibid., no date, quoted in *Catalogue raisonné*, p. 266.

21. 25 February 1917, quoted in Cassar, *Dossier Camille Claudel*, pp. 262–64, 272.

22. Montdevergues Archives, 12 March 1915, quoted in *Catalogue raisonné*, p. 264.

23. Ibid., no date, quoted in *Catalogue raisonné*, p. 264.

24. 19 March 1919, Archives Nationales.

CHAPTER 20

1. Dr. Brunet, letter to Louise Claudel, 1 June 1920, Montdevergues Archives, quoted in *Catalogue raisonné*, p. 315.

2. Madame Claudel, letter to the director of Montdevergues, June 1920, quoted in *Catalogue raisonné*, p. 271.

3. Dr. Brunet, letter to Louise Claudel, 8 June 1920, Montdevergues Archives, quoted in *Catalogue raisonné*, p. 315.

4. Camille Claudel, letter to Paul Claudel, 3 March 1927, Paul Claudel Papers, Bibliothèque Nationale de France.

5. Françoise Guilbert, *Liberté individuelle et hopitalisation des malades mentaux* (Paris: Librairies Techniques, 1974), p. 264.

6. Dr. Brunet, letter to Louise Claudel, 1 July 1920, quoted in *Catalogue raisonné*, p. 315.

7. Madame Claudel, letter to the director of Montdevergues, 9 July 1920, quoted in *Catalogue raisonné*, p. 272.

8. Madame Claudel, letter to Paul Claudel, 14 October 1920, quoted in Cassar, *Dossier Camille Claudel*, pp. 273–74.

9. Paul Claudel, 24 October 1920, *Journal*, vol. I, p. 494.

10. Montdevergues Archives, quoted in *Catalogue raisonné*, p. 315.

11. Ibid., 1 April 1922, quoted in *Catalogue raisonné*, p. 316.

12. Ibid., 27 September 1922, quoted in *Catalogue raisonné*, p. 316.

13. Elizabeth Packard, *Insane Asylum Unveiled*, (Chicago: J. N. Clarke, 1870), p. 80. Packard, a mother of six children, was committed by her husband because he objected to her interpretation of the Bible. She was released after several years of confinement, and played a major part in changing the legislation of committals in Illinois. Thanks to her testimony, the state of Illinois passed the Personal Liberty Bill, which required a jury trial of any citizen targeted for committal to an asylum.

14. The plaster of *L'Age mûr* was one of the pieces remaining in Camille's atelier after her committal. It seems that this plaster was used to make a second cast of *L'Age mûr* for Philippe Berthelot and, according to Reine-Marie Paris, the plaster may have been destroyed in the process. Camille probably heard about this transaction and thus placed Berthelot among the thieves who ransacked her atelier.

15. Camille Claudel, letter to a cousin, no date, Montdevergues Archives, quoted in *Catalogue raisonné*, p. 264.

16. Camille Claudel, letter to Paul Claudel, 3 March 1930, Paul Claudel Papers, Archives Nationales.

17. Ibid.

18. Camille Claudel, letter to Paul Claudel, no date, *Journal*, vol. 2, p. 1005. The letter was left between the pages of Paul's journal, pages dated August 1938; but the reference "ce moment des fêtes" seems to indicate that it was written around Christmas.

19. Dr. Charpenel, letter to Paul Claudel, Montdevergues Archives, quoted in *Catalogue raisonné*, p. 317.

20. Ibid.

21. Paul Claudel, 24 March 1925, *Journal*, vol. I, p. 667.

22. Camille Claudel, letter to Paul Claudel, 3 March 1927, Paul Claudel Papers, Bibliothèque Nationale de France.

23. Madame Claudel, letter to Paul Claudel, 19 November 1926, Paul Claudel Papers, Bibliothèque Nationale de France.

24. Camille Claudel, letter to Madame Claudel, 2 February 1927, Paul Claudel Papers, Bibliothèque Nationale de France.

25. Ibid.

26. Camille Claudel, letter to Paul Claudel, 3 March 1927, Paul Claudel Papers, Bibliothèque Nationale de France.

27. Paul Claudel, August 1927, *Journal*, vol. I, p. 781.

28. Ibid., September 1927, vol. I, p. 785.

29. Ibid., 14 July 1927, vol. I, p. 779.

30. Madame Claudel, letter to Paul Claudel, 20 January 1928, Paul Claudel Papers, Bibliothèque Nationale de France.

31. Dr. Jacques de Massary, letter to Paul Claudel, no date (probably 1928), Paul Claudel Papers, Bibliothèque Nationale de France.

32. Paul Claudel, 23 September 1928, *Journal*, vol. I, p. 830.

33. Ibid., 18 June 1929, p. 863.

34. Ibid., 22 June 1929, p. 864.

35. Louise Claudel, letter to Paul Claudel, 5 July 1929, Paul Claudel Papers, Bibliothèque Nationale de France.

36. Ibid.

37. Camille Claudel, letter to Paul Claudel, no date, *Journal*, vol. 2, p. 1005. Same letter left between the pages of Paul's journal, pages dated August 1938.

CHAPTER 21

1. Pirani, "Jessie: Study of an Artist," pp. 65–66.

2. Elborne Archives, 31 January 1921.

3. Ibid., 20 October 1926. From the French Embassy in Tokyo.

4. Ibid., 21 March 1927. From the French Embassy in Washington, D.C.

5. Camille Claudel, letter to Jessie Lipscomb, Elborne Archives, 11 March 1927.

6. Jessie's son and grandson remembered this anecdote.

7. Pirani, "Jessie: Study of an Artist," pp. 59–62. Interview with Sydney Elborne by Abi Pirani

8. Jessie Elborne, letter to Sydney Elborne, 21 May 1915, Elborne Archives.

9. Jessie Elborne, letter to Sydney Elborne, 8 December 1914, Elborne Archives.

10. Louise de Massary, letter to Jessie Elborne, 9 December 1929, Elborne Archives.

11. Camile Claudel, letter to Paul Claudel, 3 March 1930, Paul Claudel Papers, Bibliothèque Nationale de France.

12. Louise de Massary, letter to Jessie Elborne, 4 April 1930, Paul Claudel Papers, Bibliothèque Nationale de France.

13. Camille Claudel, letter to Jessie Elborne, 29 October 1930, Elborne archives. The reference to the Dreyfus affair is written by Camille as "the D. affair."

14. Jessie Elborne, letter to Sydney Elborne, 6 June 1939, quoted in A. Lytton Sells, "Auguste Rodin and His English Friends," *College Art Journal* 15 (Winter 1956), pp. 143–45. The presence, in the Elborne Archives, of a postcard sent from Brangues by Paul to his sister in Montdevergues and dated 19 July 1936, remains to be explained. It suggests that correspondence between Camille and Jessie may have continued through 1936, or even that Jessie may have visited Camille in 1936. With no other documentation available, we can only conjecture.

CHAPTER 22

1. Madame Claudel, letter to Paul Claudel, 29 November 1924, Paul Claudel Papers, Bibliothèque Nationale de France.

2. Paul Claudel Papers, Bibliothèque Nationale de France. The long feud between Paul and Louise is described in great detail by Jacques Cassar, pp. 307–52.

3. Ibid.

4. Paul Claudel, letter to Monsieur Moulin, 15 January 1933, Paul Claudel Papers, Bibliothèque Nationale de France.

5. Paul Claudel, 5 May 1935, *Journal*, vol. II, p. 90.

6. Ibid.

7. Ibid., 14 November 1938, p. 250.

8. Camille Claudel, letter to Paul Claudel, 4 April 1932, Paul Claudel Papers, Bibliothèque Nationale de France.

9. Interview of Yvonne Louis, anonymous article kept in the Montdevergues Archives.

10. René Diez, Interview of Marie-Thérèse Bénier, *Le Comtadin du Jeudi* (October 1991), no. 2464, p. 15.

11. Paul Claudel, September–October 1933, *Journal*, vol. II, p. 38.

12. Louis Vauxelles, "Les Arts: rétrospective Camille Claudel," *Le Monde illustré* (12 May 1934). Camille's father was from the Vosges area, hence the reference to the "rustic woman from Lorraine."

13. Judith Cladel, letter to Mathias Morhardt, 20 June 1934, Paul Claudel Papers, Bibliothèque Nationale de France. The letter mentioned by Cladel appears to be the one Camille sent to Blot on 24 May 1934, and quoted earlier: "I have fallen into an abyss. I live in a world so curious, so strange. Of the dream that was my life, this is the nightmare." Blot himself wrote to Morhardt on 21 September 1935: "I also gave to Mademoiselle Cladel several astonishing letters that she [Camille] sent me (she was still writing to me barely a year ago)." Musée Rodin Archives.

14. Eugène Blot, letter to Camille Claudel, 3 September 1932, Montdevergues Archives, quoted in *Catalogue raisonné*, pp. 283–84.

15. Judith Cladel, letter to Mathias Morhardt, 17 August 1934, Paul Claudel Papers, Bibliothèque Nationale de France.

16. Mathias Morhardt, "Sur un marbre disparu de Camille Claudel," *Le Temps* (September 1935).

17. Judith Cladel, letter to Mathias Morhardt, 17 August 1934, Paul Claudel Papers, Bibliothèque Nationale de France.

18. Paul Claudel, July 1936, *Journal*, vol. II, p. 152.

19. Paul Claudel, letter to Françoise de Marcilly, 1937, quoted in Antoine, *Paul Claudel*, p. 284.

20. Paul Claudel, letter to Daniel Fontaine, 26 February 1913.

21. René Diez, interview with Marie-Thérèse Bénier, *Le Comtadin du Jeudi* (October 1991), no. 2464, p. 15.

22. Interview with Yvonne Louis, anonymous article kept in the Montdevergues Archives.

23. Camille Claudel, letter to Paul Claudel, no date, Paul Claudel, *Journal*, vol. II, pp. 1005–6 The allusion to Jacques de Massary's death (November 1938) places the letter at the end of 1938. The holidays referred to would thus be Christmas and New Year celebrations.

CHAPTER 23

1. Dr. Izac, letter to Paul Claudel, Paul Claudel Papers, Bibliothèque Nationale de France.

2. Paul Claudel, 8 December 1942, *Journal*, vol. II, p. 426.

3. Dr. Izac, letter to Paul Claudel, 8 May 1942, Paul Claudel Papers, Bibliothèque Nationale de France.

4. Nelly Méquillet, letter to Paul Claudel, 15 August 1943, quoted in Paul Claudel, *Journal*, vol. II, pp. 456–57.

5. Paul Claudel, 20–21 September 1943, *Journal*, vol. II, pp. 460–61.

6. Ibid., 25 September 1943, vol. 2, pp. 461–62.

7. Paul Claudel, "Le Cantique des Cantiques," *Œuvres Complètes*, vol. XXII (Paris: Gallimard, 1963), p. 132.

8. Paul Claudel, *Journal*, vol. II, p. 463.

9. Cassar, *Dossier Camille Claudel*, p. 363.

10. Félix Boutin, chaplain, letter to Paul Claudel, 21 October 1943, *Journal*, vol. II, pp. 464–65. The letter, copied by Paul in his journal, is dated October 20. Considering that Camille was buried on October 21, Paul must have made a mistake when he copied the letter.

11. Nelly Méquillet, letter to Paul Claudel, Paul Claudel Papers, Bibliothèque Nationale de France.

12. Ibid.

13. Cemetery Department, letter to Pierre Claudel, 6 September 1962, Paul Claudel Papers, Bibliothèque Nationale de France.

14. Antoine, *Paul Claudel*, p. 378.

EPILOGUE

1. Paul Claudel, *Œuvres en prose*, note p. 274.

2. See the history of these works in *Catalogue raisonné*, 2nd ed., pp. 91, 111, 120, 125, 132, 134, 141, 146, 147, 160, 165.

3. Judd Tully, "The Messiest Subject Alive," *ARTnews* 94, no. 10 (December 1995), p. 112.

4. Ibid., pp. 113–14.

5. Ibid., p. 118.

6. Anonymous, "'L'Implorante' de Camille Claudel est un don du ciel pour la boulangère," *La Depêche* (October 1997).

7. Paul Claudel, "Camille Claudel statuaire," in *Œuvres en prose*, p. 276.

BIBLIOGRAPHY

ARCHIVES

Archives Nationales.

Archives Départementales d'Avignon

Camille Claudel Papers, Bibliothèque Marguerite Durand

Colarossi Family Archives

Elborne Family Archives

Judith Cladel Papers, Lilly Library, University of Indiana, Bloomington

Montdevergues Archives

Musée Rodin Archives, Paris

Ottilie McLaren Papers, National Library of Scotland, Edinborough

Paul Claudel Papers, Bibliothèque Nationale de France, Paris

Ville-Evrard Archives

BOOKS AND ARTICLES

Alcott-Nieriker, May. *Studying Art Abroad and How To Do It Cheaply*. Boston: Robert Brothers, 1879.

Allilaire, Jean-François. "Camille Claudel malade mentale" in Reine-Marie Paris, *Camille Claudel*. Paris: Gallimard, 1984.

Anonymous. "Aperçu d'une biographie de Mlle Camille Claudel." *Bulletin du Musée de Châteauroux* (1901).

_____. "Camille Claudel au musée Rodin." *Le Figaro* (13 December 1951).

_____. Interview of Yvonne Louis. Montdevergues Archives.

_____. "Les femmes et les féministes." *Revue encyclopédique Larousse* (28 November 1896).

_____. "Madame Camille Claudel." *Gil Blas* (28 Feb 1908).

_____. "Œuvres de Camille Claudel et de Bernard Hoetger." *Art et Artistes* (January 1906).

_____. "'L'Implorante' de Camille Claudel est un don du ciel pour la boulangère." *La Dépêche* (October 1997).

Antoine, Gérald. *Paul Claudel ou l'enfer du génie*. Paris: Ed. Robert Laffont, 1988.

The Art Student in Paris. Boston: Museum School, Art Student Association, 1887.

Asselin, Henry. "Camille Claudel et les sirènes de la sculpture." *La Revue française* no. 187 (April 1966): 8–12.

_____. "La Vie douloureuse de Camille Claudel." Radio Broadcasts, 1956. Typed text in Paul Claudel's Papers, Bibliothèque Nationale de France.

Asselin, Jean-Pierre. "Camille Claudel." *Bulletin de la Société Paul Claudel*. no. 21 (1st trimester 1966).

Augé de Lassus, L. "Exposition de 1889." *L'Art* (1889).

Ayral-Clause, Odile. "Camille Claudel, Jessie Lipscomb and Rodin." *Apollo* no. 424 (June 1997):

_____. "Une Partenaire anglaise; Jessie Lipscomb," in Riviere, Gaudichon, and Ghanassia, *Camille Claudel: Catalogue raisonné*: 54–57. p.21–26.

Barclay. "L'Atelier Bonnat." *Magazine of Art*. 5 (1882).

Bashkirtseff, Marie. *Journal*. Paris: Mazarine, 1980.

Barraqué, J. *Debussy*. Paris: Seuil, 1962.

Beaux, Cecilia. *Background With Figures*. Boston and New York: Houghton Mifflin, 1930.

Belloc, Marie Adelaïde. "Lady Artists in Paris." *Murray's Magazine*. 8 (1891): 371–384.

Bénézit, Emmanuel. *Dictionnaire critique et documentaire des peintres, sculpteurs, dessinateurs et graveurs*. Paris: Gründ, 1976.

Bettex, R. de. "Petites expositions, Camille Claudel et Bernard Hoetger." *La République* (5 December 1905).

Bibolet, Françoise. "Camille Claudel à Nogent-sur-Seine." *La Vie en Champagne* no. 326 (November 1982).

Birnbaum, Pierre. *L'Affaire Dreyfus*. Paris: Gallimard, 1994.

____. *La Sculpture française*. Paris: Larousse, 1945, 1963.

Blanche, J-E. *La Vie artistique sous la IIIème République*. Paris: Editions de France, 1931.

Blot, Eugène. *Histoire d'une collection de tableaux modernes*. Paris: Éditions d'Art, 1934.

Blumer, M. I. "Camille Claudel" in *Dictionnaire de Biographie française*. Paris: Letouzey et Ané, 1959.

Boime, Albert. *The Academy and French Painting in the Nineteenth Century*. London: Phaidon, 1971.

____. *Art and the French Commune*. Princeton: Princeton University Press, 1995.

____. *Hollow Icons: the Politics of Sculpture in Nineteenth Century France*. Kent, Ohio: Kent State University Press, 1987.

Boly, Joseph. "Camille Claudel, état des recherches et du rayonnement." *Société Paul Claudel en Belgique* (1989).

____. "L'Influence de Camille Claudel sur Paul Claudel et sur la genèse de 'L'Annonce faite à Marie.'" *Claudel Studies* no. 1 (1980).

Bouchot, Henri. "Les Salons de 1893: la sculpture." *La Gazette des Beaux-Arts* no. 48 (1893): 118.

Bourdeau, Lucien. "Description d'œuvres exposées aux Salons de 1893." *Revue encyclopédique Larousse* no. 65 (1893): 823.

Bouté, Gérard. *Camille Claudel. Le miroir et la nuit*. Paris: Les Éditions de l'Amateur-Éditions des catalogues raisonnés, 1995.

Braisne, Henri de. "Salon de 1892." *La Revue idéaliste*.

____. "Camille Claudel." *La Revue idéaliste* no. 19 (19 October 1897).

Bréthenoux, M. "Camille Claudel." *Claudel Studies* 15, no. 2 (1988).

Butler, Ruth. *Rodin: The Shape of Genius*. New Haven and London: Yale University Press, 1993.

Cassar, Jacques. *Dossier Camille Claudel*. Paris: Séguier, 1987.

Castelli, André. *Montdevergues les Roses terre d'asile*. Avignon: Editions Comité des œuvres sociales du personnel du Centre Hospitalier spécialisé de Monfavet, 1990.

Casteras, Susan and Linda H. Peterson. *A Struggle for Fame: Victorian Women Artists and Authors*. New Haven, Connecticut: Yale Center for British Art, 1994.

Chaigne, Louis. *Vie de Paul Claudel et genèse de son œuvre*. Paris: Maison Mame, 1961.

Champigneule, Bernard. *Rodin*. Paris: Somogy Éditions d'Art, 1994.

Champion, Pierre. *Marcel Schwob et son temps*. Paris: Grasset, 1927.

Chatain, G. "A châteauroux et Guéret, œuvres retrouvées de Camille Claudel." *L'Echo du Centre* (26 August 1982).

Chesler, Phyllis. *Les Femmes et la folie*. Paris: Payot, 1975.

Chesneau, Ernest. *L'Education de l'artiste*. Paris, 1880.

Cladel, Judith. *Rodin, sa vie glorieuse et inconnue*. Paris: Bernard Grasset, 1936.

____. *Rodin*. Paris: Terra et Aimery Somogy, 1948.

Clair, Jean. *Meduse. Contribution à une anthropologie des arts du visuel*. Paris: Gallimard, 1989.

Clarétie, Jules. *La Vie à Paris*. 5 vols. Paris: Victor Havard, 1880–84.

Claris, Edmond. *De l'Impressionnisme en sculpture*. Paris: La Nouvelle Revue, 1902.

Claudel, Paul. *Journal (1904–1932)*. vol. 1. Paris: Gallimard, 1968.

____. *Journal (1933–1955)*. vol. 2. Paris: Gallimard, 1969.

____. *Mémoires improvisés*. Paris: Gallimard, 1969.

____. *Œuvres en prose*. Paris: Gallimard, 1965.

____. *Œuvres complètes*. 29 vols. Paris: Gallimard, 1963.

____. *Théâtre*, vol. I. Paris: Gallimard, 1967.

____. *Cahiers Paul Claudel*. Vol I. Paris: Gallimard, 1959.

____. *Les Critiques de notre temps et Claudel*. Paris: Garnier, 1970.

____, Francis Jammes and Gabriel Frizeau. *Correspondance (1897–1938)*. Paris: Gallimard, 1952.

____ and François Mauriac. *Chroniques du Journal de Clichy; Claudel-Fontaine Correspondance*. Annales Littéraires de l'Université de Besançon, Paris: Les Belles Lettres, 1978.

____ and André Suarès. *Correspondance (1904–1938)*. Paris: Gallimard, 1951.

Cleemputte, Paul Adolphe van. *La Vie parisienne à travers le dix-neuvième siècle*. 3 vols. Paris: Plon, 1900–1901.

Cochin, Henri. "Quelques réflexions sur les Salons." *Gazette des Beaux-Arts* (July 1903).

Cook, Clarence. *Art and Artists of Our Time*. 3 vols. New York: Selmar Hess, 1888. reprint New York: Garland Publishing, Inc., 1978.

Coquiot, Gustave. *Rodin à l'Hôtel de Biron et à Meudon*. Paris: Librairie Ollendorf, 1917.

Daix, Pierre. "Camille Claudel au musée Rodin." *Le quotidien de Paris* (21 March 1991).

Daniel-Rops. *Claudel, tel que je l'ai connu*. Strasbourg: F.X. Le Roux, 1957.

Daudet, Léon. *Paris vécu*. Paris: Gallimard, 1969.

Dauriac, Jacques-Paul. "Poitiers musée Sainte-Croix: exposition Camille Claudel 1864–1943." *Panthéon* no. 4 (1984).

Dayot, Armand. *L'Image de la femme*. Paris: Hachette, 1899.

Debussy, Claude. *Lettres à deux amis: 78 lettres inédites à Robert Godet et Georges Jean Aubry*. Paris: José Corti, 1942.

Delbée, Anne. *Une Femme*. Paris: Presses de la Renaissance, 1982. Published in England as *Camille Claudel*, Carol Cosman, trans. New York: Mercury House, 2000.

Demont-Breton, Virginie. *Les Maisons que j'ai connues*. Vol. II. Paris: Plon-Nourrit and Co. 1926.

Descaves, Lucien, *Souvenirs d'un ours*, Paris: Les Éditions de Paris, 1946.

Descharnes, Robert, and Jean-François Chabrun. *Auguste Rodin*. Lausanne: Édita, 1967 and Paris: La Bibliothèque des Arts, 1967.

Desforges, P. "Le Silence de Camille Claudel." *Bulletin de la Société Paul Claudel* no. 114 (1989).

Le Dictionnaire des peintres, sculpteurs, dessinateurs et graveurs. Paris, 1955.

Dickens, Charles. "Artistic Professions for Women." *All the Year Round* 63, no. 1035 (29 September 1888): 296–300.

Diez, René. Interview of Marie-Thérèse Bénier. *Le Comtadin du Jeudi* no. 2464 (October 1991).

Duncan, S. James. *A Century of Statues*. Frome: Morris Singer Foundry, Ltd., 1984.

Dujardin-Beaumetz, François. *Entretiens avec Rodin*. Paris: Éditions du Musée Rodin, 1913.

Duret-Robert, François. "L'Affaire Claudel." *Connaissance des Arts*. no. 523 (Dec 1995): 108–115.

Duvernois, Henri. "La Pudeur et la Vertu." *Le Monde illustré* (12 May 1934).

Dyhouse, C. *Girls Growing Up in Late Victorian and Edwardian England*. London, 1981.

Elsen, Albert. *Rodin's Gates of Hell*. Stanford University Press, 1985.

_____. *In Rodin's Studio*. Ithaca: Cornell, 1980.

Fabre-Pellerin, Brigitte. *Le Jour et la nuit de Camille Claudel*. Paris: Lachenal et Ritter, 1988.

Fehrer, Catherine: "New Light on the Académie Julian and its Founder Rodolphe Julian." *Gazette des Beaux-Arts* 103 (1984): 207–214.

Finke, L. "Camille Claudel: A Woman of Genius." *Sculpture Review* (1990).

Fourcauld, Louis de. "La Sculpture à la Société nationale des Beaux-Arts." *Revue des Arts Décoratifs* 19 (1899): 247–57.

Fox, Shirley. *An Art Student's Reminiscences of Paris in the Eighties*. London: Mills and Boon, 1909.

Francis, E. *Un autre Claudel*. Paris: Grasset, 1973.

Frayling, Christopher. *The Royal College of Art*. London: Barnie and Jenkins, 1987.

Frederickson, Kristen. "Carving out a Place: Gendered Critical Descriptions of Camille Claudel and her Sculpture." *Word and Image* 12 (April–June 1996): 161–74.

Garb, Tamar. *Sisters of the Brush: Women's Artistic Culture in Late Nineteenth-Century Paris*. New Haven and London: Yale University Press, 1994.

_____. "L'Art féminin: The Formation of a Critical Category in Late Nineteenth-Century France." *Art History* 12 (March 1989): 39–65.

Gaudichon, Bruno. "Camille Claudel: Une femme sous influence." *Beaux-Arts Magazine* no. 15 (July-August 1984): 46–49.

Gaudichon, Bruno and Monique Laurent. *Camille Claudel (1864–1943)*. Catalogue of the 1984 exhibition, Musée Rodin and Musée Sainte-Croix, Poitiers, 1984.

Geffroy, Gustave. "Camille Claudel à Châteauroux." *Journal du Dimanche* (15 December 1895).

_____. "Çacountala." *Le Journal* (15 December 1895).

_____. "Le Salon de 1894 et le Salon de 1895." *La Vie artistique* (1895).

_____. "Le Salon de 1900: Sculpture." *La Vie artistique* (1900).

_____. "Le Salon de 1905: Sculpture." *La Vie artistique* (1905).

Gelber, L. "Camille Claudel's Art and Influences." *Claudel Studies* 1, no. 1 (1972): 36–43.

Genet-Delacroix, Marie-Claude. *Art et état sous la Troisième République: le système des Beaux-Arts*. 1870–1940. Paris: Publications de la Sorbonne, 1992.

Gibson, E. "In Search of Camille Claudel." *New Criterion*. no. 7 (November 1988): 54–60.

Gimpel, René. *Diary of an Art Dealer*. New York: Farrar, Straus and Giroux, 1966.

Godet, Henri. "Salon d'Automne." *L'Action* (1 November 1906).

Goldscheider, Cécile. *Rodin, sa vie, son oeuvre, son héritage*. Paris: Les Productions de Paris, 1962.

_____. "Camille Claudel, sculpteur." *Bulletin de la Société Paul Claudel*. no. 37 (February-April 1970).

Goncourt, Edmond. *Hokusai*. Paris: G and E Pasquelle, 1896.

_____. *Correspondance inédite d'Edmond de Goncourt et Henry Cear*. Paris: Nizet, 1965.

Goncourt, Edmond and Jules de. *Journal: Mémoires de la vie littéraire et artistique*. 3 vols. Paris: Robert Laffont, 1989.

Le Grand Larousse encyclopédique. Paris: Larousse, 1960.

Green, Alice. "The Girl Student in Paris." *The Magazine of Art* 16 (1883).

Grunfeld, Frederic. V. *Rodin: A Biography*. New York: Henry Holt and Co., 1987.

Gsell, Paul. *Auguste Rodin: L'Art*. Interviews collected by Paul Gsell. Paris: Grasset, 1911.

Guers, Marie-Josèphe. *Paul Claudel*. Arles: Actes-Sud, 1987.

Guilbert, Françoise. *Liberté individuelle hospitalisation des malades mentaux*. Paris: Librairies Techniques, 1974.

Hamel, Maurice. "Les Salons de 1905." *La Revue de Paris* (June 1905).

Hellerstein, Erna. Leslie Olafson Parker Hume and Karen M. Offen, eds. *Victorian Women: A Documentary Account of Women's Lives in Nineteenth Century England, France and the U.S.* Stanford: Stanford University Press, 1981.

Hess, T.B., and E.C. Baker. "Art and sexual Politics." *Art News* series, New York: Macmillan Press, 1973.

Hillairet, Jacques. *Dictionnaire historique des rues de Paris*. Paris: Les Editions de Minuit, 1970.

Holland, Clive. "Lady Art Students' Life in Paris." *International Studio* 30 (1904): 225–33.

_____. "Student Life in the Quartier Latin." *The Studio* 27, no. 115.

Jakovsky, Anatole. *Les Années folles de Montparnasse*. Paris: Editions Rencontre Société Coopérative, 1957.

Jeanès, J.E.S. *D'après nature. Souvenirs et portraits*. Geneva: Perrets-Gentil, 1946.

Jeanniot, G. "Le Salon du Champ de Mars." *Revue encyclopédique Larousse* no. 194 (22 May 1897).

Jopling-Rowe, Louise. *Twenty Years of My Life 1867–1887*. London: John Lane, 1925.

Kennet, Kathleen. (Lady Scott). *Self-Portrait of an Artist*. London: John Murray, 1949.

Lami, Stanislas. *Dictionnaire des sculpteurs de l'école française du XIXème siècle*. Paris: Champion, 1921.

Laparcerie, Marie. "Les Modèles." *La Presse* (15 December 1902).

Lawton, Frederick, *The Life and Work of Auguste Rodin*. London: T. Fisher Unwin, 1906.

Lecoq de Boisbaudran, Horace. *The Training of the Memory in Art and the Education of the Artist*. London: Macmillan and Co., 1911.

Lefranc, Céline. "Tribulations d'un catalogue." *Connaissance des Arts* no. 535 (January 1997): 117.

Lepage, Edouard. *Une Page de l'histoire de l'art au dix-neuvième siècle*. Paris: 1911.

Leroi, Paul. "Salon de 1887." *L'Art*. No. 43 (1887).

_____. "Salon de 1888." *L'Art*. No. 44 (1888).

_____. "Salon de 1892." *L'Art*. No. 53 (1892).

_____. "Salon de 1894." *L'Art*. No. 58 (1894).

Lethève, Jacques. *La vie quotidienne des artistes français au XIXème*. Paris: Hachette, 1968.

Mathews, Patricia. *Passionate Discontent: Creativity, Gender, and French Symbolist Art*. Chicago and London: The University of Chicago Press, 1999.

Maillard, L. *Auguste Rodin, Statuaire*. Paris: Floury, 1899.

Marx, Roger. "Beaux-Arts: la libre esthétique." *La Revue encyclopédique* (1 November 1894).

_____. "Le Salon de 1895." *Gazette des Beaux-Arts* (1895).

Mauclair, Camille. *Auguste Rodin*. Paris: La Renaissance du Livre, 1918.

May, Rollo. *Existence*. New York: Basic Books, Inc., 1958.

Michel, André. "Salon de 1888, la sculpture." *La Gazette des Beaux-Arts* (August 1888).

Michel, Pierre and Jean-François Nivet. *Octave Mirbeau. Biographie*. Paris: Séguier, 1990.

Michelet, Jules. *Journal*. Ed. Pl. Viallaneix. 2 vols. Paris, 1959.

Milner, John. *The Studios of Paris: The Capital of Art in the Late Nineteenth Century*. New Haven and London: Yale University Press, 1988.

Mirbeau, Octave. *Des artistes*. Paris: Flammarion, 1922.

_____. "Ça et là." *Le Journal quotidien littéraire, artistique et politique* (12 May 1895).

_____. *Correspondance avec Auguste Rodin*. P. Michel and J-F Nivet, eds. Tusson, Charente: Du Lérot, 1988.

_____. "Le Salon de 1885." *Revue encyclopédique*.

_____. "Le Salon de 1892." *Revue encyclopédique*.

_____. "Le Salon de 1893." *Revue encyclopédique*.

_____. "Ceux du Champ de Mars et ceux du Palais de l'Industrie." *Supplément illustré du Journal* (May 1893).

Miquel, Pierre. *La troisième République*. Paris: Fayard, 1989.

_____. *Les quatre-vingts*. Paris: Fayard, 1995.

Mitchell, Claudine. "Intellectuality and Sexuality:

Camille Claudel, the Fin de Siècle Sculptress." *Art History* 12, no. 4 (December 1989): 419–47.

Mondor, Henri. *Claudel plus intime*. Paris: Gallimard, 1960.

Monod, François. "L'Exposition de Mlle Claudel et de M. Bernard Hoetger." *Art et décoration* (January 1906).

Montebello, Roger de. "Camille Claudel: de l'image à l'œuvre." *Connaissance des Arts*, no. 442 (December 1988): 132–35.

Morand, Paul. *Mon plaisir en littérature*. Paris: Gallimard, 1980.

Morhardt, Mathias. "Mademoiselle Camille Claudel," *Mercure de France* (March 1898): 708–55.

_____. "La Bataille du Balzac." *Mercure de France* 256 (Nov-Dec 1934).

_____. "Le Banquet Puvis de Chavannes." *Mercure de France* 261 (1 August 1935).

_____. "Sur un marbre disparu de Camille Claudel." *Le Temps* (14 September 1935).

Morice, Charles. "Le Salon des Artistes Français." *Le Mercure de France* (June 1903).

_____. "Art moderne. Expositions." *Mercure de France* (15 December 1905).

Morrow, W. C. *Bohemian Paris of Today*. Philadelphia: J.B. Lippincott Co., 1899.

Nantet, Marie-Victoire. "Camille Claudel: un désastre 'fin de siècle.'" *Commentaire 42* (Summer 1988).

Natt, Phebe D. "London Art-Schools." *Lippincott's Magazine* 25 (1880): 629–35.

_____. "Paris Art-Schools" *Lippincott's Magazine* 27 (March 1881): 669–76.

Nochlin, Linda. *Women, Art and Power and Other Essays*. New York: Harper and Row, 1989, London: Thames and Hudson, 1991.

Packard, Elizabeth. *Insane Asylum Unveiled*. Chicago: J. N. Clarke, 1870.

Paris, Reine-Marie. *Camille Claudel*. Paris: Gallimard, 1984.

_____. *Camille: The Life of Camille Claudel, Rodin's Muse and Mistress*. New York: Seaver Books, Holt and Co., 1988.

_____., and Arnaud de La Chapelle. *L'Œuvre de Camille Claudel*. Paris: Adam Biro-Arhis, 1990.

Pilon, Edmond. "Camille Claudel." *Iris* (June 1900).

Pinet, Hélène. *Rodin: les mains du génie*. Paris: Gallimard, 1988.

Pingeot, Anne. "Le Chef d'œuvre de Camille Claudel: L'Age mûr." *La Revue du Louvre et des Musées de France* (October 1982): 292–95.

Pirani, Abi. "Jessie: Study of an Artist." M.A. thesis. York University, 1987.

Prendergast, C. *Paris and the Nineteenth Century*. Oxford, U.K., Cambridge, USA: Blackwell, 1992.

Renard, Jules. *Journal*. Paris: Gallimard, 1965.

Réval, Gabrielle. "Les Artistes Femmes au Salon de 1903." *Femina* no. 55 (1May 1903).

Rilke, Rainer Maria. *Rodin*. Transl. by J. Lemont and H. Transil. New York: Haskell House, 1974.

Ripa, Yannick. *La Ronde des folles: femme, folie et enfermement au XIXe siècle*. Paris: Aubier, 1986.

Rivière, Anne. *L'Interdite, Camille Claudel (1864–1943)*. Paris: Tierce, 1983.

_____. Bruno Gaudichon and Danièle Ghanassia. *Camille Claudel: Catalogue raisonné*. Paris: Adam Biro, 2000.

Rodin, Auguste. *Correspondance de Rodin*. Vol 1 (1860–99). Ed. Alain Beausire and Hélène Pinet. Paris: Éditions du Musée Rodin, 1985.

_____. *Correspondance de Rodin*. Vol 2 (1900–1907). Ed. by Alain Beausire and Florence Cadouot. Paris: Éditions du Musée Rodin, 1986.

_____. *Correspondance de Rodin*. Vol 3 (1908–12). Ed. Alain Beausire and Florence Cadouot. Paris: Éditions du Musée Rodin, 1987.

_____. *Correspondance de Rodin*. Vol 4 (1913–17). Ed. by Alain Beausire, Florence Cadouot, and Frédérique Vincent. Paris: Éditions du Musée Rodin, 1992.

Rodin et ses modèles. Paris: Éditions du Musée Rodin (Exhibition April-June 1990).

Rolland, Romain. "Les Salons de 1903." *La Revue de Paris* (1June 1903): 664.

Rousselet, Louis. *L'Exposition universelle de 1889*. Paris: Editions de Minuit, 1967.

Rousselot, Paul. *Histoire de l'éducation des femmes en France*. Paris: 1883.

Sauer, Marina. *L'Entrée des femmes à l'Ecole des Beaux-Arts. 1880–1923*. Paris: énsb-a, 1990.

Saunier, Charles. "La Sculpture aux Salons de 1893." *La Plume* (15 June 1893).

Schmoll, J. A. gen. Eisenwerth. *Auguste Rodin and Camille Claudel*. Munich and New York: Prestel Verlag, 1994.

Schwob, Marcel, *Chroniques*. Geneva: Droz, 1981.

Sells, Lytton A. "Auguste Rodin and His English Friends." *College Art Journal* 15 (Winter 1956).

Silvestre, Armand. "La Vague. La Sculpture aux salons de 1897." *Gazette des Beaux-Arts* (1897).

Slatkin, Wendy. *Women Artists in History: from Antiquity to the XXth Century*. Englewood Cliffs, N.J.: Prentice Hall, 1985.

Somerville, E. "An Atelier des Dames." *The Magazine of Art* 9 (1886): 152–57.

Soubeiran, Jean-Louis. "Histoire de l'Hôpital Psychiatrique de Montdevergues." M.D. thesis, University of Montpellier, June 1968

Stranahan, C. H. *A History of French Painting from its Earliest to its Latest Practise Including an Account of the French Academy of Painting, its Salons, Schools of Instruction and Regulations.* New York, 1888.

Symons, Arthur. *From Toulouse-Lautrec to Rodin.* London: John Lane, 1929.

Tancock, J.-L. *The Sculpture of Auguste Rodin.* Philadelphia: Philadelphia Museum of Art, 1976.

Tebbs, H. F. *Peterborough: A History.* Cambridge: The Oleander Press, 1979.

Tillier, Bernard. *Ernest Nivet, sculpteur: Des fenêtres ouvertes sur la vie.* Châteauroux: B. Tillier, 1987.

Tinayre, Marcelle. "Salon de 1904." *Revue de Paris* (1904).

Tirel, Marcelle. *The Last Years of Rodin.* New York: Haskell House Publishers Ltd., 1974.

Tully, Judd. "The Messiest Subject Alive." *ARTnews* 94, no. 10 (December 1995): 112–18.

Vallas, Léon. *Claude Debussy et son temps.* Paris: Albin Michel, 1958.

Vauxelles, Louis. "A propos de Camille Claudel: Quelques œuvres d'une grande artiste inconnue du public." *Gil blas* (10 July 1913).

____. "Les Arts: rétrospective Camille Claudel." *Le Monde illustré* (12 May 1934): 391.

____. Preface to the catalogue *Œuvres de Camille Claudel et de Bernard Hoetger* (4–16 December 1905).

Vizetelly, Ernest Alfred. *Paris and her People under the Third Republic.* Reprint edition, New York: Reprint Co., 1971.

Waszak, Peter. "The Development of Leisure and Cultural Facilities in Peterborough. 1850–1900." B.A. thesis. The Polytechnic, Huddersfield, 1975.

Weber, Eugene. *France Fin de Siècle.* Cambridge, Massachusetts: Harvard University Press, 1986.

Weiss, D. *Le Roman de Rodin.* Paris: Plon, 1965.

Wernick, R. "Camille Claudel's Tempestuous Life of Art and Passion." *Smithsonian Magazine* (September 1985).

Wilhem, J. *La Vie à Paris sous le Second Empire et la Troisième République.* Paris: Arts et Métiers Graphiques, 1947.

Woodward, Jocelyn. *Perseus, a Study in Greek Art and Legend.* Cambridge University Press, 1937.

Yeldham, Charlotte. *Women Artists in Nineteenth Century France and England.* 2 vols. New York and London: Garland Publishing, Inc., 1984.

INDEX

INDEX / PHOTO CREDITS

PHOTO CREDITS